D0463980

THE PRESIDENT'S
FIRST YEAR

**NONE WERE PREPARED, SOME NEVER LEARNED—
WHY THE ONLY SCHOOL FOR PRESIDENTS IS THE PRESIDENCY**

DOUGLAS ALAN COHN

Guilford, Connecticut

An imprint of Rowman & Littlefield

Distributed by NATIONAL BOOK NETWORK

Copyright © 2016 by Douglas Alan Cohn

British Library Cataloguing in Publication Information Available

Library of Congress Cataloging-in-Publication Data

Names: Cohn, Douglas, author.
Title: The president's first year : none were prepared, some never learned—why the only school for
   presidents is the presidency / Douglas Cohn.
Description: Guilford, Conn. : Lyons Press, 2015. | Includes bibliographical references and index.
Identifiers: LCCN 2015026143| ISBN 9781493011926 (hardcover) | ISBN 9781493023950
(e-book)
Subjects: LCSH: Presidents—United States—History. | Presidents—United States—Biography.
Classification: LCC E176.1 .C73 2015 | DDC 973.09/9—dc23 LC record available at http://lccn
.loc.gov/2015026143

∞™ The paper used in this publication meets the minimum requirements of American National
Standard for Information Sciences—Permanence of Paper for Printed Library Materials, ANSI/
NISO Z39.48-1992.

CONTENTS

(Note: Each president is preceded by the order of service.)

NOTES ON THE TEXT

1. In the text, each title (except Washington) is followed by the first year of service.
2. In the text subtitles, each president is followed by the term of service.
3. Quotes retain original spelling and grammar; sources are in the endnotes.
4. Organization is by subject; however, the first president under each heading is listed in semi-chronological order, with the first president listed under the preceding heading.
5. Tables and original charts are integral to the narrative and are accordingly referenced when applicable to more than one chapter.
6. With the Act of Union, England, Wales, and Scotland became Great Britain in 1707 and the United Kingdom following the addition of Ireland in 1801. To avoid confusion, "Britain" is used throughout the text. "England" is referenced in several quotes.
7. Military service listed in the opening biography for each president begins with the highest rank attained.

INTRODUCTION

THE FRESHMAN PRESIDENT

The only school for presidents is the presidency. This is the Presidents' Paradox.

There are long and short paths to power, though the times matter more than time to an inattentive public, which explains the broad range of presidential competencies, and why in a discussion of each president's first year in office, none come away unscathed. While George Washington, Warren G. Harding, and Harry S. Truman entered the office with justifiable trepidation, most of the others expected to hit the ground running, only to discover they hit the ground struggling. The president is the nation's chief executive, commander-in-chief, and, since 1941, leader of the free world, yet all new presidents are unqualified for this crushing combination. Bill Clinton later admitted: "I don't know that anyone feels adequate to it in the beginning." None were prepared; some never learned; few excelled.

In recognition of the legislative learning curve, first-year senators and representatives are appropriately described as freshmen, yet this condescending, though applicable, appellation has never been applied to a president. It is in that critical freshman year (which for the purposes of this book is defined as twelve to eighteen months due to different swearing-in and congressional convening dates) when a president learns—or does not learn—how to do the job. Each of them made mistakes attributable to freshman-year failings, which is why a fair analysis must separate the first year from subsequent years of every presidency, and since all presidents play to posterity, we can almost hear them pleading through the mists of time for a freshman-year exemption. Unlike monarchs of bygone

I

years—ranging in ability from Alexander the Great to far-from-great Louis XVI—who were generally trained for their future roles, democratically elected leaders, with the possible exception of John Quincy Adams, were not, an abundance of experience and innate ability notwithstanding.

No president has simultaneously been a congressionally attuned politician (LBJ), political philosopher (Jefferson and Madison), dynamic leader (Theodore Roosevelt), large-scale manager (Eisenhower), constitutional scholar (Wilson), foreign policy expert (John Quincy Adams and Buchanan), student of military strategy (the twelve general presidents), courage-tested veteran (from acclaimed soldier Washington to decorated sailor Kennedy), historian (Theodore Roosevelt, Wilson, and Kennedy), environmentalist (Theodore Roosevelt), great communicator (FDR and Reagan), or engineer (Hoover). Among other fields, sociology, science, and infrastructure should be included, and not one president was a trained economist, although through appointments, executive orders, tax initiatives, budget proposals, and vetoes, no one person has a greater impact on the financial affairs of the nation than the president. As a result, presidents must rely upon others; they must delegate. Yet, all too often our presidents lacked sufficient subject knowledge to make qualified appointments and, instead, based such decisions upon biases, partial knowledge, and uneven advice. In no field has this been more apparent than in selections for secretary of the Treasury, because presidents generally failed to distinguish between personal or even state budgets and the federal budget, the foremost differences being the national government's near limitless ability to print and borrow money and seemingly limitless ability to levy taxes, fees, and tariffs.

Several presidents—perhaps most—believed they understood the ongoing machinations of foreign governments and leaders, but generally believed a nation protected by two large moats—the Pacific and Atlantic Oceans—need not be overly concerned. They were wrong. Napoleon Bonaparte's actions directly impacted events leading to the War of 1812; Kaiser Wilhelm II's ill-advised decisions tripped one upon another until America was forced to stumble into World War I; and the theories of renowned British economist John Maynard Keynes allowed leaders and finance ministers who heeded his words to devise the economic means to fuel the massive military buildups of men and modern machines in Germany, Italy, and Japan that led to World War II (see Chapter 15, chart).

The American presidency is littered with first-year failures and missteps. Upon Franklin Roosevelt's unexpected-expected death, a stunned, self-deprecating Harry S. Truman unguardedly told a throng of astonished, grieving reporters, "Boys, if you ever pray, pray for me now. I don't know if you fellows ever had a load of hay fall on you, but when they told me yesterday what had happened, I felt like the moon, the stars, and all the planets had fallen on me." Known for bluntness and humility, Truman was only admitting what even the most egotistical and self-confident of new presidents thought or ought to have thought.

The presidency is so demanding and the burden so great that no one person could possibly be prepared for it, and of those whose areas of expertise and experience came closest, none came closer in the twentieth century than Herbert Hoover—whose one-term presidency was marred by a fatal flaw in the oxymoronic subjective science: economics.

Dwight D. Eisenhower led armies, NATO, and served as president of Columbia University, but had never run for political office, acknowledged a political affiliation, or dealt with the intricacies of global economic problems, and he admitted, "No man on earth knows what this job is all about."

Franklin Roosevelt had been governor of New York and assistant secretary of the Navy. The consummate politician, he was not an economist, political theorist, or diplomat, and his cousin, future general and Medal of Honor recipient Theodore Roosevelt Jr., derided his abilities: "Franklin is such poor stuff it seems improbable that he should be elected president."

Ulysses S. Grant was a failed businessman and successful general who too late discovered the camaraderie and trust inherent in war was not applicable to the devious machinations of political battlefields, including those of the man who straddled both endeavors, his wartime aide-de-camp and presidential private secretary.

Even precedent-setting George Washington, like Grant, was out of his element, confiding to his young friend and secretary of war, Maj. Gen. Henry Knox: "My movements to the chair of Government will be accompanied by feelings not unlike those of a culprit who is going to the place of his execution: so unwilling am I, in the evening of a life nearly consumed in public cares, to quit a peaceful abode for an ocean of difficulties, without that competency of political skill, abilities and inclination which is necessary to manage the helm." This astonishing admission was not false humility, and few who followed Washington would be as honest in self-appraisal.

It is in this context that the greatest office the nation can bestow upon an individual, the presidency, is also the greatest burden, an initially insurmountable burden. Those who emerged from their fateful first year as competent presidents possessed—or at least one or more of their closest advisors possessed—several traits in common: courage, judgment, a solid knowledge of history, mental flexibility, and one other—guile. Like the proverbial virtuous ambassadors sent abroad to lie for their country, successful presidents dissemble, a practice dubbed "plausible deniability" by the CIA in the 1960s and famously employed during the Reagan years. Indeed, national security demands as much in a world of realpolitik. Politicians lie to win; statesmen lie to govern. It was a distinction Richard Nixon failed to make and George Washington failed to embrace, which proved a hindrance for both men.

Each of our freshman presidents entered his trying first year of training and testing at the nation's expense unready for the humbling honor, though for different reasons in different periods. Although historians have defined eras through various criteria such as the party system, which relies upon political alignments as the basis for historical divisions, the following three more general eras—which are employed here to provide historical context for each president—take into account philosophical, political, technological, demographic, and economic changes that are more applicable when discussing presidential first-year errors.

From 1789 to the beginning of the Civil War in 1861, presidents were weighed down by the creation and expansion of a new nation—"A republic, if you can keep it," Benjamin Franklin said. Political philosophy, including the establishment of political parties, slavery, voting rights, a new nation's weak defenses, and equitable tariffs and taxes were among the divisive issues challenging them.

To Major General, Knox
New York.

My dear Sir,

        The Mail of the 30th brought me your favor
of the 23d — For which, and the regular information you
have had the goodness to transmit me of the state of things
in New York, I feel myself very much obliged, & thank
you accordingly.

        I feel for those Members of the New Congress,
who, hitherto, have given an unavailing attendance at the
theatre of action. — For myself, the delay may be compared to
a reprieve; for in confidence I tell you (with the world it
would obtain little credit) that my movements to the Chair
of Government will be accompanied by feelings not unlike those
of a culprit who is going to the place of his execution; so unwilling
am I, in the evening of life nearly consumed in public cares,
to quit a peaceful abode for an Ocean of difficulties, without
that competency of political skill, abilities and inclination
which is necessary to manage the helm. — I am sensible that
I am embarking the voice of the people, and a good name of my
own, on this voyage; but what returns will be made for them —
Heaven alone can foretell. — Integrity and firmness is all
I can promise, these, be the voyage long or short shall never
forsake me although I may be deserted by all men; for of the
consolations which are to be derived from these, under any

                                circumstances,

George Washington to Henry Knox, April 1, 1789

From the Civil War to America's 1917 entrance into World War I, industrialization, Robber Baron monopolization, technological advances, labor and social unrest, demographic dislocation, expanded global trade with a consequent global naval presence, and a flirtation with imperialism compounded the presidents' problems. During this period, the earlier era's idealism and debates over political philosophy came face to face with practical implementation in an increasingly complex world. Prior to the twentieth century, the White House was akin to an overworked single practitioner's understaffed, under-financed law office. From 1901 on, it increasingly began to resemble the domain of a major corporation's chief executive officer, including its corresponding staff, budget, and perquisites.

The modern era began with World War I, the war to end wars, which, while horribly failing in its purpose, did change the world map, not always for the better as arbitrary boundaries in the Balkans (Yugoslavia in particular) and the Mideast would later reveal. Empires were destroyed and countries created. At least fifteen million people died in the conflict and at least fifty million more perished from the subsequent Spanish Flu pandemic. These horrors spawned the peacetime euphoria and excesses that led to the Great Depression, which in turn led to World War II and another spurt in technological advances. Its aftermath compelled a unity of purpose and had a liberating and empowering effect upon women, minorities, and young citizens, dramatically enlarging the workforce, college enrollments, and the electorate. With World War I, the United States became a major world player; with World War II, the world leader. And because the president has greater reach in foreign affairs than in any other aspect of the constitutionally defined position, presidential duties mushroomed—as did the Presidents' Paradox.

CHAPTER 1

THE MODEL OTHERS FAILED
TO FOLLOW

GEORGE WASHINGTON—PRECEDENTS
1789–1797

Born/Died: 1732 Pope's Creek, VA–1799 Mount Vernon, VA
Education: No formal education
Occupation: Planter
Political Party: Aligned with Hamilton and others who would form the Federalist Party
Government Service: President of the Constitutional Convention 1787, Delegate to the Continental Congress 1774–1775
Military Service: General and Commander in Chief of the United Colonies; American Revolution, Virginia Militia in the French and Indian War

If leadership is a form of genius, George Washington was a genius. No military genius, Washington lost more battles than any other American general. No political theorist, Washington required tutoring from his young friend James Madison. No deep thinker, Washington relied upon the minds of others, especially Madison, Alexander Hamilton, and

President George Washington as a general during the American Revolution, depicted in *Washington Crossing the Delaware*
EMANUEL LEUTZE, COURTESY OF THE METROPOLITAN MUSEUM OF ART

Thomas Jefferson. Undereducated, the first president found an ally in silence. He had more judgment than intelligence, the sort of judgment that led him to appoint people he knew to be more intelligent and better read than himself. It was mental inflexibility that led to his freshman-year mistakes, a deficiency he would eventually overcome as he and the office grew. However, none of his successors fully followed his model, a model combining restrained political ambition with honest self-appraisal and unquestioned courage.

George Washington was many people. He may not have stood up in the boat while leading troops across the Delaware as depicted in the famous Leutze painting, though the calm aloofness portrayed in that work captured his military mask. A year later, in the body- and mind-numbing winter of 1777-78, he strode beneath the literal and figurative clouds darkening Valley Forge, surrounded by his suffering troops, yet he was alone. It was there, where more men succumbed to disease than died in all of his battles, that he perfected the façade which would lift him a man above men.

There had always been a distant side to his makeup. A jovial, comfortable conversationalist at home in Virginia or among friends in the parlors of Philadelphia and New York, he could become serious, silent, and stoic when issues of consequence were at hand. Washington merged this formidable, nearly unapproachable persona with a statue-like bearing that seemed to make his towering (for the time) six-plus feet even taller. When in this mode, a slightly raised eyebrow, slim smile, pursed lips, or hint of frown was sufficient to convey expectation or opinion. So effective and unnatural was this technique, it is almost certain that like an actor getting into character, he consciously developed it over time. It was an image reinforced by the implied threat of an infrequently employed, but explosive temper.

Washington had been a surveyor, sometime soldier, part-time legislator, successful land speculator, lifelong planter, and one of an eventual twelve slave-holding presidents. As a young colonial militia officer, he had tried and failed to gain a commission in the regular British Army, a fortuitous rejection that would change the course of world history. Years later, when the American colonies revolted, Washington once again played his hand for promotion, arriving in Philadelphia as a member of the Continental Congress attired in full military uniform. The Revolution had begun in the northern colonies, and John Adams of Massachusetts, ever the calculating attorney and desperately needing southern support, lobbied Congress to appoint the tall, taciturn Virginian as commander of the Continental Army. It was an alignment of stars. The politics of geography had conspired to bind these two dissimilar men, the general and his advocate, later to become the president and vice president/presidential successor.

Washington's service as a colonel of colonial militia during the French and Indian War had simultaneously won him fame for courage and disparagement for amateurish and impetuous tactics. His dismal performance in the ensuing years of the Revolution would confirm the doubts of detractors, but Adams never wavered. Between the successful 1775 Siege of Boston and the war-ending 1781 Siege of Yorktown, most of Washington's battles were lost, but he understood the larger picture. Protracted warfare could wear down the enemy; survival rather than tactical victories could win the war. To implement such a strategy, the initially untried, poorly trained, poorly equipped, underfed, rarely paid army of regulars and unreliable militia had to remain viable and in the field, no small goal when confronting the larger, professional, dominant British Army and an all-powerful British Navy capable of projecting its reach to most of the colonies' significant cities.

Washington epitomized the power of personality in war, for leadership, not generalship, kept his army together. His unimaginative and defective tactical dispositions at the Battles of Long Island and Brandywine cost him, respectively, New York and Philadelphia. Conversely, his complex plan for the Battle of Germantown entailed a nighttime concentration of multiple columns on the battlefield similar to his smaller-scale successes at Trenton and Princeton ten months earlier. On this larger scale, the difficult maneuver proved to be beyond the ability of Washington and his subordinates alike. Still, his commanding presence and innate leadership motivated the troops, despite his tactical and their military shortcomings. Likewise, leadership, rather than legislative, philosophical, or political expertise, would be the cornerstone of his presidential success, despite a near fatal failing.

The American Revolution came to a successful close with the signing of the Treaty of Paris in 1783, and Washington could have continued as the commanding general of the new country's army or become the nation's king or president—both were offered. He wanted none of it. He simply wanted to return to Mount Vernon and his wife, Martha. Meanwhile, America's first attempt at self-government imploded. The loose union of thirteen states created by the Articles of Confederation had simply not worked, and Washington was called upon to preside over the Constitutional Convention where it was hoped a new, stronger federal union could be created. As always, he followed the dictates of duty.

The convention proceeded with virtually no input from Washington, a man clearly more comfortable presiding than debating, and the Constitution was drafted and ratified by eleven of the thirteen states. George Washington was then unanimously chosen as the first president by the new Electoral College.

He was not pleased.

He had never held high political office and believed himself unqualified by meager education and experience to do so. Further, he looked upon himself as a gentleman planter whose vocation was running his Mount Vernon plantation. To him, military and political services were civic duties.

As the failed government faded through the winter of 1789 and the Constitution brought a new government to life with the coming of spring, the new nation's reluctant father—perpetually land-rich and cash-poor—borrowed the necessary money and traveled to New York to be sworn in as the first president of the United States of America. Martha Washington, even more hesitant than her husband, would follow later, expressing her disappointment in a letter to Mercy Otis Warren, the famed patriot writer and wife of Gen. James Warren: "I will not, however, contemplate with too much regret disappointments that were enevitable, though the generals feelings and my own were perfectly in unison with respect to our predilctions for privet life, yet I cannot blame him for having acted according to his ideas of duty in obaying the voice of his country." Clearly, George and Martha Washington were the nation's most reluctant First Couple.

The new president understood what he was being called upon to do, though not necessarily how to do it, lamenting rather than bragging, "I walk on untrodden ground. There is scarcely any part of my conduct which may not hereafter be drawn into precedent."

Aware of his shortcomings, and relying upon a superb ability to judge talent, he brought together some of the finest minds the country would ever witness, minds he knew to be far superior to his own. It was a congregating of talent Franklin Roosevelt would attempt to emulate with his Depression-era "Brain Trust" 144 years later.

Secretary of the Treasury Alexander Hamilton, Washington's wartime military aide, born of humble origins in the West Indies, was a self-made man who received a college education, practiced law, entered New York society, and assumed an aristocratic air. Intelligent, handsome, and brave, he was proposed for the Cabinet position by his future political foe, Thomas Jefferson's good friend, member of the House of Representatives, and "Father of the Constitution," James Madison. So successful did Hamilton prove to be, he could rightly have laid claim to being the "Financial Father of the Country."

Jefferson, himself, only agreed to serve as secretary of State at the behest and persistent prodding of the president-elect, for, like Washington, he preferred the serene comforts of a gentleman farmer on his Virginia estates. This tall, good-looking, gangling cavalier was America's Renaissance man, a scientist, architect, inventor, multilingual graduate of William & Mary, and primary author of the Declaration of Independence (derived in part from John Locke's *The Second Treatise of Civil Government*).

The Washington, Jefferson, Madison, and Hamilton relationships were intertwined and complex. The first three were Virginia aristocrats, friends, and slaveholders. Hamilton, ill at ease among Jefferson and Madison, was close to Washington, the general he had served throughout the trials of the long war. Yet, it was Washington, comfortable among landed gentry and rough-hewn troops alike, who was reticent during philosophical discussions. In contrast to his college-educated associates, he barely had the equivalent of an elementary school education.

All four were fervent patriots and ardent Federalists (those who supported ratification of the Constitution, not to be confused with members of the future Federalist Party). Hamilton and Madison, along with future Chief Justice of the Supreme Court (known as Chief Justice of the United States after 1866), Washington's friend, John Jay, had authored the Federalist Papers, those well-argued philosophical documents written to ensure the Constitution's ratification and which to this day continue to provide a window into the Founding Fathers' original intent. The only other common thread—minor, yet interesting—was red hair, though it was the non-redhead, Princeton-educated Madison, the youngest and, at 5'4", by far the shortest, who wielded the most influence, leading what would become the Democratic-Republicans in the House of Representatives while counseling, advising, and tutoring the new president, nineteen years his senior. To New York society, the towering, political pupil and his diminutive tutor must have looked like father and son. Onlookers could not have perceived the role reversal they were watching.

General Washington was the man to execute a plan with single-minded determination and vigor; President Washington was not. He took the Constitution's separation of powers to heart, even to extreme. After an embarrassing attempt visiting Congress to seek "advice and consent" as required by the Constitution for an executive appointment, he realized he was out of his league amid those educated, experienced legislators from colonial days who questioned and debated him, he who was accustomed to giving orders. For some time thereafter, Washington refused to lobby Congress on his own proposals, and the executive branch accordingly began to diminish for lack of an advocate. A bill establishing uniform weights and measures and another establishing a mint did not initially pass, and Congress even refused to impose increased tariffs on Britain as a means of forcing British troops from their posts on the western frontiers as required by the Treaty of Paris.

By standing aside, Washington was setting the new government and its new Constitution on a collision course with failure. He came to the conclusion that it was his prerogative to propose, but only Congress could dispose, omitting the obvious corollary of presidential proposal power: advocacy, those arm-twisting arguments later to be known as using the bully pulpit by President Theodore Roosevelt or jawboning by Presidents John F. Kennedy and Lyndon Johnson. Thankfully, Washington's ill-conceived non-precedent lacked legs and ended with his presidency. Meanwhile, it was this same freshman-year flaw of inflexibility that nearly allowed the weight of three words to collapse the new republic: Residence, Funding, and Assumption.

Residence: Where would the nation's permanent capital be established? During the Revolution, the Continental Congress met in Philadelphia when British troops occupied New York. Then, with the war won and the Constitution in place, the first United States Congress was able to meet in New York, the political and financial capital of the country, and northern financiers wanted to keep it that way. The agrarian South, fearful of undue financial influence on the government, did not. This issue pitted New Yorker Hamilton against Virginians Jefferson and Madison. Their fellow Virginian, the president, was barely engaged.

Funding: The 1781 surrender of General Cornwallis's British Army to American and French forces at Yorktown brought Revolutionary War hostilities to an end two years before the peace treaty was signed, leaving the Continental Congress free to concentrate on domestic troubles. Unable to pay the troops in full, Congress issued certificates in place of money. During the ensuing years, many veterans—probably most veterans, including Washington himself—sold some or all of their certificates for pennies (five cents in Washington's case) on the dollar to speculators, who included Abigail Adams, his future vice president's wife. Having actively purchased certificates for years through her uncle due to laws restricting women's rights to hold property, she wrote him on January 17, 1790, eight days after Treasury Secretary Hamilton issued his first report to Congress: "I have thought whether it would not be best to sell the indents [state bonds] & purchase [deep discount] certificates."

Speculators often resold these certificates, especially to America's financial allies, the Dutch. America's sole foreign minister in 1787, Thomas Jefferson, then serving in Paris, assured foreign creditors America would stand behind its debts. So, by 1790 with the Constitution and Congress in place, Hamilton introduced the Funding Bill authorizing Congress to redeem the certificates. Madison countered with legislation called "Discrimination," so called because it would redeem the certificates at less than face value and only pay the original holders, the Revolutionary soldiers who had won the war. While Washington's heart was with Madison and the veterans, Hamilton convinced him otherwise. A nation must honor its financial obligations or face the devastating consequences of default. After all, the certificates were negotiable instruments, not unlike modern treasury bills, which the US Department of the Treasury guarantees are "backed by the full faith and credit of the U.S. government."

Assumption: Simultaneously, an even larger issue had gone unresolved. During the Revolution, the states had incurred substantial debts to support the war effort. Some, like Virginia, had subsequently paid most of their obligations; others in New England and the Carolinas remained heavily encumbered. To thwart the fiasco of multiple state defaults, Hamilton introduced the Assumption Bill authorizing Congress to assume the states' debts. Whereas the funding of government-issued certificates to soldiers was clearly a federal obligation, the assumption of state debts was not, and this created a congressional impasse.

For five months in 1790, the Funding and Assumption bills languished in Congress. Speculators became uneasy when the inability of Congress to pass Assumption threatened Funding, and they began selling and buying certificates with each congressional gyration. Foreign lenders became unsettled. Would the young nation honor its debts or would it default? Meanwhile (and not for the last time), the New England states and South Carolina threatened to leave the Union if Assumption failed, while Rhode Island had still not joined the Union. The United States of America had become disunited in the first year of its constitutional existence. In the crisis, Washington spoke up—only in private—writing to his friend David Stuart on June 15, 1790:

> *I do not mean however, from what I have here said, to justify the conduct of Congress in all its movements; for some of these movements, in my opinion, have been injudicious and others unseasonable, whilst the questions of Assumption; Residence and other matters have been agitated with a warmth and intemperance; with prolixity and threats; which it is to be feared has lessened the dignity of that body and decreased that respect which was once entertained for it. . . .*
>
> *As an evidence of it, our reputation has risen in every part of the Globe; and our credit, especially in Holland, has got higher than that of any Nation in Europe (and where our funds are above par) as appears by Official advices just received. But the conduct we seem to be pursuing will soon bring us back to our late disreputable condition. . . .*
>
> *The question of Assumption has occupied a great deal of time, and no wonder; for it is certainly a very important one; and, under proper restrictions, and scrutiny into Accounts will be found, I conceive to be just. The Cause in which the expenses of the War were incurred, was a Common Cause. The States (in Congress) declared it so at the beginning and pledged themselves to stand by each other. If then, some States were harder pressed than others, or from particular or local circumstances contracted heavier debts, it is but reasonable when this fact is ascertained (though it is a sentiment I have not made known here) that an allowance ought to be made them when due credit is given to others. Had the invaded, and hard pressed States believed the case*

would have been otherwise; opposition in them would very soon, I believe, have changed to submission; and given a different termination to the War.

With the nation teetering on the edge of the abyss, the man who led the Continental Army to victory and chaired the Constitutional Convention was publicly silent. The absence of message comported with his evolved view of the president's constitutional powers and limitations. He was not a member of Congress, and he had no interest, right, or desire to join in that body's debates, nor did he believe he was qualified to do so. On the other hand, his Cabinet members had a constitutionally mandated duty to report to Congress, and he and the nation were saved by them.

While out walking at the height of the crisis, Jefferson ran into Hamilton, who was uncharacteristically disheveled and distraught because his former Federalist Papers' collaborator, the president's mentor and Jefferson's personal friend and political ally James Madison, was leading the opposition to his debt plans. The nation was in jeopardy. Jefferson quickly stepped in where Washington had stepped out, inviting the two men for dinner, perhaps the most famous dinner in American history. Among the Founding Fathers, these three were the Founding Patriarchs—three brilliant patriots who devised a nation-saving compromise over a meal. Madison would not drop his personal objections to the Hamilton Funding and Assumption plans, while simultaneously ensuring enough votes for their passage. In exchange, Hamilton agreed to throw his support behind the effort to establish the nation's permanent capital along the banks of the Potomac River between Maryland and Virginia, far away from the influence of his financial friends in New York. While some historians give less credit to the dinner, and Jefferson later claimed he was duped, the fact remains that the men met, a compromise was reached, and the president was not present.

The great crisis of 1790 did create a negative precedent. The president's aloof silence, whether motivated by insecurity, idealism, or even ill-fitting false teeth, was a mistake, and never again would a president choose to disengage from the political debate. One way or another, presidents would make their views known. Even President Calvin Coolidge, "Silent Cal," was loud compared to Quiet George.

The amity of "The Dinner" did not last. Washington refused to accept the rise of what Madison called factions (which we know today as political parties), especially after the ideological split between Hamilton's Federalists (not to be confused with the Constitution-supporting Federalists) and the new Jefferson-Madison Democratic-Republicans became libelous and vicious, mostly through surrogate newspaper editors. Yet, as in the Revolution, Washington equated survival with victory. As he had once kept the army intact, so he kept the government intact. It was the key to his success both as a general and as a president. Despite the fact that he was more aligned with Hamilton's strong central government concepts, he remained closest to Madison. When Madison urged him to serve a second term, Washington confided he "found himself deficient in many of the essential qualifications, owing to his inexperience in the forms of public business, [and] his unfitness to judge of legal questions arising out of the Constitution." Even so, Hamilton and Jefferson joined Madison, imploring him to serve.

Washington was unique among successful presidents. His courage counterbalanced educational shortfalls and political naiveté, and although his sound Cabinet appointees more than made up for his lack of guile, he struggled with inflexibility. As president he was slow in adapting to the political environment, and while he eventually grew with the office, it was in the intangible attribute of leadership he excelled. This quality, more than any other, lifted him to the pinnacle of the presidential pyramid.

His erstwhile Revolutionary War foe, King George III, twice dubbed him the "greatest character of the age," first after Washington relinquished his military command in 1783 and again after refusing to run for a third term as president in 1796. Further perspective came fifteen years after Washington's death. It was 1814, James Madison was president, the War of 1812 was not going well, the British blockade had brought foreign trade to a standstill, and the New England states were talking secession and a separate peace. In the midst of the crisis, Washington's friend-turned-foe, Thomas Jefferson, saw the first president in legacy's light:

His mind was great and powerful, without being of the very first order; . . . It was slow in operation, being little aided by invention or imagination, but sure in conclusion. Hence the common remark of his officers, of the advantage he derived from councils of war, where hearing all suggestions, he selected whatever was best. . . . But if deranged during the course of the action . . . he was slow in re-adjustment. The consequence was, that he often failed in the field, and rarely against an enemy in station, as at Boston and York[town]. He was incapable of fear, meeting personal dangers with the calmest unconcern.

Perhaps the strongest feature in his character was prudence, . . . refraining if he saw a doubt, but, when once decided, going through with his purpose, whatever obstacles opposed. His integrity was most pure, his justice the most inflexible. . . . He was, indeed, in every sense of the words, a wise, a good, and a great man. . . .

In public, when called on for a sudden opinion, he was unready, short and embarrassed. Yet he wrote readily, rather diffusely, in an easy and correct style. This he had acquired by conversation with the world, for his education was merely reading, writing and common arithmetic, to which he added surveying at a later day. . . .

On the whole, his character was, in its mass, perfect, in nothing bad, in few points indifferent; and it may truly be said, that never did nature and fortune combine more perfectly to make a man great. . . . For his was the singular destiny and merit, of leading the armies of his country successfully through an arduous war, for the establishment of its independence; of conducting its councils through the birth of a government, new in its forms and principles, until it had settled down into a quiet and orderly train.

CHAPTER 2

WITCH HUNTERS: SEDITION AND MCCARTHYISM

JOHN ADAMS (1797) AND DWIGHT D. EISENHOWER (1953)

John Adams and Dwight D. Eisenhower were of similar minds. Adams, the attorney, and Eisenhower, the athlete, hated to lose—which their displays of temper amply demonstrated. Both men could be congenial until things went awry. When they did, Adams could become overbearing, stubborn, argumentative, and surly. Eisenhower's pate would turn red, his mood would sour, and he would pound his desk or display some other form of immature displeasure. Eisenhower put on a better face with his famous warm smile and outgoing personality, but beneath the façade an Adams-like volcano was merely awaiting eruption.

Adams was a courtroom brawler, Eisenhower an aggressive almost scientific poker and bridge player, who became a predatory card player after an injury ended his West Point football career. Later, he took up golf, displaying a competitive immaturity, in one instance throwing his entire bag of clubs at a fellow player, his doctor. And when he won, whether in golf, poker, or bridge, his overt gleefulness was described as childlike.

The Adams-Eisenhower bad behaviors emanated from wills to win. Both men were canny, clever, perceptive, knowledgeable, honorable patriots with full faith in their own judgments, and most of their peers readily agreed. What stood in contrast was their limited ability to absorb defeats, unusual for a general who knows the loss of a single soldier is tragic and the loss of a battle potentially catastrophic, though neither event can be allowed to hamper decision-making. Casualties come with war. Likewise in concept if not in scale, most attorneys know unpleasant compromises and negative court decisions come with their profession. Eisenhower, the athlete turned general, and Adams, the attorney turned statesman, were not of these molds, and both brought a petulant brilliance to the presidency that would impact each man's freshman year.

JOHN ADAMS—SEDITION
1797–1801

Born/Died: 1735 Braintree (now Quincy), MA–1826 Quincy, MA
Education: Harvard College (became Harvard University in 1780)
Occupation: Lawyer
Political Party: Federalist
Government Service: Vice President 1789–1797, Ambassador (Britain) 1785–1788, and (Dutch Republic) 1782–1788, Diplomat (France) 1778–1782, MA Delegate to the Continental Congress 1774–1778
Military Service: None
Preceded by: George Washington (finances placed on sound footing; established precedents such as two terms; put down Whiskey Rebellion without conflict; maintained peace)

On March 2, 1796, Napoleon Bonaparte, twenty-seven years old, was placed in command of the French Army of Italy, commencing a nineteen-year period of fame, power, and failure that would affect three American presidents, beginning with sixty-one-year-old John Adams, elected president of the United States on November 4, 1796 (and confirmed by the Electoral College in December). Napoleon's subsequent stunning military successes in Italy influenced the continental powers of Europe

as well as geopolitical relations between France, Britain, and the United States. In
1798, the French government
formed the Army of England
preparatory to a cross-channel
invasion of its most intracta-
ble enemy and placed Napoleon in command.

On June 24, 1796, just
over four months before the
election of Adams, the United
States ratified the Jay Treaty
(named for US Supreme
Court Chief Justice John Jay),
ironing out problems left over
with Britain from the American Revolution and establishing limited commerce rights
between the two nations.
Pro-British Federalists such

President John Adams
GILBERT STUART, LIBRARY OF CONGRESS

as Vice President John Adams and former Secretary of the Treasury
Alexander Hamilton hailed it; President George Washington was uncer-
tain and had sought advice from Hamilton before signing it; pro-French
Democratic-Republicans including former Secretary of State Thomas
Jefferson and Virginia Rep. James Madison claimed the United States
was unwisely taking sides in the British-French belligerency, a segment
of what would come to be known as the Napoleonic Wars. Certainly, the
French took this view.

Then, as quickly as he took the oath of office in March 1797, President Adams was confronted with France's ongoing response, the capture
of 316 US merchant ships between July 1796 and June 1797 by French
privateers (a form of government-sanctioned piracy—memorably used
by English Queen Elizabeth I against Spanish gold ships in the sixteenth
century—shrouded in deniability, albeit, implausible deniability). The

Timeline: XYZ Affair, Sedition Act, Quasi War, and Louisiana Purchase

	Year		Americans	French
June 24	1795		Jay Treaty with Britain ratified; France views as enemy alliance	
	1796	Mar. 2		Napoleon appointed commander of the French Army of Italy
		July →		French privateers seize 316 U.S. merchant ships
Nov. 4			John Adams elected president; Thomas Jefferson vice president	
Mar. 4	1797		Adams and Jefferson sworn in	
May		June	Adams sends envoys to France	
		June 7		French Consul General Létombe informs Paris of Jefferson's recommendation to drag out peace negotiations
		Oct. 26		Napoleon placed in command of the French Army of England for cross-channel invasion
Mar. 4	1798		Adams receives envoys' message of French extortion attempts	
Mar. 21			Jefferson urges patience to give Napoleon time to invade Britain	

	Americans			French
Apr. 3	Adams reports extortion attempts as the XYZ Affair to Congress			
July 7	Congress revokes the 1778 Treaty of Alliance with France; Quasi War with France begins			
July 14	Congress passes the Sedition Act			
		1799	Nov. 10	Napoleon becomes First Consul—leader of France
Sep. 30	Convention of 1800 ends Quasi War	1800		
Mar. 4	President Thomas Jefferson sworn in	1801	Oct. 1	Preliminary Treaty of Amiens
		1802	Mar. 25	Treaty of Amiens between France and Britain
			Aug. 1	Napoleon becomes First Consul for Life
Apr. 30	Napoleon sells Louisiana Territory to U.S. (acquired by Spain from France in 1764 and France from Spain in 1800)	1803		

president soon sent emissaries to explain the Jay Treaty and seek peace. He should have looked over his shoulder. There was a problem. A flaw in the Constitution—one which would soon be remedied with ratification of the Twelfth Amendment—provided for the runner-up in a presidential election to serve as vice president, because the Constitution's framers had not foreseen the rise of political parties, though they soon would as the political fissures widened almost from the start of Washington's presidency. By the election of 1796, this oversight meant John Adams, a Federalist, would have Thomas Jefferson, a Democratic-Republican, serving as vice president, an awkward situation at best, a near-traitorous one at worst, as Adams was about to discover.

Jefferson, his longtime friend from their 1776 Declaration of Independence collaboration, was now Adams's political opponent, the man he had just barely defeated for the presidency. There would be no collaborating this time; Jefferson took little interest in the vice presidency and a great deal of interest in leadership of the opposition. He and his fellow Democratic-Republicans were overtly and, in the case of Jefferson, covertly pro-French, whereas the Federalists, and especially the more elitist High Federalists, were staunchly pro-British, a schism pitting the two parties not just on opposing sides in general, but on opposing sides in a war.

In this vein, French Consul General Philippe-Henry-Joseph de Létombe, writing from Philadelphia, then the US capital, sent an astonishing communication to his superiors in Paris. In a letter dated June 7, 1797, de Létombe claimed Vice President Jefferson told him: "Mr. Adams is vain, suspicious, and stubborn, of an excessive self-regard, taking counsel with nobody. . . . But his presidency will only last five years [*sic*]; he is only president by three [Electoral College] votes. . . . It is for France, great, generous, at the summit of her glory, to pretend to take no notice, to be patient, to precipitate nothing, and all will return to order. . . . [D]rag out the negotiations at length, and mollify them by the urbanity of the proceedings."

We cannot know if Jefferson actually said such things. We do know the sentiments were correct as Jefferson confirmed in his March 21, 1798, letter to James Madison: "As to do nothing, and to gain time, is everything with us [Democratic-Republicans], I propose that they [Congress] shall come to a resolution of adjournment 'in order to go home and consult their constituents on the great crisis of American affairs now existing.' Besides gaining time enough by this to allow the descent [Napoleon's invasion, which was soon called off as impractical because Britannia ruled the seas] on England to have its effect here as well as there, it will be a means of exciting the whole body of people."

Due to these exhortations or greed or both, the peace negotiators sent by Adams were met with deceit. Three French intermediaries, dubbed X, Y, and Z by Adams, attempted to extort bribes as a condition of peace (see Chapter 3's section on Jefferson for a discussion of Talleyrand, the man behind the scandal). The Americans refused, and Adams received the coded information one year to the day after his inauguration on March 4, 1798. The following month, under congressional pressure, he exposed the gambit known as the XYZ Affair to Congress in executive (closed) session. It immediately became public and just as quickly the *casus belli* for the Quasi War. The majority of Americans, who until then had felt a sense of indebtedness to France for its crucial assistance during the American Revolution and who, in many cases, sported the tri-color symbol of the French Revolution, suddenly turned hostile. War fever was afoot, and on July 7, 1798, Congress revoked the 1778 Treaty of Alliance with France, an act viewed by both the French and Vice President Thomas Jefferson as a declaration of war. One week later, on Bastille Day, the 1789 day celebrated as the beginning of the French Revolution, Congress passed the Sedition Act.

When on the receiving end, freedom of speech is the most difficult of all freedoms to stomach. So it was for thin-skinned John Adams, who, in a direct assault on the First Amendment, signed the short-lived Sedition Act. In an instant, a right had been wronged when it became a federal crime to "write, print, utter or publish . . . any false, scandalous and malicious writing or writings against the government of the United States . . . the Congress . . . or the president . . . with intent to defame."

As an elitist who championed the common man, there was a dichotomy to his thinking. For example, as vice president he had strongly lobbied to have the president addressed as "His Majesty the President," or the title initially passed by a congressional committee: "His highness, the

President of the United States of America, and Protector of the Rights of the Same." The result was derision and rebuke, with Washington opting instead for "The President of the United States," or simply, "Mr. President." All this gave fodder to his political opponents, who claimed Adams was a monarchist.

Actually, he was a lawyer and owner of a small farm in Braintree, Massachusetts. Unlike Washington, he relied upon the power of argument rather than the power of personality. A lawyer through and through, his combative advocacy often blinded him to the tempo of the times or the sensibilities of contemporaries. As such, it was difficult to dissuade him once his course was set. In 1798 it was set, albeit reluctantly, on what came to be known as the Quasi War, America's undeclared naval war with France.

Toward that end, the Sedition Act was rationalized as a wartime measure. Aimed at French émigrés and their Jeffersonian allies, the new law sought to quell free speech, and fourteen people, mostly newspapermen and pamphleteers, were prosecuted, fined, and jailed for such statements as declaiming Adams's "continued grasp for power," calling him "a repulsive pedant, a gross hypocrite and unprincipled oppressor," characterizing him as "a continual tempest of malignant passions," and calling for "downfall to the tyrants of America."

There is no question Adams faced vicious attacks from pro-French Jeffersonians, nor is there any question that his Federalist allies responded in kind. Such unrestrained emanations rooted in the First Amendment's free speech clause were common during the nation's first seventy years, leading to violent altercations, fights, duels, and lawsuits, even in the halls of Congress. (More than fifty years later, on March 4, 1849, Massachusetts Whig Rep. Horace Mann wrote, "There were two regular fist-fights in the House, in one of which blood flowed freely; and one in the Senate.") The amendment had spawned what could be called America's Anti-Decorum Age, and despite his attempts, Adams was not the man to thwart it.

With his sensitive and prickly personality, Adams equated overblown free speech with sedition and made the situation worse. In fairness, he—like all the Founding Fathers—was treading new waters. Of them, only Washington showed restraint, for there was nothing restrained about the writings and speeches of Jefferson, Madison, and Hamilton, especially of those filtered through surrogates. In many respects Adams was the most moderate of them all, constantly seeking consensus, usually falling short.

He kept Washington's Cabinet members as his own, another clear first-year error since they actually answered to Hamilton. He did generally adhere to Washington's precedents, only veering from the path of moderation when the vitriol of his opponents exceeded the limits of his toleration. This and his wife's prompting led him to sign a law that struck at the core of civil liberties, and neglected to distinguish between name-calling and defamation. His acknowledged chief advisor and wife, Abigail Adams, gave him the excuse if not the logic: "Yet daringly do the vile incendiaries keep up in Bache's [news]paper the most wicked and base, violent and culminating abuse [and] nothing will have effect until Congress passes a Sedition Bill." Democratic-Republican newspaper editor Benjamin Franklin Bache, who had written of "the blind, bald, crippled, toothless, querulous Adams," was arrested in 1798 for violating the Sedition Act.

Between the Adams presidency and the Civil War, presidents generally practiced restraint on the subject of free speech. War and Abraham Lincoln changed this. With states seceding following his election and more after his call for military action, Lincoln suspended habeas corpus and imprisoned several thousand people who were "guilty of any disloyal practice," which led to the arrest of newspaper editors critical of his war policies.

The issue would finally come to a head with the 1964 *New York Times v. Sullivan* case, when the Supreme Court ruled: "[T]he First Amendment protects the publication of all statements, even false ones, about the conduct of public officials except when statements are made with actual malice (with knowledge that they are false or in reckless disregard of their truth or falsity)."

In conjunction with the Sedition Act, three Alien Acts were also passed. Of these, only the Alien Enemies Act was significant. Although never actually enforced by Adams, it remains on the books and has been appropriately and inappropriately used to detain or deport people considered "dangerous to the peace and safety of the United States," including the unjust detention of Japanese-Americans during World War II.

The most reactive responses to the Alien and Sedition Acts were anonymously written by Vice President Thomas Jefferson and future

President James Madison in their Kentucky and Virginia Resolutions, the postulates being that states had the right to ignore what they deemed to be unconstitutional laws, setting the stage for the near secession of the New England states during the War of 1812, the anti-tariff Nullification Crisis of 1832, and southern secession in 1860-61.

A more tolerant president could have resolved the issues in 1797. Instead, tolerance came from an unexpected quarter. On November 10, 1799, Napoleon Bonaparte became First Consul of France, and soon after sought an end to the undeclared war with America. Peace came the following year on September 30 with the Convention of 1800, and just over a month later, Thomas Jefferson, the unabashed ally of the French, was elected president of the United States. The despised Alien and Sedition Acts were terminated or ignored as quickly as possible, and people convicted of sedition were pardoned.

Adams had become an isolated president, facing hostility from every direction. His own Federalists were led by a disdainful Alexander Hamilton, not him, while his principal opponent and leader of the opposition was his vice president and former (and future) friend, Thomas Jefferson. He sought conciliation and moderation only to end up fighting a needless war and signing some of the most controversial and obviously unconstitutional acts in American history, all in his first year in office, which left him seeking extrications for the balance of his one-term presidency.

DWIGHT D. EISENHOWER—MCCARTHYISM
1953–1961

Born/Died: 1890 Denison, TX–1969 Washington, DC
Education: US Military Academy (West Point)
Occupation: Professional Army officer
Political Party: Republican
Military Service: General of the Armies (five star); Supreme Allied Commander in European Theater of Operations World War II, under General MacArthur in the Philippines in 1930s, stateside World War I

Gen. Dwight D. Eisenhower at a press conference
LIBRARY OF CONGRESS

Preceded by: Harry S. Truman (FDR dies at beginning of fourth term; allows Soviet occupation of Eastern Europe; atomic bombs used; World War II ends; Marshall Plan rebuilds Europe; General MacArthur rebuilds Japan; Cold War begins; Truman Doctrine saves Greece; NATO and UN established; Korean War begins 1950; armed forces integrated by executive order; fires MacArthur)

One hundred fifty-four years after John Adams's inauguration, Gen. Dwight D. Eisenhower, widely known as Ike, was running for president and Wisconsin Republican Sen. Joe McCarthy was running amok, trampling on free speech in his self-serving witch hunt for communists, even denouncing Ike's old boss: "[Gen. George C.] Marshall should not be confirmed [as Secretary of State] unless and until he convinces the Senate that he has learned the facts of life about communism."

Then, one month before the election, Ike's campaign came to Wisconsin, McCarthy's home turf, and the candidate's prepared remarks came to Marshall's defense. At that point, Eisenhower, in the lowest

29

Sixth Draft - Communism and Freedom

To defend freedom, in short, is -- first of all -- to respect

freedom. That respect demands another, quite simple kind of

respect -- respect for the integrity of fellow citizens who

enjoy their right to disagree. The right to question *challenge* a man's

judgment carries with it no automatic right to question his

honor.

Here I have a case in mind.
~~With respect to one case I shall be quite specific. I~~

~~know that~~ Charges of disloyalty have in the past been levelled

against General George C. Marshall. *I am not now discussing* Any ~~of his alleged~~ errors in

judgment *he may have made*, while serving in capacities other than military, ~~I am~~

~~not here discussing.~~ But I was privileged throughout the years

of World War II to know General Marshall personally, as Chief

of Staff of the Army. I know him, as a man and a soldier, to be

dedicated with singular selflessness and the profoundest

patriotism to the service of America. ~~Here we have a sobering~~

~~lesson of the way freedom must not defend itself.~~

Armed with this *our* clear and uncompromising respect for

freedom, how then shall we defend it?

Stet

Draft page, "Sixth Draft" of Eisenhower speech given on October 3, 1952, in
Milwaukee, Wisconsin, on "Communism and Freedom"

point of his distinguished career, chose to omit the pertinent phrase from his speech.

The expurgated portion of Eisenhower's October 3, 1952, speech:

"Here I have a case in mind. Charges of disloyalty have in the past been levelled against General George C. Marshall. I am not now discussing judgment he may have made while serving in capacities other than military. But I was privileged throughout the years of World War II to know General Marshall personally, as Chief of Staff of the Army. I know him, as a man and a soldier, to be dedicated with singular selflessness and profoundest patriotism to the service of America."

Why did Eisenhower omit this paragraph?

Born in Denison, Texas, Eisenhower was soon transplanted to Abilene, Kansas, where he grew up. Appointed to the US Military Academy at West Point, he graduated in 1915 in the "Class the Stars Fell On," so named because he and more than one-third of his classmates became generals during World War II, not unlike the Class of 1846 in the Civil War. He did not see action in World War I, and although highly regarded, he was still a major at the age of forty-five. Like Marshall, he served under the influential Gen. Fox Connor as well as Gen. John J. "Black Jack" Pershing, who had commanded the American Expeditionary Force (AEF) in World War I. His longest and most contentious service was as an aide to Gen. Douglas MacArthur, first in Washington, DC, and then the Philippines, a mutually unpleasant experience.

General Marshall kept a little black book filled with the names of promising officers, Eisenhower among them. When the United States entered World War II following the December 7, 1941, Japanese attack on Pearl Harbor, Marshall called upon Eisenhower to assist him in Washington after his first choice was killed in an airplane accident. Once again, Eisenhower excelled in staff work, and Marshall told him he would remain there. Not this time. Ike proved so adept at dealing with the British and was so attuned to Marshall's thinking, he was soon bound for London and eventual command of Allied forces in Europe.

Upon arriving in Britain, he was assigned a British driver, Kay Summersby.

Private lives are only of interest here when assessing presidential first-year failings, and Eisenhower's personal relationship with Summersby may have had something to do with his failure to defend Marshall against McCarthy's attacks.

Kay was Ike's pert, pretty Irish driver, near telepathic bridge partner, and constant companion. Her association with the "boss" was well known at headquarters, which included Eisenhower's son, John, just graduated from West Point on June 6, 1944, D-Day. It was the final year of World War II, and he was visiting the Supreme Headquarters Allied Expeditionary Forces in the European Theater of Operations (ETO), his father's command. Soon after, Ike had him accompany Kay on a trip to Washington and New York.

Decades later, then Brig. Gen. John D. Eisenhower and this author were conducting research for our respective books at the Military History Institute in Carlisle, Pennsylvania, when I asked if he had any thoughts about Summersby's new book, *Past Forgetting: My Love Affair with Dwight D. Eisenhower*, to which he matter-of-factly replied, "She gave him solace." In later interviews, John denied knowledge of an affair, or at least of a physical affair, and perhaps his term "solace" simply meant "comfort." The evidence is otherwise.

Ike's documented, handwritten, signed note to Summersby is particularly poignant: "Good night! There are lots of things I could wish to say—you know them. Good night." And Ike's classmate, friend, confidant, and highest-ranking American subordinate in the ETO, Gen. Omar N. Bradley, wrote:

> *Their close relationship is quite accurately portrayed, as far as my personal knowledge extends, in Kay's second book,* Past Forgetting. *Ike's son John published his father's personal letters to Mamie, in part to refute Kay's allegation that she and Ike were deeply in love. Many of those letters are obviously Ike's replies to probing letters from Mamie about his relationship with Kay. To my mind, Ike protests too much, thus defeating John's purpose. . . . [H]owever, I do not believe the story Harry Truman allegedly told Merle Miller for his book* Plain Speaking *that Ike wrote Marshall that he wanted to divorce Mamie to marry Kay.*

When the war in Europe ended, Ike returned to the United States. Kay, by then a US Army captain, was the only member of his staff not brought back to Washington, which is where the story gets murky, but significant. Why would he leave a trusted officer and companion behind? Merle Miller quoted President Harry S. Truman as saying Ike had written Army Chief of Staff General Marshall, informing him of plans to divorce his wife, Mamie, and marry Kay. According to Truman, Marshall erupted and threatened to ruin Ike's career. Although this version of events is debated by Bradley and others, another is documented. In a 1991 oral history, Truman's cousin, Lt. Gen. Louis W. Truman, confirmed:

So when I would come down I would go over to the White House and contact him [President Truman], I guess about every month or so, something like that. I mentioned to a man this morning, that that was when President Truman, Cousin Harry, mentioned the fact that he had offered support to Eisenhower to run for president, for the Democratic Party. Eisenhower turned him down. He also showed me the letter that he had written to Eisenhower. He had written that certain things would have to happen about his driver friend, or he was going to kick him [General Eisenhower] out. You probably have a letter here.

JOHNSON [interviewer]: He did make an issue of that [the relationship between General Eisenhower and Kay Summersby].

TRUMAN: Yes, he did, very definitely. He told me about that.

This may explain the animus that impelled Ike to leave Marshall at McCarthy's slanderous mercy. Otherwise, it was out of character. Eisenhower was an honorable man, and Marshall had been his mentor, the man who recommended his promotion from colonel to brigadier general to major general to lieutenant general to general in less than seventeen months (September 29, 1941–February 11, 1943). Both Eisenhower and Marshall and several other senior Army generals and Navy admirals were later promoted to five-star rank.

Eisenhower also claimed to personally know Marshall. It was not so. The aloof and upright Marshall revealingly said, "I have no feelings except those I reserve for Mrs. Marshall." Such an attitude, especially to the extent it encompassed the Summersby matter, may have been sufficient for Ike to rationalize a temporary lapse of loyalty when faced with the exigencies of a presidential campaign. Ike believed he needed Wisconsin's electoral votes, and his political advisors warned him not to cross swords with Senator McCarthy in the midst of the Second Red Scare (the first Red Scare over Soviet communism occurred at the end of World War I during the Wilson Administration) and in the midst of the Korean War then being waged against Chinese and North Korean communists (and, as we now know, Soviet fighter pilots).

Persisting in this vein as president, Eisenhower refused to confront McCarthy, believing the senator would simply fade away: "Nothing will be so effective in combating his particular kind of trouble-making as to ignore him." So, McCarthy carried on with the erroneously perceived blessing of the president, ruining in his wake innocent lives and promising careers, not once providing proof for any of his allegations.

Eisenhower did fume in private, perhaps realizing or not that his favorite film, *High Noon*, was an allegory on McCarthyism. He played it three times in the White House and must have known the film's screenwriter, Carl Foreman, had appeared before the House Un-American Activities Committee and admitted to having been a member of the Communist Party. His membership had been ten years in Foreman's past, and while disavowing an ongoing connection, he refused to name names. Blacklisting was the punishment. No Hollywood studio would employ him, and he departed for Britain.

So here was Eisenhower, certainly no communist sympathizer or witch-hunting zealot, in the midst of a shooting war with communists in Korea, contending with McCarthy's demagoguery and Hollywood's blacklisting (see chart below), enjoying an evening at the movies in the White House, listening to Gary Cooper and Grace Kelly delivering the words of a blacklisted former communist. All the while, he remained publicly silent about McCarthyism, certain it would burn itself out, not comprehending that like the seventeenth-century Salem Witch Trials, lives would be burned before it was over.

Clearly, this was a mistake—a freshman-year mistake made by a political neophyte, following on the heels of the Marshall mistake during the campaign. Having dealt in World War II with President Franklin Roosevelt, British Prime Minister Winston Churchill, Gen. Charles de Gaulle (Churchill's French liaison Major General Spears famously said of the irascible leader, "The only cross I have to bear is the Cross of Lorraine," the symbol of de Gaulle's Free French Army), British Field Marshal Bernard Law Montgomery, Gen. George Patton, and a host of other personalities, Ike was viewed as a political general, and he undoubtedly believed himself adept in the political arena. Now, he was confronted with a nastier, career-before-country game completely foreign to him and his high-level wartime politics.

And where did he turn for help? Not unlike an earlier general-turned-president, Ulysses S. Grant, he turned to a group of political advisors, including those who had urged him to cut the defense of General Marshall from his campaign speech, but also to one individual, a man who reveled in political in-fighting, Sen. Richard M. Nixon of California. When Ike, after years of reluctance, finally decided to run for the presidency in 1952, he was late to the party. Ohio Republican Sen. Robert A. Taft, the son of former president and former Chief Justice of the United States William Howard Taft, had already lined up a sufficient number of delegates to win the nomination. Enter Nixon. Already known as "Tricky Dick," Nixon succeeded in having enough Taft delegates removed and replaced with Eisenhower delegates to swing the nomination on the first ballot to Ike, and, in the process, securing the vice presidential nomination for himself.

In this, Ike made a common (pre-)first-year error—selecting or allowing the convention to select a running mate for the wrong reasons. The right reason, of course, is to name someone qualified to be president, and in 1952, that was not Eisenhower's view of Nixon. Realizing this, the president made a fumbled attempt to replace his vice president when running for reelection in 1956. Seven times before the Eisenhower presidency and twice since, vice presidents acceded to the presidency upon the president's death or resignation (in the case of Nixon in 1974). And this does not include at least two occasions when the vice president should have taken control after the president became disabled: Woodrow Wilson due to a stroke in 1919 and Eisenhower himself in 1958 after he suffered a heart attack and stroke.

Well-Known Names from the Hollywood Blacklists

Eddie Albert	Judy Holliday
Richard Attenborough	Lena Horne
Harry Belafonte	Langston Hughes
Leonard Bernstein	Kim Hunter
Charles Chaplin	John Ireland
Lee J. Cobb	Burl Ives
Aaron Copland	Sam Jaffe
Howard Da Silva	Gypsy Rose Lee
Ossie Davis	Burgess Meredith
Ruby Dee	Arthur Miller
Dolores del Río	Henry Morgan
Howard Duff	Zero Mostel
Frances Farmer	Dorothy Parker
José Ferrer	Paul Robeson
Jerry Fielding	Edward G. Robinson
Carl Foreman	Pete Seeger
John Garfield	Artie Shaw
Barbara Bel Geddes	William L. Shirer
Harold Goldman	Allan Sloane
Lee Grant	Howard K. Smith
Uta Hagen	Sam Wanamaker
Dashiell Hammett	Orson Welles
Robert P. Heller	Michael Wilson
Lillian Hellman	Martin Wolfson

Because the presidency merges a monarch's living embodiment of nationhood with the managerial and political duties of a prime minister, some occupants of the office came to downplay the last of these assignments and believed they were above the fray. Among them were Dwight D. Eisenhower and George Washington, the two presidents to enter the office with unassailable prestige, which endowed them with more power than they employed, a generally admirable but occasionally misplaced restraint. Both eventually and reluctantly would come to the realization that the presidency is indeed a political office. For Ike, it would take McCarthy, McCarthyism, and Nixon to finally make the point.

Eisenhower, a political moderate, was normally a consensus builder, who once he became president often found more common ground with Democrats than Republicans. Except for the 1953–1955 period, he faced a Democratic majority in Congress, which meant dealing with two fellow Texans from the opposite party, Senate Majority Leader Lyndon B. Johnson and Speaker of the House "Mr. Sam" Samuel T. Rayburn, political relationships that led to several notable successes, including establishment of the Interstate Highway System. Influenced in part by the impression Germany's Autobahn made on him during the war and in part by the perceived need for rapid evacuation routes in the event of nuclear attack, such a massive, expensive, unprecedented project could never have come to pass during an Eisenhower Administration had he not learned political lessons from the Marshall, McCarthy, and Nixon mistakes in his first year.

CHAPTER 3

THE LONERS

THOMAS JEFFERSON (1801), JIMMY CARTER (1977), AND BARACK OBAMA (2009)

Many presidents believed they were the smartest people in the room, and Thomas Jefferson, Jimmy Carter, and Barack Obama probably were, a problem unintentionally identified by President John F. Kennedy when hosting a dinner honoring Nobel Prize winners: "I think this is the most extraordinary collection of talent, of human knowledge, that has ever been gathered together at the White House, with the possible exception of when Thomas Jefferson dined alone." The intended compliment actually revealed a significant flaw. The three Loner Presidents should have heeded the humble key to business success immortalized by H. Ross Perot, the erratic and quirky billionaire who garnered 19 percent of the vote as a third-party presidential candidate in 1992: "I hire people who are much smarter and far more talented than I am." The Loners' failure to either hire or fully utilize people more knowledgeable and talented than themselves started all three of them out on the wrong foot with both Congress and the electorate.

The contrast with presidents who did the opposite brings to light the stark contrasts of the problem. FDR had his famous "Brain Trust"; Truman heavily relied on Gen. George C. Marshall as secretary of State; Eisenhower gave substantial leeway to the Dulles brothers—John Foster at State and Allen at the CIA; Kennedy had his own "Brain Trust" as well as his brother Bobby to help guide him through the Cuban Missile Crisis; and Nixon practically made Secretary of State Henry Kissinger a coequal. Such standout Cabinet members were not to be found among the loner presidents either because the loners did not select them or fully use them when they were selected.

THOMAS JEFFERSON—LOUISIANA PURCHASE
1801–1809

Born/Died: 1743 Goochland (now Albemarle) County, VA–1826 Charlottesville, VA
Education: The College of William & Mary
Occupation: Lawyer, planter
Political Party: Democratic-Republican
Government Service: Vice President 1797–1801, Secretary of State 1790–1793, Diplomat/Ambassador (France) 1784–1789, VA Delegate to the Congress of the Confederation 1783–1784, Governor (VA) 1779–1781, VA Delegate to the Continental Congress 1775–1776, Member of the VA House of Burgesses 1769–1775
Military Service: Brief non-combat militia service
Preceded by: John Adams (Quasi War at sea with France following French demand for bribes in XYZ Affair; Sedition Act inhibits free speech; Jay Treaty marks tilt toward Britain during Napoleonic Wars)

Dissembling may not have been in George Washington's political arsenal; it certainly was in Jefferson's, and he made extensive use of the weapon through surrogate writers. The most notorious of these was Jefferson ally James T. Callender, a journalist adept at scathing articles and alleged exposés of John Adams, Alexander Hamilton, and Federalists in general. In *The Prospect Before Us*, he described Adams as a "continual tempest of malignant passions . . . , repulsive pedant, a gross hypocrite and an unprincipled oppressor." As a result, Callender was fined and imprisoned under the Sedition Act. Jefferson, who was not revealed as the instigator and was not prosecuted, promptly pardoned Callender upon assuming the presidency in 1801. Then, when Jefferson refused to provide Callender with a position, the writer turned on him with poison-penned vengeance, detailing the president's long-term relationship with his slave Sally Hemings, a fact later proven through modern DNA testing.

So, what Jefferson wrought, Jefferson endured when attacks against him were spiked with vulgar, personal, and criminal accusations sufficient to make modern political dirty-tricksters blush. Freedom of speech ran amok as though early-nineteenth-century Americans did not quite know what to make of or how far to go with this new constitutionally guaranteed right. Jefferson thought it had gone far enough. Ever the pragmatist and ignoring his anti–Sedition Act stance, he had arranged to have Supreme Court Justice Samuel Chase impeached. Although the Federalist judge had been railing against Jefferson, enough members of the president's own party joined the opposition and acquitted the justice. This was a direct outgrowth of Jefferson's first-year campaign to repeal the Judiciary Act of 1801.

In a precursor to Franklin Roosevelt's court-packing scheme more than one hundred years later, John Adams had sought to fill the new lower court openings created by the Judiciary Act, in what were tantamount to midnight appointments. Jefferson was furious, and upon taking office, he immediately thwarted the maneuver by withholding eleven of the Adams judgeships, while having his allies in Congress move to repeal the act.

In an ironic twist, William Marbury appealed the withholding of his appointment as a justice of the peace for the District of Columbia only to have fellow Federalist Supreme Court Chief Justice John Marshall rule against him, declaring the original Judiciary Act of 1789 allowing the Supreme Court to issue writs of mandamus (such as compelling Jefferson's Secretary of State James Madison to confirm Marbury's appointment) to be unconstitutional. This monumental decision in *Marbury v. Madison* established the Supreme Court's right of judicial review, the right to invalidate an act of Congress. As often occurred during his tenure,

Jefferson's errors and successes were intermingled and interdependent.

Like Adams before him, Jefferson struggled in the presidency. Despite the admirable example Washington eventually set, both men tended to concentrate on the first president's mistakes, though from opposite poles. Adams, like Washington, believed in a strong central government—too strong, his opponents claimed—whereas Jefferson was the great advocate of decentralization, a view that brought about his break with both Washington and Adams

President Thomas Jefferson
LIBRARY OF CONGRESS

and inhibited the latitude of his later executive actions. Washington tried to remain above the fray. Jefferson reveled in it. In foreign affairs, Washington strove for neutrality, Adams tilted toward Britain, and Jefferson was an unabashed Francophile.

Jefferson had been the ambassador to France when it was a monarchy, and through education—and a love of the arts and feminine company—the tall, redheaded aristocratic widower was admired and accepted by French society. Here was a cultured, Renaissance man from a land many Europeans stereotyped as an uncouth frontier. Even so, when the French Revolution erupted in 1789, Jefferson, the idealist, embraced it. When Napoleon Bonaparte emerged as the protector of the revolution and, in 1804, Emperor of the French by plebiscite, Jefferson regarded him an autocrat, though still preferable to the British. Whether ruled by a king, revolutionaries, or an emperor, they were French, and Jefferson was enamored with France, its people, its culture, its refinement, a mutual admiration that led to both his greatest errors and his greatest achievement.

Adams had already ended the 1798–1800 Quasi War with France, a war his vice president, Jefferson, had opposed from the start, even to the extent he at first refused to believe agents of France had actually demanded a bribe for peace in the XYZ Affair. Jefferson's old foe from the Washington Administration, Alexander Hamilton, had been given command of the army, and although it never saw action in this purely naval war, the political action was intense. Hamilton was not only the Federalist leader, but as a general, his influence was significant, much to the chagrin of Adams, a less pure Federalist, and to Jefferson, who was philosophically opposed to a large standing army.

While Jefferson supported the peace overtures and performed the vice president's only constitutional function, presiding over the Senate debate, no one was pleased with the outcome, especially since Adams agreed to have the United States assume $7 million in American merchantmen claims against France. It cost him reelection, his opponent being Vice President Jefferson. The young nation's politically awkward turn-of-the-century politics involved a good deal of elbowing as the democratic experiment progressed.

Jefferson was a man of eclectic opinions. He had a slaveholder's ambivalence about slavery that impelled him to favor the Northwest Ordinance barring slavery from what would become America's Midwest, a president's distrust of power that did not constrain him from unilaterally declaring war on the Barbary Pirates, and an aristocrat's belief in the rights of the common man that he enshrined in the Declaration of Independence. He was a strict constitutional constructionist whose rationalized deviations from the Constitution included the constitutionally questionable purchase of the Louisiana Territory and the clearly unconstitutional granting of citizenship to its inhabitants. He had a lifelong debtor's disdain for government debt and said government debts should be limited to nineteen years so as not to pass them on to the next generation. He was both the man of peace who all but disbanded the Army and reduced the Navy and the president who established the US Military Academy at West Point and threatened war with Spain over New Orleans.

It was this eclecticism, not initially found in less flexible presidents such as John Adams, J. Q. Adams, Jackson, Lincoln, Wilson, Coolidge,

Louisiana Purchase, Mexican Cession, and Oregon Territory
NATIONALATLAS.GOV, 1970 PRINT EDITION, LIBRARY OF CONGRESS

Hoover, Reagan, and G. W. Bush, that provided him with the nimbleness to adapt to circumstances, occasionally with poor results, more often with critical successes, none more so than the Louisiana Purchase and its doubling of the nation's land mass. The transaction represented the largest peaceful transfer of territory in human history, but as with most Jeffersonian decisions, it had a downside.

Jefferson's first year in office was one of sorting out his conflicting voices. He opposed the earlier Jay Treaty's move toward amicable relations with Britain, including a large increase in trade with the former mother country, with an antipathy bordering on belligerence. Despite the treaty, British ships were accosting US merchant vessels on the high seas in search of deserters, and for a time, Jefferson considered war, thought better of it, and decided to return the deserters only to discover he would be returning a quarter to a half of all American merchant mariners. He had no choice but to back down; he had no Navy of consequence. His party had undermined naval shipbuilding, reducing the number of frigates under construction from six to three, and upon becoming president, Jefferson opted instead for a small fleet of coastal gunboats, all but abandoning the idea of a blue-water navy. At the end of his first year in office, he even exulted how he and his majority party in Congress had "reduced the army and navy to what is barely necessary." This was a double-edged error. While simultaneously tilting US foreign policy in favor of France—soon to be the losing side in the Napoleonic Wars—and virtually disarming the Army and Navy vis-à-vis Britain—soon to be the winner in the Napoleonic Wars—he bequeathed a losing scenario to his successor, James Madison, and the ill-advised War of 1812.

At first, Jefferson's disarmament policy seemed prudent and financially beneficial, when one year after his 1801 inauguration, France and Britain signed the Treaty of Amiens (see Chapter 2, Timeline) on March 25, 1802 (preliminarily signed October 1, 1801), bringing what would turn out to be a one-year truce in the Napoleonic Wars. During this period of peace, British and American visitors flocked to Paris. America's renewed friendship with France on the heels of the Adams Administration's Franco-American Quasi War perfectly suited Jefferson and certainly influenced Napoleon's sale of the 828,000-square-mile Louisiana Territory to the United States the following year. After all, had America been a British ally—which the Jay Treaty implied—the sale might never have occurred, especially considering the often overlooked character lurking in the background, the master diplomatic puppet master and deal maker extraordinaire whom Napoleon described as "immorality personified."

This was Napoleon's Machiavellian minister of foreign affairs, Charles Maurice de Talleyrand, the driving force behind both the XYZ Affair and the Treaty of Amiens who was also the foremost French opponent of the pending sale of Louisiana to the United States. He had become rich extorting bribes for political favors and was perfectly capable of dealing further with Britain if the United States had persisted in its British tilt under the Jay Treaty. In such a scenario, Talleyrand might have struck a better deal with the British on the Louisiana Territory as a means of driving a wedge between that nation and the United States. With Anglo-French peace established by the Treaty of Amiens, even if tenuous and temporary, the timing for an Anglo-French territorial transaction could not have been better. So quite simply, the US-French deal probably could not have occurred with an Adams Administration, and America's westward expansion would have been stunted or stopped before it began.

In the most convoluted early-nineteenth-century fashion, America did make the deal, but the ultimate cost was far more than $15 million, because the Franco-American friendship sowed the seeds for the costly Anglo-American War of 1812. How much of this was rational statecraft? It is interesting to ponder the roles played by the Anglophile and Francophile biases in America's foreign policy decisions of the era.

What was not stopped was the spread of slavery. In 1784, Jefferson had proposed a bill forbidding slavery (except in Kentucky) west of the Appalachian Mountains. It missed passage by just one vote, a single vote that would yield devastating consequences during the coming decades. However, it did succeed in laying the groundwork for the Northwest Ordinance's anti-slavery clause three years later. A similar bill proposed for the land encompassed by the Louisiana Purchase in 1804 was narrowly defeated as, this time, President Jefferson stood aside. Why? A decade-long slave revolt was raging in what is today Haiti and the Dominican Republic on the island of Hispaniola (France had freed the slaves, but did not offer them full citizenship rights, and then appeared to reverse the process). Taking advantage of the temporary peace with Britain, Napoleon sent an army led by his brother-in-law to reassert control, only to see half of the troops and their commander fall victim to yellow fever. This, combined with the looming prospect of renewed British hostilities, caused Napoleon to lose interest in a North American empire and the Hispaniola sugar trade supporting it. With a belligerent Britain all-powerful at sea, New Orleans and the Louisiana Territory just reacquired from Spain could not be defended. Fearing American military designs on the region, a sale seemed prudent.

The problem for Jefferson was that many of the French and Spanish, as well as free people of color, in Louisiana were slaveholders. Before the Louisiana Purchase was finalized, word was received about Napoleon's insistence that the treaty not be amended in any manner, including the insertion of an anti-slavery clause. After the territorial transfer had taken place, Congress did pass the Act of March 26, 1804, banning the importation of slaves from outside the United States, this nearly four years before the US Constitution allowed such a ban to take place for the existing states and territories. To do more, such as an outright ban on slavery, would have risked alienating the territory's inhabitants and, in turn, caused Napoleon—who was already having second thoughts about the deal Talleyrand always opposed—to renounce the treaty.

In time, posterity would scan the tumultuous half century before the Civil War and discover Jefferson, along with James Monroe and Zachary Taylor—slaveholders all—had the greatest opportunities to stop and strangle the spread of slavery. Jefferson tried and faltered, Monroe tried not at all, and Taylor died trying.

In the end, Jefferson's greatest success, the Louisiana Purchase, was built upon his first-year failures. During the euphoria of the false peace created by the Jay Treaty, the end of the Quasi War, and the Anglo-Franco Peace of Amiens, he had emasculated the Navy, leaving the nation's merchant fleets unprotected, and he had reduced the Army to an inconsequential level. Then, in response to Britain's bullying of US ships in search of deserters, he imposed an embargo that undermined New England's commerce and led to the near secession of that region and finally to the costly and pointless War of 1812. Further, his acceptance of slavery in the Louisiana Purchase lands would contribute to an even greater cost in lives and fortune a half century later when the Civil War devastated the nation.

What might he have done differently? Jefferson's clear objective was to expand the nation's territory without expanding slavery, a view he had repeatedly stated and that he could have accomplished had he played his hand with more astuteness. Almost one-third of all US exports traveled through New Orleans, and on April 18, 1802, Jefferson wrote to Robert Livingston, then in Paris negotiating the purchase of Louisiana: "The day that France takes possession of New Orleans . . . we must marry ourselves to the British fleet and nation." Spain had created no impediment to US trade, but with France about to take control, unexpected consequences could follow. So here was Jefferson, distrustful of Napoleon's designs while realizing the French were militarily impotent in Louisiana in the face of British sea power. Under these circumstances, a substantial show of force could have brought Louisiana into America's hands at very little cost and with no strings (i.e., slavery) attached, and all before France could have struck a deal with Britain. In short, most of the $15 million paid for the territory would have been better spent on a viable military establishment. Certainly, the Jeffersonian idea of a defenseless nation was not only a mistake, it was irresponsible. Jefferson was living in a philosophical world of his own making, not the real world of early-nineteenth-century realpolitik.

In this he was ill served by his two most prominent Cabinet members, Secretary of State James Madison and Treasury Secretary Albert Gallatin. Both of them helped put the country at risk by failing to question Jefferson's antipathy toward debt, with the result that the Army and Navy were virtually gutted. The price would be paid later by the nation's poor performance during the War of 1812.

JIMMY CARTER—STAGFLATION
1977–1981

Born: 1924 Plains, GA
Education: US Naval Academy (Annapolis)
Occupation: Peanut farmer
Political Party: Democratic
Government Service: Governor (GA) 1971–1975, State Senator (GA) 1963–1967
Military Service: Navy Lieutenant; Korean War
Preceded by: Gerald Ford (Nixon Pardon; Vietnam War ends; OPEC oil embargo causes inflation and shortages)

"I can't deny that I am a better ex-president than I was a president." There was a reason for Carter's self-assessment. An intelligent, hardworking, upstanding individual, he lacked sufficient expertise in economics when he took office.

He began as an outsider, ran as an outsider (keeping his campaign headquarters in Atlanta), and remained an outsider inside the White

President Jimmy Carter and First Lady Rosalynn Carter
LIBRARY OF CONGRESS

House. Carter was a micro-manager who neglected to hire high-profile, experienced, Washington-based political operatives, and his top aides, Hamilton Jordan and Frank Moore, made matters worse, alienating members of his own party, including the powerful Speaker of the House, Democrat Tip O'Neill of Massachusetts. Renowned political commentator Jules Witcover wrote "the trouble began with Carter, whose unfamiliarity with Washington and the affairs of state at home and abroad cast him as an uncertain and indecisive figure from the start of his presidency"—a loner. Carter had been a state senator and governor in Georgia, where he ran a peanut farm, but like all other presidents, he was not an economist. In 1977, it was his misfortune to enter office at a time of increasingly significant economic challenges caused by the 1973 OPEC oil embargo and subsequent four-fold increase in oil prices. Completely misjudging the potential for oil discoveries, production, and demand, he predicted the nation's oil needs would outrun supply within a decade, stating such in a speech on April 18, 1977, that proved to be so wrong in so many ways. Coming just three months after his inauguration, the overwrought oratory seemed to be founded on preconceived misconceptions:

With the exception of preventing war, this is the greatest challenge our country will face during our lifetimes. . . . We simply must balance our demand for energy with our rapidly shrinking resources. . . . This difficult effort will be the moral equivalent of war. . . . The oil and natural gas we rely on for 75 percent of our energy are running out. In spite of increased effort, domestic production has been dropping steadily at about six percent a year. Imports have doubled in the last five years. Our nation's independence of economic and political action is becoming increasingly constrained. Unless profound changes are made to lower oil consumption, we now believe that early in the 1980s the world will be demanding more oil than it can produce. . . . Because we are now running out of gas and oil, we must prepare quickly for a third change, to strict conservation and to the use of coal and permanent renewable energy sources, like solar power. . . . If we do not act, then by 1985 we will be using 33 percent more energy than we do today. . . . We can't substantially increase our domestic production, so we would need to import twice as much oil as we do now. Supplies will be uncertain. The cost will keep going up. . . . Now we have a choice. But if we wait, we will live in fear of embargoes. We could endanger our freedom as a sovereign nation to act in foreign affairs. Within ten years we would not be able to import enough oil—from any country, at any acceptable price. . . .

We will feel mounting pressure to plunder the environment. We will have a crash program to build more nuclear plants, strip-mine and burn more coal, and drill more offshore wells than we will need if we begin to conserve now. Inflation will soar, production will go down, people will lose their jobs. Intense competition will build up among nations and among the different regions within our own country.

If we fail to act soon, we will face an economic, social and political crisis that will threaten our free institutions.

Lacking both knowledge and the help of experts with knowledge, his assessments were wrong, which made his solutions wrong—except his fallacious foreboding overrode reality, and inflation did soar. The benchmark prime rate banks offer their most creditworthy customers (see chart on opposite page) reached historic highs, topping out at 21.5 percent in 1980 after the 1979 Iranian Revolution—which began in October 1977—ushered in an anti-US regime of religious zealots who used oil as a weapon, possibly taking their cue from Carter's erroneous admission of natural resource weakness. As a result, as in 1973-74, an oil crisis occurred, and the long lines at gas pumps returned. Meanwhile, young Iranian revolutionaries acting with the obvious support of the new government attacked the US embassy in Tehran.

The US Department of State, Office of the Historian, described how President Carter overruled advisors and mishandled the crisis:

> On November 4, 1979, Iranian students seized the embassy and detained more than 50 Americans. . . . The Iranians held the American diplomats hostage for 444 days. . . . [T]he Iran hostage crisis undermined Carter's conduct of foreign policy. . . . and made the Administration look weak and ineffectual. . . . Carter's foreign policy team often seemed weak and vacillating.
>
> The Administration's vitality was sapped, and the Soviet Union took advantage of America's weakness to win strategic advantage for itself. In 1979, Soviet-supported Marxist rebels made strong gains in Ethiopia, Angola, and Mozambique. Vietnam fought a successful border war with China and took over Cambodia from the murderous Khmer Rouge. And, in late 1979, the Soviet Union invaded Afghanistan to support its shaky Marxist government.
>
> In light of these challenges to global stability, President Carter significantly altered his view of both the Soviet Union and the advice of his own advisers.

Carter initially favored Secretary of State Cyrus Vance's policy of negotiation, but by 1980 was more receptive to National Security Advisor Zbigniew Brzezinski's more confrontational stance. Once again the

National Security Council and the Department of State were in open conflict. The issue came to a head when Secretary Vance opposed a mission to rescue the hostages in Iran—a move championed by Brzezinski. Vance had been correct—the 1980 mission was a debacle.

Fast forward thirty-five years, and it is clear how wrong Carter's energy predictions were. True, conservation measures such as increased fuel standards for cars and trucks did make a difference, but Carter was otherwise wide the mark. His freshman-year long-term predictions underestimated the ability of modern technology to find and extract oil in such quantities that the United States could actually become energy independent.

Meanwhile, the words "malaise" and "stagflation"—a British linguistic import describing stagnation and inflation—crept into the public lexicon. Carter may have thought he was speaking in the same vein as British Prime Minister Winston Churchill, who famously announced to

Prime Rate 1955–2014
(Highest average rate for banks' most creditworthy short-term business borrowers)

1955	3.50%	1971	6.75%	1985	10.75%	1999	8.50%
1956	4.00%	1972	6.00%	1986	9.50%	2000	9.50%
1957	4.50%	1973	10.00%	1987	9.25%	2001	9.50%
1958	4.50%	1974	12.00%	1988	10.50%	2002	4.75%
1959	5.00%	1975	10.25%	1989	11.50%	2003	4.25%
1960	5.00%	1976	7.25%	1990	10.50%	2004	5.25%
1961	4.50%	1977	7.75%	1991	9.50%	2005	7.25%
1962–64	4.50%	1978	11.75%	1992	6.50%	2006	8.25%
1965	5.00%	1979	15.75%	1993	6.00%	2007	8.25%
1966	6.00%	1980	21.50%	1994	8.50%	2008	7.25%
1967	6.00%	1981	20.50%	1995	9.00%	2009	3.25%
1968	6.75%	1982	17.00%	1996	8.50%	2010–14	3.25%
1969	8.50%	1983	11.50%	1997	8.50%		
1970	8.50%	1984	13.00%	1998	8.50%		

SOURCE: BOARD OF GOVERNORS OF THE FEDERAL RESERVE

Parliament in 1940: "I have nothing to offer but blood, toil, tears, and sweat." Britain was at war then, a nation-at-risk shooting war, the war of Carter's coming-of-age years. It was not 1977, and to claim America faced anything approaching what Churchill and Britain had faced, calling it "the moral equivalent of war," was a misreading of the situation and a misreading of the mood of the American public.

Carter went on to later successes such as the Panama Canal Treaty, Israeli-Egyptian peace through the Camp David Accords, as well as the promotion of women's rights, being the first president to have his wife, the intelligent and warmly charming Rosalynn, attend Cabinet meetings, a significant step considering most presidents never even invited their vice presidents to do so.

We will never know how much his words motivated the Iranians. We do know it never pays to sell the American dream short, and it never pays to erroneously do so as he did in his misfired first year in office. Three years later, he lost reelection in a landslide to Ronald Reagan, whose optimistic 1984 ads proclaiming, "It's morning again in America," were equally descriptive of Reagan's sunny outlook in the 1980 campaign.

BARACK OBAMA—OBAMACARE
2009–2017

Born: 1961 Honolulu, HI
Education: Occidental College (transferred), Columbia University, Harvard Law School
Occupation: Lawyer
Political Party: Democratic
Government Service: Senator (IL) 2005–2008, State Senator (IL) 1997–2004
Military Service: None
Preceded by: George W. Bush (9/11 terrorist attacks; Afghanistan and Iraq Wars commence; appoints Bernanke head of Federal Reserve; Great Recession begins; housing prices collapse; further terrorist attacks prevented)

Barack Obama is a study in contrasts: a private public person, personable with a few close friends, a self-assertive introvert, canny politician who eschews politics, an articulate poor communicator, and social network guru wholly lacking in networking skills. Leon Panetta, who served as Obama's director of the Central Intelligence Agency for twenty-eight months before becoming secretary of Defense, where he served another eighteen months, wrote: "[the president's] decision-making apparatus was centralized in the White House" far more than

President Barack Obama

PETE SOUZA, THE WHITE HOUSE OFFICIAL SITE

that of any other administration he had seen, reducing the importance of Cabinet posts. And he criticized Obama for "playing it cool" and as "disdainful of Congress generally." While just one man's observation, it goes to the heart of Obama's image as a loner most at ease with his own counsel.

Todd Purdum, writing in *Vanity Fair*, took note of this smartest-man-in-the-room phenomenon: "Obama has surrounded himself mostly with a team of loyalists. . . . 'He's a total introvert,' the former adviser told me. 'He doesn't need people.'" Then, in an anecdote that seamlessly meshed with Kennedy's Nobel Prize dinner quip, Purdum went on: "Obama's energy secretary, Steven Chu, may have a Nobel Prize in physics, but that counted for little when he once tried to make a too elaborate visual presentation to the [cerebrally confident] president. Obama said to him after the third slide, as one witness recalls, 'O.K., I got it. I'm done, Steve. Turn it off.'"

This aspect of Obama's personality was manifested as soon as he took office and made the momentous decision to ask Congress to pass the Affordable Care Act, which would come to be known as Obamacare. Providing near-universal health care coverage for America's citizens, it was a policy first advocated by Harry S. Truman and spectacularly botched by Bill and Hillary

Clinton in 1993. This time, Obama was certain that Democratic majorities in the House and Senate could deliver, and they did, only to see passage followed by a disastrous computer-glitch rollout. The Affordable Care Act went on to pass muster with the US Supreme Court and appeared to be working, albeit with the acknowledged need for significant tweaking.

Political fallout was another matter; it was devastating and contributed to gridlock, preventing passage of almost all of the balance of the Obama agenda, from immigration reform to tax reform. And it led to the eventual Republican takeover of both houses of Congress.

All of this took place amid the backdrop of the worst financial crisis since the Great Depression. Dubbed the Great Recession, it began in December 2007, just over a year before Obama took office, and picked up steam during the following year, with declining home prices destroying much of middle-class America's net worth. The Dow Jones Average fell by 50 percent, unemployment soared, banks and major companies—General Motors among them—filed bankruptcy. Meanwhile, the country was bogged down in Afghanistan and Iraq, fighting wars the new president had promised to end.

James P. Pfiffner, Professor of Public Policy at George Mason University, wrote:

> *Thus, in economic policy making, since Obama had no honest broker to lead policy discussions, he acted as his own orchestrator of debate and interrogator of his aides. He read the briefing papers, mastered the details of policy, and acted as his own honest broker. In this way his style more closely resembled the policy analytic approach of Presidents Nixon, Carter, and Clinton than those of Reagan and George W. Bush, who tended to delegate the details of policy to their staffs. Obama's approach contrasted most starkly with that of President Bush, who let Vice President Cheney frame the issues, conduct detailed analysis, and dominate the policy process.*

In short, by the time Obama was sworn into office in January 2009, he was facing economic and military challenges greater than any faced by a president since the cataclysmic events of the Depression, World War II, and the Korean War, or the singular Cuban Missile Crisis. To confront and contend with it all would require an experienced savvy politician. Obama was neither. Having no managerial or military experience, and not even a completed term in the US Senate, he was among the least prepared presidents in American history.

He did press for continuation of the economic stimulus proposals put in place by his predecessor, George W. Bush, but it was Chairman of the Federal Reserve Ben Bernanke, a student of the Great Depression, who saved the day, convincing the independent Federal Reserve Board to pump billions of dollars into the economy through a program of Quantitative Easing, a euphemism for what *The Economist* calls "electronic cash." Instead of having money printed, the Fed purchased federal debt (T-bills) and mortgage-backed securities with electronic transfers, dramatically increasing the money supply in the process. Such a program had never been attempted on so massive a scale, but it worked, and in 2009, Obama nominated Bernanke for a second term as Fed chief, crediting him with preventing another Great Depression.

As a result, Obama's first year in office was largely successful, masking the freshman-year errors embedded in those successes. MIT economist Dr. Jonathan Gruber, who was an advisor on both the Massachusetts health care plan and Obamacare, revealed in a 2011 speech that "economists have called for 40 years to get rid of the regressive, inefficient and expensive tax subsidy provided for employer-provided health insurance." He explained that beginning in 2018 Obamacare would assess a 40 percent tax on so-called employer-provided Cadillac health care plans, but the threshold for the tax would be increased each year based upon the consumer price index instead of the higher medical inflation rate, which would mean that over time all employer-provided health care plans would be forced to pay the tax.

When his speech reached the public domain in 2014, a political shock wave resulted. His comments were diametrically opposite of what the president had said when the bill was wending its way through Congress in 2009. Gruber, an advocate of the bill, was acknowledging what the bill's sponsors understood: The tax deduction for employer-provided health insurance plans was bad tax policy that had to go, a feat only to be accomplished by blindsiding Congress and the public. Whether or not this was good policy, Obama was caught dissembling, that necessary presidential quality no president ever wants to acknowledge.

Similarly, Obama's war-extrication policies came under fire. He pulled troops out of Iraq, inadvertently laying the foundation for the rise of extreme ISIS zealots who would overrun significant parts of Syria and Iraq. Next, he began the withdrawal of US forces from Afghanistan before the Afghan Army was prepared to confront its enemies, leaving a void that a resurgent Taliban began to fill.

Once again, Iraq became a battleground. The work of Gen. David Petraeus in the "Sunni Awakening" had done much to reconcile Iraq's Sunnis with the country's Shiite majority and its Shiite-led government. One-time political advisor to the US military command in Iraq, Emma Sky later wrote of a snag: "Too often, Mr. [Iraqi Prime Minister Nuri Kamal al-]Maliki has misinterpreted American backing for his government as a carte blanche for uncompromising behavior." Maliki, a Shiite, who spent his exile years in Iran while Saddam Hussein controlled Iraq, was effectively given a bye from the Obama Administration as he excluded and arrested Sunni opponents and increasingly assumed dictatorial powers. His actions unraveled the "Sunni Awakening," and many disaffected Sunnis eventually joined or sympathized with ISIS fighters who could not have captured Mosul, Iraq's second-largest city, Anbar Province, and several other large swaths of Iraqi territory without their support.

These situations were exacerbated because Obama the loner began by inadequately communicating with Congress and the public. His insular and inward-looking White House planted the seeds sown by Obamacare dissembling, the improperly executed military withdrawals from Iraq and Afghanistan, and the failure to exert greater influence on the political affairs in those countries. His job approval rating plummeted as those problems surfaced during his second term, and caused his party to suffer grievous losses in the 2014 election, including control of the US Senate.

However, halfway through his second term, a steadily improving economy combined with succinct messaging previously missing from the Obama White House began to be reflected in rising poll numbers. The learning curve had been long; the problems enormous.

CHAPTER 4

CONFLICTS THEY MIGHT HAVE PREVENTED, AVOIDED, OR WON: 1812, VIETNAM, 9/11, AFGHANISTAN, AND IRAQ

JAMES MADISON (1809), LYNDON B. JOHNSON (1963), AND GEORGE W. BUSH (2001)

Following in the Francophile footsteps of his friend and predecessor, Thomas Jefferson, James Madison began his term in 1809 by also betting on the losing side in the Napoleonic Wars, a bet that would eventually lead to the War of 1812. In contrast to the American Revolution, when a French army and fleet turned the tide in America's favor, the United States found itself alone once Napoleon was defeated and exiled in 1814. Madison might have won and even annexed Canada had the war been fought in 1809, if it was necessary to fight at all.

Lyndon B. Johnson was a domestic-issues president, whose knowledge of military matters was limited. And so the Johnson presidency was two presidencies, and history will likely judge them separately, awarding high marks for his role in civil rights, social safety nets, and the welfare of the common man, while giving him entirely different marks for his conduct of the Vietnam War, a war he fought the wrong way with the wrong people.

Following the 9/11 terrorist attacks in 2001, newly inaugurated President George W. Bush targeted al Qaeda training camps in Afghanistan and claimed Saddam Hussein in Iraq was also harboring terrorists. With covert US assistance, the Afghani Northern Alliance quickly overthrew the Taliban rulers of Afghanistan and routed al Qaeda forces there. Bush then proceeded to put boots on the ground and embroil American forces in an ongoing conflict with insurgents.

Two years later, Bush ordered the invasion of Iraq, mistakenly claiming the country was engaged in the development of weapons of mass destruction. While as in Afghanistan, the military campaign was brief and successful, in both countries Bush changed the mission of the US military to the rooting out of Islamist guerrilla forces, effectively interposing America in two civil wars.

JAMES MADISON—THE WAR OF 1812
1809–1817

Born/Died: 1751 Port Conway, VA–1836 Orange County, VA
Education: College of New Jersey (later Princeton University)
Occupation: Planter
Political Party: Democratic-Republican
Government Service: Secretary of State 1801–1809, Rep. (VA) 1789–1797, VA Delegate to the Congress of the Confederation 1781–1783
Military Service: Non-active militia service
Preceded by: Thomas Jefferson (reverses Adams's pro-British policies; tilts toward France, which makes Louisiana Purchase possible; fails to prohibit slavery in the acquired lands; tensions build with Britain; Embargo and Non-Intercourse Acts stifle trade)

As Father of the Constitution, an author of *The Federalist Papers*, George Washington's mentor, Thomas Jefferson's collaborator and secretary of

State, and influential member of the House of Representatives during that institution's first eight years, James Madison was seemingly prepared for the presidency. The new nation's preeminent political philosopher, Madison was the person most responsible for forming the institutional bedrocks of America, and his experiences in Congress and the Cabinet should have been sufficient to dispel the notion of him as more thinker than doer. Yet, when his career is looked upon in component parts, the truth of the notion becomes clear.

President James Madison
LIBRARY OF CONGRESS

His philosophical thinking was macro; his pre-presidential career was micro, consumed by the minutiae of governance. He had never held an executive position, and his tenure as secretary of State did not qualify because in the early 1800s, the position was more bureaucratic than managerial, especially when serving under Thomas Jefferson, a man who believed himself adept at handling a broad spectrum of tasks.

The University of Virginia's Miller Center described this phenomenon: "He is said to have been a master of the small arena. Studious, keenly political, and a perceptive judge of men and issues, Madison could shape constitutions and influence legislation with few peers, but he was too cautious for the kinds of presidential leadership that left clear marks upon the political landscape."

By 1809, the Napoleonic Wars dominated the Western world. The French threat to the British homeland had disappeared with Admiral Horatio Nelson's famous 1805 naval victory over the French and Spanish fleets at Trafalgar, leaving Britain free to stand as Napoleon's most constant enemy. Britain was the banker of the anti-Napoleon coalitions as well as the primary military opponent of French armies in Spain, roles that consumed men and treasure alike. Meanwhile, Napoleon increased his hold on the continent with the stunning victory at Austerlitz, also in 1805, after which he congratulated his troops and identified the enemy not present: "a Russian [and Austrian] army of 76,000 men, hired by the gold of England, was annihilated by you on the plains of Olmutz." It appeared the history of Europe was being written by two men in two battles. To Madison it must have looked like stalemate.

This situation was all too tempting not to be turned to advantage by a hostile America, which is to say, a hostile American government. Most people in the New England states did not share the anti-British views of Thomas Jefferson and his protégé/successor, because New England was the shipping center of the United States, and most ocean trade was conducted with Britain. New Englanders had vehemently opposed Jefferson's ill-begotten Embargo Act. It had halted trade with both Britain and France, bringing the New England economy to a standstill. By 1809, that act had been repealed, only to be replaced by the Non-Intercourse Act, which due to Napoleon's feigned compliance, targeted only Britain, so New England Yankee resentment remained.

The groundwork for the War of 1812 was set in 1809-10, Madison's first year in office. During the American Revolution, military campaigns had tried and failed to take Canada from Britain. Now, with Britain embroiled in what appeared to be costly and never-ending wars with Napoleon, Madison revived the idea. Jefferson concurred, writing him on April 27, 1809, just weeks after his inauguration: "They [Britain] never made an equal commercial treaty with any nation. . . . We should . . . include the North [Canada] in our confederacy, which would be of course in the first war, and we should have such an empire of liberty as she has never surveyed since the creation: and I am persuaded no constitution was ever before so well calculated as ours for extensive empire and self government."

In fact, the opportunity was at hand in 1809; the means were not, or so it seemed. As president, Jefferson had not seen the necessity of a standing army and neither did his then–secretary of State, James Madison. Both had mistakenly interpreted and thought to emulate Napoleon's method of calling up men by class (military age) as a call-up of militia. But while French conscripts may not have been lifelong professional soldiers, they were trained and drilled as regulars to serve for fixed periods, a harbinger of the twentieth century's large national armies. Militia, on the other hand, were made up of poorly trained temporary soldiers who had repeatedly been outmatched by regulars during the American Revolution. Madison and Jefferson believed they were following Napoleon's lead, basing America's ability to fight Britain upon militia. It would prove a fateful thought. In 1809 and 1810, President Madison wavered about war while rattling imaginary sabers, confident the British could not respond. It was a bad bluff, and the English called it by continuing to stir up Indian tribes west of the Appalachians. In fact, it need not have been a bluff.

Annexing Canada was a version of Manifest Destiny (see Chapter 10, Polk), and had Madison succeeded, he would have been hailed as one of three presidents who dramatically increased the land mass of the nation, the others being Thomas Jefferson with the Louisiana Purchase and James K. Polk, who precipitated the Mexican-American War and turned America into a sea-to-sea nation. But Madison ignored a bedrock line from the Constitution's first paragraph: to "provide for the common defence." He allowed the Army and Navy to languish at unviable levels, and his timing was terrible. In 1809-10, there were few British troops in Canada, so few (under five thousand) that even a large militia force might have succeeded against them. Instead, waiting until pressed hard by the War Hawks in Congress, Madison finally launched his war in 1812, three years too late.

It seemed propitious. By then, Napoleon was nearing mastery of continental Europe and was massing troops for the invasion of Russia, Britain's last major ally. So, on June 18, 1812—three years to the day before Napoleon would meet final defeat at the hands of Prussia's Blucher and Britain's Wellington at Waterloo—the US Congress, upon Madison's request, declared war on Britain. Six days later, Napoleon and his allies began crossing the Neman River into Russia.

Within months, the French Grande Armée dissolved in a disaster of epic proportions amid Russia's snow-swept expanses; the following year, Napoleon and a new army were defeated at Leipzig; in 1814, the Allies invaded France, and Napoleon was forced to abdicate. (He would return in 1815 for The Hundred Days and Waterloo.) Madison had not only bet on the wrong side; he bet on the wrong side at the wrong time, because the British Army and Navy were now free to turn their attention and strength against America.

Madison's forces had already achieved a few successes, most notably twenty-seven-year-old Captain (later Commodore) Oliver Hazard Perry's naval victory on Lake Erie, but all attempts to invade and hold Canada had been unsuccessful. Poorly trained and poorly led troops did what such troops do, they retreated or surrendered, and the war was about to get worse. In 1814, British reinforcements on land and sea fell on unready America, striking at multiple locations, including the nation's heart, Washington, DC. The American Army, with Madison present, was quickly defeated at Bladensburg. As the only sitting American president ever to take part in a battle, the defeat was his war in microcosm. (Abraham Lincoln did observe some of the action in Lt. Gen. Jubal Early's 1864 Confederate Raid on Washington.) Word of the defeat quickly came to his wife, Dolley, who packed up the White House silver and ordered the Gilbert Stuart portrait of George Washington to be brought safely away. British troops arrived shortly thereafter and put most of the public buildings to the torch. Strong winds did the rest, devouring the balance of the city in flames.

No one wants to be the last soldier killed in a war, much less the last soldier killed after the war is already over, but that is what happened at New Orleans on January 8, 1815, when Maj. Gen. Andrew Jackson defeated the Duke of Wellington's brother-in-law, Lt. Gen. Sir Edward Pakenham, a veteran of the Napoleonic Wars. Pakenham died there, and his army was severely mauled, neither side knowing the Treaty of Ghent ending the war had been signed on December 24, 1814. What the battle did do was create an illusion of victorious war, a perceived reality that caused Madison's popularity to soar and catapulted Jackson into the political spotlight and eventually the presidency.

All the while, New England simmered. Down along the shores of the Potomac, the new capital had arisen across from Virginia, and was beginning to look as if its most prominent residents, the presidents, were going to perpetually be Virginians. Except for the single term of John Adams, so it was from Washington to Jefferson to Madison to Monroe, known as the Virginia Dynasty. Indeed, northerners would only occupy the highest office for nineteen of the seventy-two years from 1789 to 1861. As a result, the idea of northern secession arose on several occasions, most notably at the Hartford Convention of 1814-15, when the New England states actually advocated separation from the Union in opposition to the War of 1812, dubbed by them "Mr. Madison's War." Among their demands for foregoing disunion was a one-term limit for presidents and a requirement that a successor president could not come from the same state as a sitting president. In one respect New England had already seceded because the region had continued its trade with Britain throughout the war, and the Hartford Convention was an obvious next move in the sequence of events.

Delegates from Massachusetts, Connecticut, Rhode Island, the New Hampshire Counties of Cheshire and Grafton, and the Vermont County of Windham met at Hartford, Connecticut, from December 15, 1814, to January 4, 1815, and issued a series of resolutions, including (boldface is the author's):

> *Finally,* **if the Union be destined to dissolution***, by reason of the multiplied abuses of bad administrations, it should, if possible, be the work of peaceable times, and deliberate consent.—****Some new form of confederacy should be substituted among those States****, which shall intend to maintain a federal relation to each other.—Events may prove that the causes of our calamities are deep and permanent. They may be found to proceed, not merely from the blindness of prejudice, pride of opinion, violence of party spirit, or the confusion of the times; but they may be traced to implacable combinations of individuals, or of States, to monopolize power and office, and to trample without remorse upon the rights and interests of commercial sections of the Union. Whenever it shall appear that these causes are radical and permanent,* **a separation by equitable arrangement, will be preferable to an alliance by constraint***, among nominal friends, but real enemies, inflamed by mutual hatred and jealousies, and inviting by intestine divisions, contempt, and aggression from abroad.*

In fact, the war envisioned by Jefferson, Madison, and the War Hawks ended with the status quo ante, except more than twenty thousand lives had been lost and the national debt jumped from $45 million to $127 million, which was probably the primary cause of America's first major financial crisis, the Panic of 1819. Prisoners and lands taken were exchanged. Only the native tribes, the pawns in the affair, were affected as Britain discontinued supporting and arming them in exchange for an American promise of their fair treatment, a promise ignored from the moment it was written in the Ninth Article of the treaty:

"The United States of America engage [*sic*] to put an end immediately after the Ratification of the present Treaty to hostilities with all the Tribes or Nations of Indians with whom they may be at war at the time of such Ratification, and forthwith to restore to such Tribes or Nations respectively all the possessions, rights, and privileges which they may have enjoyed or been entitled to in one thousand eight hundred and eleven previous to such hostilities."

Britain and the war with Britain consumed most of Madison's eight years in the White House, and the aura of victory brought him a popularity not found at the beginning of his two terms. History has been less generous. His first term's first-year errors created his second term's debacle, made worse because his broad range of expertise did not include even a subset of military knowledge.

James Madison was the last of three presidents to be affected by Napoleon, adversely in his case. Unlike Adams, whom Napoleon bailed out of the Quasi War with the Convention of 1800, or Jefferson, whose presidency was saved by Napoleon's sale of the Louisiana Purchase, Madison became the victim of Napoleon's defeat.

That defeat was immortalized in Tchaikovsky's *1812 Overture*, which has become a mainstay of Fourth of July celebrations, although few people see the irony of Americans applauding a musical piece written to commemorate a Russian victory that led to an American defeat. Although the War of 1812, Mr. Madison's War, certainly did not end with America victorious, it could have been had it been the War of 1809.

LYNDON BAINES JOHNSON—THE VIETNAM WAR
1963–1969

Born/Died: 1908 Stonewall, TX–1973 Stonewall, TX
Education: Southwest Texas State Teachers College
Occupation: Rancher, professional politician
Political Party: Democratic
Government Service: Vice President 1961–1963, Senator (TX) 1949–1961, Representative (TX) 1937–1949
Military Service: Navy Lieutenant Commander; World War II
Preceded by: John F. Kennedy (Bay of Pigs fiasco; Cuban Missile Crisis prevents nuclear war; Apollo Space Program commenced to land man on the moon; civil rights reforms; major tax cut increases tax revenues; advisory role in Vietnam continued)

On November 22, 1963, President John F. Kennedy was assassinated, and Vice President Lyndon B. Johnson inherited his position and his problems, including the US military advisory role in South Vietnam. Less than a year later, LBJ countered the growing threat posed by South Vietnamese communist Viet Cong guerrillas and communist North Vietnamese regulars with US and allied air, sea, and ground forces. Unlike the wars in 1812 and 1950, there was ample US strength, just not an equivalent plan, and the conflict devolved into a war of attrition, a form of warfare America would not win.

Gen. William C. Westmoreland, who had distinguished himself in World War II, was selected to command the effort. What LBJ failed to understand was that not all generals are military historians or even military strategists. While the American method of promotion was not as inept as the old British method of purchasing rank, neither was it geared toward elevating military philosophers, strategists, and tacticians to the highest levels. Before World War II, Gen. George C. Marshall began logging names in a little book (see Chapter 2, Eisenhower)—names of

President Lyndon B. Johnson and Gen. William C. Westmoreland
YOICHI OKAMOTO, LBJ LIBRARY

officers he believed would make good general officers in the war he was certain was coming. Yet, even that little book had to stand the test of combat, and often came up short, requiring relieving, shuffling, and promoting until finally the right generals were placed in the right jobs.

Gen. Harold K. Johnson succeeded Gen. Earl G. Wheeler as Chief of Staff in 1964, and neither of them had a little book like Marshall's. But they did have efficiency reports of officers who had served in World War II and Korea. Still, none of those officers had served as generals or led independent commands in combat. Generals Johnson and Wheeler simply lacked sufficient input to evaluate a general's ability to lead a large army with strategic and tactical acumen in such an unfamiliar political, military, and physical environment.

LBJ's own military experience in World War II was as a junior officer who saw very limited service. Further, he was no student of military history. As a result, he relied upon the judgment of General Johnson and a few others in the selection of Westmoreland. It was the great error of

LBJ's first year in office. "Westy," as he was known, looked the part and acted the role, but he was not the general for the job and neither was LBJ the president to manage him or the war.

LBJ was a domestic-issues president, and he would achieve landmark successes in civil rights, Medicare, and his War on Poverty. The Vietnam War was an unwanted distraction on the one hand and an increasingly consuming interest on the other. Like Lincoln in the Civil War, a military neophyte was at the helm, and he could not resist the role, meddling and agonizing and meddling some more as the situation deteriorated. Unlike Lincoln, who tended to replace generals as soon as they exhibited battlefield incompetence, LBJ stuck with Westy for three and a half years, prolonging and worsening his freshman-year error.

LBJ needed at his side a military philosopher/historian/strategist, someone who could put the war in context. Neither General Johnson nor Secretary of Defense Robert McNamara was that man. While researching at the Military History Institute, the renowned military theorist Col. Harry G. Summers Jr. reiterated to me what he had written in *On Strategy: A Critical Analysis of the Vietnam War*, his tie-in to Carl von Clausewitz's nineteenth-century classic *On War*: "Instead of concentrating attention on military strategy which had become unfashionable after World War II . . . , there was an increased emphasis on technical, managerial, and bureaucratic concerns. Instead of being experts in the application of military force to achieve the political ends of the United States, we became neophyte political scientists and systems analysts and were outclassed by the civilian professionals who dominated national security policy under Secretary of Defense Robert S. McNamara. It is no wonder that the president turned to these civilian professionals rather than the military for strategic advice."

That advice turned into group-think as all of them fell into the attrition trap, believing that killing enough North Vietnamese soldiers would compel North Vietnam to pull its troops out of South Vietnam. This was a fundamental mistake. The North Vietnamese had a dramatically higher threshold for casualties than did Americans. Meanwhile, LBJ took an invasion of the North off the table, a reasonable decision to avoid an escalation that might bring China into the conflict, but once that decision was made, it was incumbent upon him to seek a strategic alternative.

Establishing a cordon barrier across the narrow neck dividing North and South Vietnam extending west through Laos to the Thai border would have blocked the Ho Chi Minh Trail, effectively stopping the flow of North Vietnamese regulars and supplies into the South. Colonel Summers wrote: "U.S. forces should have been committed to isolate the battlefield by sealing off South Vietnam from North Vietnam . . . [and] such a strategy was proposed in 1965 by South Vietnamese General Cao Van Vien. His plan entailed fortifying a zone along the 17th parallel from Dong Ha in Vietnam to Savannakhet on the Lao-Thai border. . . . [The] plan paralleled a concept proposed by the [US] Joint Chiefs of Staff in August 1965." Colonel Summers went on to say that Westy agreed with the plan only if the president would mobilize the reserves. Westmoreland's demand forced another critical mistake, because the president was not going to call up the reserves and he knew it. Westmoreland also should have realized he already had sufficient forces to seal the border, because, once sealed, the fighting in the South would have been relegated by the communists to the Viet Cong guerillas, a force the ARVN (Army of the Republic of Vietnam) was equipped to handle.

Instead, LBJ agreed to the establishment of the McNamara Line, primarily manned by unreliable mechanical sensors that were expected to detect enemy movements, a program about which this author had first-hand knowledge. The sensors did detect movements, including swaying trees, animals, and distant artillery, as well as men and machines, and only if the sensors were properly placed and working. So North Vietnamese men and materiel continued to flow into South Vietnam, where Westmoreland assured the president he could defeat them in pitched battles.

Thus, the conflict went on as a war of attrition, the outcome succinctly explained by a Colonel Summers anecdote on point. He told a North Vietnamese colonel after the war: "You know you never defeated us on the battlefield," to which the enemy colonel replied, "That may be so, but it is also irrelevant."

Westmoreland harkened back to World War II, and clung to a game of big battles, but exchanging lives was a losing proposition, and nothing was more irrational than the high command's penchant for assaulting hilltops for no other reason than to engage and kill enemy soldiers. To them, it was part of the strategic plan of attrition; for the troops on the ground it was something else.

A personal anecdote puts the face on one gallant officer who paid the price:

Hilltops and the Price of Attrition

US MILITARY ACADEMY, WEST POINT, NY, 1964—Spying an untouched apple pie at the end of breakfast during plebe year, restraint was impossible. In nearly one motion at dismissal it was napkin to chest, pie to napkin, scarf and coat wrapped around it. With my left hand barely pressed against the coat just below the pie, my right hand was free for saluting upperclassmen on the way to the barracks. Up the stairs, slamming against the wall as upperclassmen passed, squaring the corners to the third floor, and turning for home, gloating bubbled to the surface just inches from success, when from down the hall came:

"Cohn! Halt! What do you have there, Mister?"

"An apple pie, sir."

"A whole apple pie?"

"Yes, sir."

My heart raced. A pause. Then came this, a mild response with a hint of congratulatory pride: "Carry on, Mister."

That was Pete Lantz, two years ahead of me in the Class of '66. In 1967, Pete would die at Dak To, a lieutenant leading his platoon in the 173rd Airborne Brigade, assaulting a hill defended by entrenched North Vietnamese troops, a hill that would be abandoned as soon as it was taken.

Three of us from '68 joined his widow, Dagmar, and the daughter he never knew, at the Academy for the presentation of his Silver Star.

The pain of this poignant story has not diminished with time or telling.

LBJ believed he was prepared for the presidency, and in many respects he was. But he was not prepared for war, and he never overcame the deficiency. Domestic issues were another matter, and his War on Poverty, passage of landmark civil rights legislation, and Medicare are among the initiatives that will continue to improve his standing as the pain and sacrifices suffered by the Vietnam War generation begin to fade beneath the whitewash of history.

GEORGE W. BUSH—9/11, AFGHANISTAN, AND IRAQ
2001–2009

Born: 1946 New Haven, CT
Education: Yale University, Harvard Business School
Occupation: Businessman
Political Party: Republican
Government Service: Governor (TX) 1995–2000
Military Service: 1st Lieutenant; Texas Air National Guard, stateside during the Vietnam War
Preceded by: William Clinton (universal health care defeated; tax increase; surplus budgets; seeks Republican help to pass North American Free Trade Agreement, welfare reform, and gutting of Glass-Steagall Act that had prevented banks from speculating in equity markets, which will eventually contribute to Great Recession of 2007–2009)

In 1876 Lt. Col. George Armstrong Custer made his last stand on the Little Big Horn and Samuel J. Tilden made his last stand in Florida. Tilden, the Democratic candidate, had won the popular vote over Republican nominee Rutherford B. Hayes, but the Florida vote was disputed and finally decided in favor of Hayes by a Republican majority panel and a compromise agreement (see Chapter 9, Hayes). Vice President Al Gore met the same fate 124 years later, when, once again, the Democrat won the popular vote by a solid margin. This time the disputed Florida vote, undergoing a recount, was halted by a 5–4 US Supreme Court vote, and George W. Bush, the Republican, was elected. Clearly, neither the election of 1876 nor the election of 2000 were models of democracy, and the latter

President George W. Bush and First Lady Laura Bush
COURTESY GEORGE W. BUSH PRESIDENTIAL LIBRARY AND MUSEUM

event in particular undermined the nation's moral high ground, soon to be recaptured when the horrific events of September 11, 2001, unfolded.

Earlier that year, this author's family had spent an evening at "The Top of the World" restaurant atop one of New York's World Trade Center Twin Towers, taking for granted that sense of security Americans then enjoyed. Not since the Japanese attacks in December 1941 had US territory been struck such a significant blow. The warning signs were there, such as Saudi nationals taking flight training in the United States, while foregoing landing instructions. Of more significance was either the absence of a military protocol addressing the appropriate reaction to thwart a civilian plane under the control of hijackers or a reluctance to employ it.

On 9/11 two planes were intentionally crashed into the Twin Towers, a third struck the Pentagon, and a fourth was brought down in rural Pennsylvania when brave passengers attacked the attackers. On that day, more than three thousand people, mostly Americans, died in those attacks, and questions soon surfaced. Why had fighter planes not intercepted the hijacked planes, and if they had, who would have issued the orders to shoot down planes filled with civilians, including children and infants?

9/11 Comparative Time Sequence

TWIN TOWERS	PENTAGON	PENNSYLVANIA	PRESIDENT & VICE PRESIDENT
American Airlines (AA) Flight 11 (Boston to L.A.)	**American Airlines Flight 77 (DC to L.A.)**	**United Airlines Flight 93 (Newark to San Francisco)**	
United Airlines (UA) Flight 175 (Boston to L.A.)			
7:59 Takeoff (AA 11)			
8:14 Takeoff (UA 175)	8:20 Takeoff		
8:19 Flight attendant notifies AA of hijacking			
8:21 Transponder turned off			
8:38 Boston Center* notifies NEADS* of hijacking		8:42 Takeoff	
8:46 NEADS scrambles Otis fighter jets			
8:46 AA 11 crashes into 1 WTC* (North Tower)			
8:47 Transponder code changes			
8:52 Flight attendant notifies UA of hijacking			
8:55 New York Center suspects hijacking	8:54 AA 77 makes unauthorized turn south		8:55 President informed small plane struck a Twin Tower; he enters Sarasota, FL, school
	8:56 Transponder is turned off		

9:03 UA 175 crashes into 2 WTC (South Tower)	9:05 AA headquarters is aware that Flight 77 is hijacked		9:05 President informed of 2nd plane strike
9:15 New York Center advises NEADS UA 175 is second aircraft to crash into WTC			9:15 President briefed, confers with VP et al.
9:16 AA headquarters aware AA 11 has crashed into WTC			
9:21 Boston Center advises NEADS AA 11 is airborne heading for Washington			
9:24 NEADS scrambles Langley fighter jets in search of AA 11			
	9:25 Herndon FAA* Command Center grounds all flights (Ground Stop)		
	9:34 FAA advises NEADS that AA 77 is missing	9:34 Herndon FAA Command Center advises FAA H.Q. UA 93 is hijacked	9:35 President motorcade departs for airport
		9:36 Flight attendant notifies UA of hijacking	9:37 VP enters Pres. Emergency Op. Ctr. below White House
	9:37 AA 77 crashes into the Pentagon		9:38 President informed of Pentagon attack
		9:41 Transponder is turned off	
		9:57 Passenger revolt	9:54 President departs on Air Force One
		10:03 UA 93 crashes in field in Shanksville, PA	10:10 VP authorizes shootdown of planes

*Center: Air Traffic Control Center
*NEADS: Northeast Air Def. Sector
*WTC: World Trade Center
*FAA: Federal Aviation Admin.

SOURCE: THE 9/11 COMMISSION REPORT

Lee H. Hamilton, co-chairman of the 9/11 Commission, told reporters "there's no documentary evidence" that Vice President Cheney conferred with Bush before issuing the shoot-down order.

In their 2007 book, *Without Precedent*, 9/11 Commission chairmen Hamilton and Thomas Kean wrote of the growth of 9/11 conspiracy theories:

> *If the military had had the amount of time they said they had . . . and had scrambled their jets, it was hard to figure out how they had failed to shoot down at least one of the planes. . . . In this way, the FAA's and NORAD's inaccurate reporting after 9/11 created the opportunity for people to construct a series of conspiracy theories that persist to this day. . . . The tape recordings . . . from the day were extremely important—they provided a real-time record of what was happening that enabled our staff to relive the day, instead of relying solely on people's memory or their hurried notes of what took place. (See chart on preceding pages)*

In fact, chaos reigns when events on the magnitude of 9/11 occur. In these cases the military chain-of-command is so critical in ensuring the rapid, clear dissemination of accurate information to the responsible decision-making officers, and, conversely, from those officers back to the implementing forces. Further, the president as commander-in-chief of the Armed Forces, who is at the top of the chain, must be continually updated and advised. Such did not occur on 9/11, in part due to a delay in communications from civilian air traffic controllers to their FAA (Federal Aviation Administration) superiors and on to the appropriate military command, NORAD (North American Air Defense Command).

At the time, President Bush was reading a book to schoolchildren in Sarasota, Florida, and instead of breaking off once he understood the crashing planes were not accidents, he continued on with the class. In fact, there is no evidence that he issued any orders or instructions. Vice President Dick Cheney, who was at the White House, took it upon himself to take charge, and it was he who authorized the shooting down of hijacked commercial airliners. However, he failed to issue the orders through the correct chain, and the pilots received them too late to prevent the attack on the Pentagon. It was the head of the FAA's Ground Center who took the unprecedented step of grounding all flights, once again without the president in the loop.

In fairness, the president is not expected to assert operational control of a military response. The president's job is to ensure that the correct protocols and guidelines are in place, to keep informed, and to intervene when necessary, especially when confusion fouls bureaucracy. President Bush did not do this. Instead, he seemed content to leave Cheney in charge. A seasoned president would never have behaved in this way, and Bush certainly did not when other crises erupted later in his presidency. The great unheralded success of his presidency was the fact that somehow he prevented the generally anticipated second shoe from dropping. The country was not struck by another major terrorist attack.

Is the Vice Presidency the Best Preparation for the Presidency?

History is our guide. Were eighteenth- and nineteenth-century Vice Presidents John Adams, Thomas Jefferson, Martin Van Buren, John Tyler, Millard Fillmore, Andrew Johnson, and Chester Arthur or twentieth-century Vice Presidents Theodore Roosevelt, Calvin Coolidge, Harry Truman, Lyndon Johnson, Richard Nixon, Gerald Ford, and George H. W. Bush better prepared than most of the other non–vice presidents who became presidents? The answer is more complex than it appears. First, the presidency became far more complex in the twentieth century, which is why the vice presidents are divided by centuries. Even so, all of the vice presidents who became presidents had one element in common. None of them were brought into the inner circles of the Oval Office and almost never into Cabinet meetings. Truman had not even been briefed on the Manhattan Project. Rarely have vice presidential candidates been selected by their party or presidential candidates because they were expected to make good successors. Rather, they were typically chosen for demographic and/or factional balance.

The vice president's only designated function is to preside over the Senate and cast tie-breaking votes, neither of which duty has regularly been performed, and vice presidential literature is littered with the occupants' scorn for the constitutional irrelevance of the office:

John Adams: "My country has, in its wisdom, contrived for me the most insignificant office that ever the invention of man contrived or his imagination conceived."

Thomas Jefferson: "[It is a] tranquil and unoffending station" and "a splendid misery."

Thomas Marshall: "Once there were two brothers: one ran away to sea, the other was elected vice-president—and nothing was ever heard from either of them again." And "[the vice presidency is like] a man in a cataleptic fit; he cannot speak; he cannot move; he suffers no pain; he is perfectly conscious of all that goes on, but has no part in it."

John Nance Gardner: "[Taking the job] was the worst damn fool mistake I ever made."

Harry Truman: "Look at all the vice presidents in history. Where are they? They were about as useful as a cow's fifth teat."

Conversely, there was this from Dick Cheney, a vice president who did not become president: "President Bush gave me a tremendous opportunity to serve as the vice president. I enjoyed very much having the opportunity to be a part of his team. He told me at the outset, he wanted me to sign on to be a part of his team—and he was true to his word, kept it." Interestingly, Cheney was criticized for being too powerful.

Therefore, the answer to the question is that the vice presidency could be the best preparation for the presidency if the president believes the vice president to be qualified, if the vice president is given important responsibilities, and if the vice president is given full access to the inner workings of the presidency, all historically unlikely occurrences.

CHAPTER 5

AMERICA'S ORIGINAL SIN: SLAVERY

JAMES MONROE (1817), ZACHARY TAYLOR (1849) AND MILLARD FILLMORE (1850), FRANKLIN PIERCE (1853), JAMES BUCHANAN (1857), AND ANDREW JOHNSON (1865)

Slavery was a national, not a regional sin, manifested in several forms. By 1817, slavery and its horrors and, to a lesser degree, indentured servitude, child labor (slavery by another name), and impoverished factory labor provided the backs upon which the new nation was being built. Even the self-sufficient yeoman farmers, whom Thomas Jefferson idealized as the backbone of America, those independent landowners free from masters to face the vicissitudes of nature and markets, typically survived through the uncompensated labor of their large families. James Oakes wrote of the phenomenon: "Given his continued dependence on the labor of his sons, the typical yeoman farmer sought to exercise extensive control over his patrimony. . . . Far from rearing their children to individual autonomy, yeoman society depended heavily on the perpetuation of intergenerational dependency."

Racial, biblical, cultural, and bigoted justifications were used to perpetuate slavery. Slaves received food, clothing, and housing from cradle to grave, but were subject to the dictates of masters, who could mistreat them at will, unenforced laws to the contrary notwithstanding. Indentured servitude, a form of time-limit slavery—so prevalent in Colonial America—was rapidly being replaced by yeoman families and slavery primarily due to a shortage of manpower available from Britain. Child labor, the slavery of the voiceless, was the great thief of childhood and guarantor of shortened lives. Factory workers, the economic slaves of industry, were guaranteed nothing, often worked in unhealthy environments, and barely survived, malnourished and in squalor, but they were free to leave, free to starve. Alexis de Tocqueville, who traveled and made a famously insightful study of America in 1831, was motivated to compare "equality in slavery to inequality with freedom." He continued:

I see that in a certain portion of the territory of the United States at the present day, the legal barrier which separated the two races is tending to fall away, but not that which exists in the manners of the country; slavery recedes, but the prejudice to which it has given birth remains stationary. Whosoever has inhabited the United States must have perceived that in those parts of the Union in which the negroes are no longer slaves, they have in no wise drawn nearer to the whites. On the contrary, the prejudice of the race appears to be stronger in the States which have abolished slavery, than in those where it still exists; and nowhere is it so intolerant as in those States where servitude has never been known.

. . . The electoral franchise has been conferred upon the negroes in almost all the States in which slavery has been abolished; but if they come forward to vote, their lives are in danger. If oppressed, they may bring an action at law, but they will find none but whites amongst their judges; and although they may legally serve as jurors, prejudice repulses them from that office. The same schools do not receive the child of the black and of the European. In the theatres, gold cannot procure a seat for the servile race beside their former masters; in the hospitals they lie apart; and although they are allowed to invoke the same Divinity as the whites, it must be at a different altar, and in their own churches, with their own clergy. . . .

In the South, where slavery still exists, the negroes are less carefully kept apart; they sometimes share the labor and the recreations of the whites; the whites consent to intermix with them to a certain extent, and although the legislation treats them more harshly, the habits of the people are more tolerant and compassionate. In the South the master is not afraid to raise his slave to his own standing, because he knows that he can in a moment reduce him to the dust at pleasure. In the North the white no longer distinctly perceives the barrier which separates him from the degraded race, and he shuns the negro with the more pertinacity, since he fears lest they should some day be confounded together.

As the post–Civil War century unfolded, slavery would be outlawed, though continued through other means, including the enforced labor of falsely accused convicts and sharecroppers stripped of rights by America's form of serfdom. Labor unions emerged, but worker rights, wages, and working conditions did not dramatically improve until the early twentieth century's Progressive Movement brought about legal changes.

These then were the myriad forms of American slavery that should be remembered in the context of the following six presidents' responses and reactions to the enslavement of African Americans.

The Twelve Slaveholding Presidents

George Washington	Andrew Jackson	James K. Polk
Thomas Jefferson	Martin Van Buren	Zachary Taylor
James Madison	William Henry Harrison	Andrew Johnson
James Monroe	John Tyler	Ulysses S. Grant

JAMES MONROE—MISSOURI COMPROMISE OF 1820
1817–1825

Born/Died: 1758 Westmoreland County, VA–1831 New York City, NY
Education: The College of William & Mary
Occupation: Planter
Political Party: Democratic-Republican

Government Service: Secretary of State 1815–1817, Secretary of War 1814–1815, Secretary of State 1811–1814, Governor (VA) 1799–1802, 1811, Ambassador (Britain) 1803–1808, (France) 1794–1796, Senator (VA) 1790–1794, VA Delegate to the Congress of the Confederation 1783–1786
Military Service: Major; Continental Army 1775–1778, wounded at the Battle of Trenton
Preceded by: James Madison (Napoleon's near mastery of continental Europe ties up British forces; creates opportunity for United States to take Canada; maneuvers toward war with Britain; launches War of 1812 as Napoleon invades Russia; Napoleon defeated in Russia; British troops free to attack United States; Washington, DC, attacked and burned; New England's Hartford Convention threatens secession; Battle of New Orleans unknowingly fought after war ends, makes hero of Gen. Andrew Jackson and falsely implies US victory in the war; national debt dramatically increased to support war leads to Panic of 1819)

Like fellow Virginians Washington, Jefferson, and Madison before him— the Virginia Dynasty—President James Monroe was a slaveholder who understood slavery to be a dying institution. By the time he took the oath of office in March 1817, slavery had been outlawed in many European and New World countries. And, one by one, several US states were ending the practice, with New York freeing all slaves less than four months after Monroe's inauguration. Monroe responded by supporting the American Colonization Society, which led to the founding of Liberia. Its capital, Monrovia, was named in his honor. It was an idea with little meaning for American slaves who had American roots going back more than a dozen generations, and transporting them to Africa was as impractical as it was immoral. Even so, it was a view espoused by Abraham Lincoln as late as 1862 (see Chapter 11, Lincoln).

In acknowledgment of a European trend, the US Constitution authorized an end to the slave trade after 1808, and Thomas Jefferson, president at the time, promptly signed a bill in 1807 (he had already signed such a bill in 1804 for the Louisiana Purchase lands) turning that option into law.

Madison, of the same mind as his predecessor, was too consumed by the War of 1812 and the events leading up to it to give proper attention to the issue.

Such should not have been the case when James Monroe was inaugurated. Dubbed the Era of Good Feeling, Monroe's presidency began in a time of inventive disruption particularly applicable to an expanding and increasingly expansive nation. Eli Whitney patented the cotton gin in 1794, allowing the mechanical seed separation of short staple cotton at a rate

President James Monroe
LIBRARY OF CONGRESS

seventeen times as fast as could be accomplished by hand. Further, short staple cotton could be grown at a variety of elevations, which opened substantial lands to cotton agriculture, and before long, cotton exports surpassed the total dollar value of all other US exports combined, becoming the primary product fueling the Industrial Revolution then sweeping Britain and the Northeast United States.

This increased use of the soil was supported by increased means of transportation. James Finley built the first suspension bridge at Uniontown, Pennsylvania, in 1801; Robert Fulton initiated maritime steam power with his successful test of the *Clermont* in 1807; construction of the Erie Canal commenced in 1817; and steam-powered railroads were developed in Britain in 1811.

This world awaiting the presidency of James Monroe was a changed world he seemed not to see. These inventions altered the dynamics of the nation, a nation that jumped from nineteen states at his inauguration to twenty-four states by the summer of 1821, including Mississippi (1817), Illinois (1818), Alabama (1819), Maine (1820), and Missouri (1821), each addition maintaining the balance between free and slave states and their representation in the US Senate.

By 1817, cotton production was soaring and well on its way to becoming "King Cotton." Northern mills as well as British mills relied upon the crop as did New York financiers and shipping interests so long as slave labor kept the price per bale competitive, this despite a growing international condemnation of what was referred to in America as the "peculiar institution."

Inventions, national expansion, intertwined economics, and moral outrage set the stage for competing policies. It was time for a new president to understand the dynamics and take the bold steps necessary to cope with them despite the political price. James Monroe was not such a president. Already, the New England states had come close to secession during the War of 1812. Would not the South do likewise over the abolition or restriction of slavery? Would not the cotton-connected interests in the North oppose any action impacting the cost of the product? Would an evenly split Senate ever concur?

What could Monroe have done? With five territories applying for statehood, he could have vetoed the admission of any of them as slave states. (Future presidents would use the veto to delay or prevent the admission of states, including President Taft, who vetoed Arizona's first attempt at statehood, and Lincoln, who wavered before signing West Virginia's application.) In 1817, the uproar could have been deafening, since political power, more than slavery, was at stake.

The first protective tariff had just become law in 1816, setting off a dispute with far-reaching consequences, because it protected northern industries against foreign imports at the expense of southern exports that were dependent upon two-way trade with Europe. A mill owner in New England who was buying cotton from the South did not want to face competition from English mills buying cotton from the same source, whereas cotton planters needed both customers. The Mason-Dixon Line also became a tariff line, and only political parity could keep it that way, which is why the slave states needed to maintain a political balance in the Senate. Whether or not the new states would become cotton-plantation states or not was irrelevant. For example, Florida (1845), Kansas (1861), Nevada (1864), Oklahoma (1907), and New Mexico (1912) never became significant cotton-producing states, yet, as territories, they provided fodder for the expansion-of-slavery disputes confronting the nation until 1860.

Still, if Monroe had vetoed Mississippi's application for statehood as a slave state in 1817—his first year in office—the expansion-of-slavery issue could have been settled or at least delayed then and there, and Monroe would have lost his bid for reelection in 1820. What is more, he had two more opportunities to make the same courageous and historic move, in 1818 when the eastern portion of the Mississippi Territory came into the Union as Alabama and again in 1819 when the issue came like a thunderclap over Missouri. Northerners wanted it to come in as a free state. Southerners objected. Monroe believed it was up to the citizens of the prospective state, a foreshadowing of the flawed popular sovereignty principle advocated by Illinois Democrat Sen. Stephen Douglas and others three decades later. He finally agreed to what became known as the Missouri Compromise of 1820. Missouri would come in slave; Maine would come in free; and future states entering from the Louisiana Purchase would enter the Union as slave below the 36°30' parallel (Missouri's southern border), and free above it. In reality, the compromise made matters worse, because it codified the extension of slavery, and led to future disputes over Texas and the Southwest (see Chapter 10 and map in Chapter 3), which were then part of Mexico and could not be included in the Missouri Compromise without implying aggressive intent. In fact, Texas would become the nation's largest cotton producer.

Monroe was less compromising in foreign affairs. Enunciating what would come to be known as the Monroe Doctrine, he warned the powers of Europe not to interfere with the newly independent nations of Central and South America, at the time an apparently bold and toothless statement because the United States had neither the Army nor Navy to back it up. In fact, just eight years after the conclusion of its war with the United States (the War of 1812), Britain offered its Navy in support, and the reason may be found in the realm of international trade.

Cotton was becoming "King." In 1900, Worthy Putnam Sterns wrote in *The Foreign Trade of the United States from 1820 to 1840*: "The crop of 1824 was 30 million pounds larger than that of 1823. . . . It came upon the market just in time to reap the benefit of the abnormal demand resulting from the great speculative movement in England in 1824 and 1825. . . . The value exported to England in 1824 was 15 million dollars, in 1825 30 million dollars."

Monroe may have seemed oblivious to the new age of steam and machine, but whether by accident or design, he was relying upon commerce to defend the nation, which may explain his failure to interfere with slavery, the labor driving that commerce.

ZACHARY TAYLOR AND MILLARD FILLMORE—COMPROMISE OF 1850

ZACHARY TAYLOR
1849–1850

Born/Died: 1784 near Barboursville, VA–1850 Washington, DC
Education: No formal education
Occupation: Professional Army officer
Political Party: Whig
Government Service: US Army 1808–1849
Military Service: Major General; Mexican-American War, Second Seminole War, Black Hawk War, War of 1812

MILLARD FILLMORE
1850–1853

Born/Died: 1800 Summerhill, NY–1874 Buffalo, NY
Education: Limited formal education
Occupation: Lawyer

Political Party: Whig
Government Service: Vice President 1849–1850, Comptroller (NY) 1848–1849, Representative (NY); 1837–1843
Military Service: Federal Major, Home Guard during the Civil War
Preceded by: James K. Polk precedes Taylor and Fillmore (reduces tariff; places federal funds in US Treasury instead of state banks; instigates and wins Mexican-American War; settles Oregon Territory boundary with Britain; Mexican Cession and Oregon Territory create sea-to-sea nation as envisioned in concept of Manifest Destiny)

Maj. Gen. Zachary Taylor is one of the overlooked gems of American history. Uneducated and politically disinterested, he was an unlikely candidate for president and knew it. Despite the view of his predecessor, James K. Polk, that he was "wholly unqualified for the station," as a hero of the Mexican-American War, Taylor was viewed in the politically marketable mold of Generals Andrew Jackson and William Henry Harrison. In fact, he was more akin to future President Ronald Reagan, another nonintellectual executive with strong, unbending opinions, opinions in Taylor's case that would come as a surprise. Massachusetts Whig Rep. Horace Mann wrote of him: "He really is a most simple-minded old man. He has the least show of pretension about him of any man I ever saw; talks as artlessly as a child about affairs of State, and does not seem to pretend to a knowledge of any thing of which he is ignorant. He is a remarkable man in some respects; and it is remarkable that such a man should be President of the United States."

He was a large Louisiana slaveholder, one-time father-in-law (his daughter died soon after her marriage) of future Secretary of War and future Confederate President Jefferson Davis, and father of future Confederate Lt. Gen. Richard Taylor. He was also a staunch opponent of protective tariffs, those discriminatory taxes so opposed by his fellow planters. For all this, in 1850 he declared, "People of the North need have no apprehension of the further expansion of slavery."

True to his word, he proposed admitting the lands from New Mexico to California, just acquired from Mexico, as free states or territories. Slavery expansionists were in shock, threatened secession, and were further stunned in February 1850 when Taylor declared if they were "taken in rebellion

President Zachary Taylor as a major general in the Mexican-American War, 1846–1848
LIBRARY OF CONGRESS

against the Union, he would hang [them] . . . with less reluctance than he had hanged deserters and spies in Mexico." A week later, the general in him saw it differently. In a significant precursor to Lt. Gen. Winfield Scott's Anaconda Plan in the Civil War (see Chapter 11, Lincoln, and Appendix B), Taylor said: "[S]end a fleet to blockade their harbors, levy duties on all goods going into the South, and prevent any goods from coming out. I can save the Union without shedding a drop of blood. It is not true, as reported in the North, that I said I would march an army and subdue them: there would be no need of any."

Here was just the person to end both the expansion of slavery and the question of secession as issues, but he did not survive to see his will asserted, dying in July before he could deliver his promised veto of the Compromise of 1850.

Clearly, Taylor had his heart in the right place; his head was out of place. He was simply out of his element, and except for the all-important slavery issue, he was virtually a caretaker president, a form of failure for a general in the field and no less so for the nation's chief executive. He knew nothing of foreign affairs and delegated this important presidential function to Secretary of State John M. Clayton, a former senator from Delaware and Yale graduate, who did negotiate the Clayton-Bulwer Treaty with Britain as an initial attempt at "facilitating and protecting the construction of a ship canal between the Atlantic and Pacific Oceans" across Central America. Otherwise, Clayton's lack of diplomatic experience proved to be a hindrance in America's foreign relations.

Vice President Millard Fillmore, the New Yorker who succeeded him, promptly reversed Taylor's vision and placed the Union back on a two-nation course.

Sen. Stephen Doug-
las, the great advocate
of popular sovereignty,
took over the floor debate
when Sen. Henry Clay—
the Kentucky Democrat
known as the Great Com-
promiser—fell ill, break-
ing the compromise bill
into five politically pal-
atable parts: California
would enter the Union a
free state; the slave trade
(not slavery) was ended in

President Millard Fillmore as a candidate, 1852
LIBRARY OF CONGRESS

Washington, DC; New Mexico and Utah Territories would decide their
own paths on slavery; Texas would relinquish claims to territory in New
Mexico in exchange for the US assumption of Texas debts; and the Fugitive Slave Act would be reinforced and enforced. The floodgates were
opened, and Fillmore justified it on December 2, 1850, in his first message to Congress, unabashedly standing as the anti-Taylor: "They were
adopted in the spirit of conciliation and for the purpose of conciliation."

The Mexican Cession, encompassing all or part of the future states of
New Mexico, Arizona, Nevada, Utah, and Colorado, would be affected,
although in reality none of these lands were conducive to slave-labor
crops such as cotton. What Taylor stood to stop, Fillmore perpetuated,
and more trouble would come four years later with the next tranche of
states through the Kansas-Nebraska Act of 1854.

Fillmore was only slightly better educated than Taylor, and mostly
through apprenticeships in the law. He did send Commodore Matthew C.
Perry to open trade with Japan, the two most significant results of which
were its inspiration for one of the world's great operas, Giacomo Puccini's
Madama Butterfly, and as the instigator of modernization for Japanese
industry and its military, modernizations that would eventually stun the
world when Japan emerged victorious in the Russo-Japanese War fifty
years later.

As an anti-slavery, pro-protective tariff Whig, Fillmore had opposed admitting Texas into the Union as a slave state in 1845, which makes his actions in 1850 all the more confusing. He immediately replaced Taylor's Cabinet and proceeded to confound supporters and opponents alike, so upsetting the balance of his party, especially by supporting the Fugitive Slave Act, that he set the Whigs upon a path to fragmentation and dissolution. He would be the last Whig president.

Neither Taylor nor Fillmore was as qualified as ten of their eleven unqualified predecessors (Andrew Jackson being their equally unqualified exception), but had he lived, posterity might have shined on Zachary Taylor for his innate hard-headed, no-nonsense common sense, instead of his inconsequential occupancy of the office. Had this southern slaveholder lived, the Civil War might have been the stuff of fiction rather than reality.

FRANKLIN PIERCE—KANSAS-NEBRASKA ACT OF 1854
1853–1857

Born/Died: 1804 Hillsborough (now Hillsboro), NH–1869 Concord, NH
Education: Bowdoin College
Occupation: Lawyer
Political Party: Democratic
Government Service: Senator (NH) 1837–1842, Representative (NH) 1833–1837
Military Service: Brigadier General; Mexican-American War 1846–1848, NH Militia 1831–1846
Preceded by: Millard Fillmore, successor after Zachary Taylor's death (reverses Taylor's attempt to inhibit spread of slavery and signs Compromise of 1850, which Taylor had promised to veto; Compromise brings California in free and opens New Mexico Territory for potential slave state admissions; supports Fugitive Slave Act; opens trade with Japan; last Whig president)

Franklin Pierce was a man of superlatives. He was the northernmost man ever elected president; the youngest man up to that time to become president; the only president to go from private to brigadier general in a year and then go on to run for the presidency against his old commanding officer (Whig candidate Maj. Gen.—later Lt. Gen.—Winfield Scott). More rounds of voting—forty-nine—were required to nominate him than to nominate any other successful candidate for the office, making him America's quintessential dark horse nominee; he was the first president to recite his more than three-thousand-word inaugural address from memory (which means he was probably the only president with an eidetic memory); he was the only elected president to serve an entire term without a vice president (his running mate died after taking the oath of office in his hometown); he was the only person to run for president against a schoolmate (John P. Hale, Bowdoin Class of 1827 ran as a Free Soil candidate against Pierce, Class of '24); and, most significantly, Franklin Pierce was a thorough anti-slavery Yankee, born, raised, and educated in New Hampshire, who was—with apparent incongruity—among the strongest states' rights advocates ever to become president, a fact made clear from the outset in his inaugural address:

President Franklin Pierce as a brigadier general during the Mexican-American War, 1846–1848
LIBRARY OF CONGRESS

> *If the Federal Government will confine itself to the exercise of powers clearly granted by the Constitution, it can hardly happen that*

its action upon any question should endanger the institutions of the States or interfere with their right to manage matters strictly domestic according to the will of their own people. . . .

I believe that involuntary servitude, as it exists in different States of this Confederacy, is recognized by the Constitution. I believe that it stands like any other admitted right, and that the States where it exists are entitled to efficient remedies to enforce the constitutional provisions. . . . I believe that the constituted authorities of this Republic are bound to regard the rights of the South in this respect as they would view any other legal and constitutional right, and that the laws to enforce them should be respected and obeyed, not with a reluctance encouraged by abstract opinions as to their propriety in a different state of society, but cheerfully and according to the decisions of the tribunal to which their exposition belongs.

Pierce's states' rights view led him to embrace the concept of popular sovereignty, allowing the citizens of each state or prospective state to choose free or slave status, a mainstay of the Compromise of 1850, also reiterated in his inaugural: "I hold that the laws of 1850, commonly called the 'compromise measures,' are strictly constitutional and to be unhesitatingly carried into effect."

That compromise along with the 1854 Kansas-Nebraska Act eviscerated the Missouri Compromise. No longer would there be a North-South 36°30' demarcation line. Pierce believed slavery was enshrined in the Constitution solely as a state right, a view driven by his strict constructionist adherence to the document.

He was ten years old when the New England states threatened secession at the Hartford Convention during the War of 1812, and much older in 1844, when the Massachusetts legislature passed a resolution introduced by Charles Francis Adams Sr., son of President John Quincy Adams and grandson of President John Adams, asserting: "The Commonwealth of Massachusetts faithful to the compact between the people of the United States, according to the plain meaning and intent in which it was understood and acceded to by them, is sincerely anxious for its preservation; and that it is determined, as it doubts not other States are, to submit to undelegated powers in no body of men on earth; and that the project of the annexation of Texas, unless resisted on the threshold, may tend to drive these States into a dissolution of the Union."

Coming of age in the hotbed of these New England secessionist movements, Pierce did not ascribe to force as a solution to secession. Unlike Andrew Jackson and Zachary Taylor, he believed in accommodation rather than the threat of military coercion to keep the nation whole.

Toward that end, Pierce supported passage of the 1854 Kansas-Nebraska Act, allowing those territories to decide whether or not to allow slavery. Since Nebraska was certain to come in free, the issue came down to Kansas, and opposing sides sent outsiders there to influence the election. This was the result from the misguided concept of popular sovereignty perpetuated by Sen. Stephen Douglas.

The division of the nation over slavery had come to the forefront again, and the compromise of 1854 made matters worse. Instead of seeing an end to hostility over slavery, Pierce saw the situation grow worse. As should have been anticipated, violence erupted. Not anticipated was the president's ideologically driven reluctance to interfere in a "local" issue.

Pierce also made a move to buy Cuba from Spain, which not only failed but caused a domestic and international uproar when news leaked that his administration was considering war to take the island if it could not be bought. Apparently, the public was coming to grips with the nation's similar precipitation of the recent Mexican-American War.

The failure of the Kansas-Nebraska Act to diffuse the slavery issue was Pierce's downfall. Unlike Jefferson and Monroe, who had the opportunity to prohibit slavery in the Louisiana Purchase, and Taylor, who had the opportunity to do so in the Mexican Cession, Pierce was left to seek another solution. Popular sovereignty, which aligned with his strict constructionist view of the Constitution, was the wrong solution, though this begs the question: What was the correct solution? There is the conundrum. We know why he failed; we can only guess how he or anyone under the circumstances might have prevailed. It would be for his successor, James Buchanan, to address the few available options.

JAMES BUCHANAN—SECESSION
1857–1861

Born/Died: 1791 Cove Gap, PA–1868 Lancaster, PA
Education: Dickinson College
Occupation: Lawyer, professional politician
Political Party: Democratic
Government Service: Ambassador (Britain) 1853–1856, Secretary of State 1845–1849, Senator (PA) 1834–1845, Ambassador (Russia) 1832–1833, Representative (PA) 1821–1831
Military Service: Private; Pennsylvania State Militia, War of 1812
Preceded by: Franklin Pierce (1854 Kansas-Nebraska Act institutes "popular sovereignty" allowing advocates to vote for admittance of states as free or slave; leads to small civil war in "Bleeding Kansas")

After the Whig Party's disintegration in 1854, only the Democratic Party remained as a national party. Republicans had emerged from the ashes of northern Whigs, though only as a regional entity. Formed in the North, Republicans ran in the North, and their first presidential candidate, the famed "Pathfinder of the West," John C. Fremont (whose wife, Jessie Benton, was a friend of Franklin Pierce), was overwhelmed by Buchanan and the nationwide Democratic Party in the election of 1856. His electoral success goes far in explaining why Buchanan, a northerner from Pennsylvania, strove to hold on to the Democrats' southern branch, lest the party go the way of the Whigs or the regional route of the Republicans. In the latter scenario, a northern Republican Party facing a southern Democratic Party would have meant a) Republicans, with their larger population base, would win every election, and b) a nation divided North and South along party lines would dissolve and possibly suffer civil war. Therefore, Buchanan's first priority upon taking office was to ensure Democratic unity. It was not that he was putting party above nation. He was preserving the nation by preserving the party.

It may have been an impossible task. The slave-state, free-state designations were in reality not about the spread of slavery, because the peculiar institution had nowhere to economically spread. It was about political power. If Kansas, New Mexico, Arizona, and Nevada could enter the Union as slave states even though few slaves would populate them (see chart on pages 95–97), their political loyalties would be with the other slave states. If, on the other hand, Thomas Jefferson had succeeded in his pre-presidential effort to prohibit slavery west of the Appalachians, or President Monroe had prevented Mississippi, Alabama, and Missouri from coming

President James Buchanan as candidate, 1856
LIBRARY OF CONGRESS

in slave, or Zachary Taylor had lived to advance his no-slave policy in the Mexican Cession states and territories, the whole issue of slavery would have been contained, confined, and deprived of political power until it vanished. Now, in 1857, it was too late.

The truth is that the much-maligned President James Buchanan of Pennsylvania inherited a mess. Five other presidents from northern states had already served, and neither they nor the presidents from southern states had been able or willing to solve the slavery issue. Colonization did not and could not work. Popular sovereignty seemed practical, only to result in an undeclared mini-war in Kansas. Then, two days after Buchanan's inauguration, the US Supreme Court handed down the Dred Scott decision invalidating the various compromises altogether, when it opined that a master could take a slave anywhere, slave state or free state. It did not matter. The slave would remain a slave. Buchanan blamed the inflaming passions of northern abolitionists and southern "fire eaters" for sidelining moderates, although like Pierce, his strict interpretation of the Constitution stymied all attempts to coalesce around a centrist majority.

By 1857, the North-South divide was becoming critical, and infrastructure wasn't helping. Forty years earlier, migration into cotton-producing lands had been enhanced by the steam engine, an invention that also helped move slavery's center of gravity deeper into the Deep South. By the time Buchanan took office, those demographic changes were reversing the dynamic with distance and impediments. There were more paths than roads, more fords than bridges, and trains were operating on seven different track widths—gauges—with the three north-south railroads, in particular, having different gauges on opposite sides of the Ohio and Potomac Rivers, a situation that could only contribute to delays and disarray, if not disunity. The large majority of southerners were not directly involved with slavery, but great distances, different climates, and distinct heritages had created diverse, insulated cultures, causing people North and South, including the North's rising star, Abraham Lincoln, to refer to the nation in the plural: "The United States are . . ." That would become singular over the decades following the Civil War. Buchanan either did not understand any of this or refused to admit it.

The nation's remaining links were between cotton growers, northern mills, and New York bankers and shippers as well as the communications and commerce prevalent among border-state citizens. On the other hand, regional alienation between the Deep South and the North increased. The Dred Scott decision and Kansas-Nebraska Act made it worse, facts Buchanan ignored. Despite the ongoing troubles in Kansas, Buchanan naively exulted in his Inaugural Address: "The whole Territorial question being thus settled upon the principle of popular sovereignty—a principle as ancient as free government itself—everything of a practical nature has been decided." This was Buchanan's great first-year mistake, made on his first day in office.

Unable to identify the problem, Buchanan was unable to form a solution. While his predecessors missed or lost their opportunities to restrict the spread of slavery, Buchanan thought he was left with only three choices: embrace popular sovereignty, acknowledge both the legality and irrelevance of the Dred Scott decision (at the time of his inauguration, he had already been told of the Supreme Court's verdict in the Dred Scott case), or confront the South. He chose the first, realizing that to choose confrontation risked secession. As ill-conceived as the Supreme Court decision was, it had no practical effect. Over the next four years, slaveholders did not flock to free states with their slaves, nor did they even migrate to Kansas or Nebraska, and the Rocky Mountain territories were certainly not conducive to the slaveholding economies.

As the following chart indicates, slavery was hardly a growth industry. Almost all civilized nations had prohibited slavery. The march of history was against it, and various schemes, including compensated emancipation, were on the table. Even the hated protective tariff could have been selectively increased to stifle cotton exports by undermining foreign trade. In short, there were alternatives to passivity, confrontation, secession, or bloody war, but it would have taken a greater mind and bolder makeup than Buchanan possessed to embrace them.

Slavery, Census, and Secession

Notes:

1. The four seceding Upper South states that had voted against secession voted for secession following President Lincoln's call for seventy-five thousand volunteers to force the seven seceding states back into the Union.
2. There were virtually no slaves in Kansas and Nebraska, confirming that the Kansas-Nebraska Act of 1854 and expansion of slavery to the Louisiana Purchase and Mexican Cession territories concerned political power, not slavery.
3. After the cotton gin was patented in 1794, the slave population swelled 70 percent between 1790 and 1810 and another 60 percent from 1810 to 1830 as the nation expanded, after which the rate began to slow as slavery concentrated in the Cotton Belt of the Deep South. Maryland and the District of Columbia actually saw a decrease in their slave population after 1810, while in Virginia the rate of increase for the fifty years from 1810 to 1860 was 24 percent against a 232 percent increase for the same period nationwide.
4. Slavery was prevalent in Rhode Island and Connecticut until 1800 and in the Mid-Atlantic states until the 1820–1840 period.

SOURCES: CREATED BY THE AUTHOR FROM THE US CENSUS BUREAU

Slave Population by Year

	1790	1800	1810	1820	1830	1840	1850	1860
Total	697,624	893,602	1,191,362	1,538,022	2,009,043	2,487,355	3,204,313	3,953,760
New England								
Maine	-	-	-	-	2	-	-	-
New Hampshire	157	8	-	-	3	1	-	-
Vermont	-	-	-	-	-	-	-	-
Massachusetts	-	-	-	-	1	-	-	-
Rhode Island	958	380	108	48	17	5	-	-
Connecticut	2,648	951	310	97	25	17	-	-
Northern States								
Ohio	-	-	-	-	6	3	-	-
Indiana	-	28	237	190	3	3	-	-
Illinois	-	107	168	917	747	331	-	-
Michigan	-	-	24	-	1	-	-	-
Wisconsin	-	-	-	-	31	11	-	-
Iowa	-	-	-	-	-	16	-	-
Mid-Atlantic								
New York	21,193	20,903	15,017	10,088	75	4	-	-
New Jersey	11,423	12,422	10,851	7,557	2,254	674	236	18
Pennsylvania	3,707	1,706	795	211	403	64	-	-
Delaware	8,887	6,153	4,177	4,509	3,292	2,605	2,290	1,798

Western States									
Utah Territory		-	-	-	-	-	-	26	29
Nebraska		-	-	-	-	-	-	-	15
Kansas		-	-	-	-	-	-	-	2
Upper South (Divided Loyalty)									
Maryland & DC		103,036	107,707	115,056	111,917	107,499	93,057	94,055	90,374
Kentucky		12,430	40,343	80,561	126,732	165,213	182,258	210,981	225,483
Missouri		-	-	2,875	10,222	25,091	58,240	87,422	114,931
Upper South	Seceded								
Virginia	4/17/61	292,627	346,968	394,357	427,005	471,371	450,361	472,528	490,865
Arkansas	5/6/61	-	136	1,617	4,576	19,935	47,100	111,115
North Carolina	5/20/61	100,783	133,296	168,824	204,917	245,601	245,817	288,548	331,059
Tennessee	6/8/61	3,417	13,584	44,535	80,107	141,603	183,059	239,459	275,719
Deep South	Seceded								
South Carolina	12/20/60	107,094	146,151	196,365	258,475	315,401	327,038	384,984	402,406
Mississippi	1/9/61	-	2,995	14,523	32,814	65,659	195,211	309,878	436,631
Florida	1/10/61	-	-	-	-	15,501	25,717	39,310	61,745
Alabama	1/11/61	-	494	2,565	41,879	117,549	253,532	342,844	435,080
Georgia	1/19/61	29,264	59,406	105,218	149,656	217,531	280,944	381,682	462,198
Louisiana	1/26/61	-	-	34,660	69,064	109,588	168,452	244,809	331,726
Texas	2/1/61	-	-	-	-	-	-	58,161	182,566

ANDREW JOHNSON—RECONSTRUCTION
1865–1869

Born/Died: 1808 Raleigh, NC–1875 Carter's Station, TN
Education: No formal education
Occupation: Tailor
Political Party: Democratic and National Union Party
Government Service: Vice President 1865, Senator (TN) 1857–1862, 1875, Federal Military Governor of TN 1862–1865, Governor (TN) 1853–1857, Representative (TN) 1843–1853
Military Service: Federal Brigadier General; Civil War, Tennessee Militia in 1830s
Preceded by: Abraham Lincoln (fails to hold on to the Upper South; leads to long Civil War; Thirteenth Amendment frees slaves; proposes mild Reconstruction policy; assassinated)

There is an overlooked truth about Andrew Johnson and his predecessor. Had Abraham Lincoln lived, he likely would have acted as Johnson acted. Certainly, there would have been differences in details and degrees, but their big-picture views coincided. Both men advocated a conciliatory Reconstruction policy for the defeated South.

Lincoln chose Johnson, a Democrat, the only senator from a seceding state (Tennessee) to remain in the Senate, as his second-term running mate on a National Union ticket in 1864—precisely what Lt. Gen. Winfield Scott had advocated three years earlier (see Chapter 11, Lincoln). Then, within a month of their inauguration in 1865, with the Civil War ending, Lincoln was assassinated, and Johnson became president. Intemperate in politics, speech, and alcohol, Johnson alienated members of Congress to such a degree that his plans for rapid restoration of the southern states to the Union were thwarted.

It was left to Johnson to clean up the catastrophe bequeathed to him by five decades of presidential and congressional mismanagement of the slavery issue. The Radical wing of the Republican Party controlled

Congress and was insisting on the imposition of a harsh peace, including military occupation of the South. While such an attitude is not unusual for victors throughout history, it was not Lincoln's attitude, and he said so in his Second Inaugural Address, most aptly captured in the phrase: "With malice toward none and charity for all."

Meanwhile, the most dynamic demographic change in American history was taking place. Four million slaves were suddenly free, and almost all of them were illiterate, not by choice but by a system that imposed it. Yet a movement was afoot to provide former male slaves the vote. Both Johnson and Lincoln were contaminated with the bigotry of the times (see Chapter 11, Lincoln), although posterity has only attached the sentiment to the former, and they, like most white people North and South, opposed African-American suffrage. The tide of history dictated otherwise, and Johnson remained out of step with it, as had Lincoln. This issue would culminate with passage of the Fifteenth Amendment during his last month in office, on February 26, 1869, and ratification in 1870—a right that would be denied the female half of the nation's population for another fifty years.

President Andrew Johnson
LIBRARY OF CONGRESS

The war had completely devastated the South, eliminating any possibility of a resumption of hostilities, and while there was a legitimate concern for the welfare of former slaves, they were not well served by a harsh military occupation. Rather, the compassionate approach for all citizens advocated and practiced by such officers as Maj. Gen. Winfield S. Hancock (see Chapter 12, Garfield) was clearly the appropriate course, and it was the course Johnson tried to follow, but a course his successor, Ulysses S. Grant, reversed.

Where Johnson stumbled was in his unpolitic dealings with a hostile Congress, a Congress that would have been equally opposed to the same Reconstruction initiatives from Lincoln. The difference was that Johnson the politician could not measure up to the acquired political acumen of the martyred president he succeeded. Lincoln had been more akin in methodology to future President Lyndon Johnson, who knew how to jawbone, cajole, coerce, flatter, threaten, finagle, and impose his will on an unwilling caucus. As the war progressed, Lincoln had become increasingly uninhibited by constitutional constraints. Andrew Johnson, on the other hand, was not equipped to deal with a hyper-partisan, vengeance-charged Congress in the wake of a bloody war, and as a result, he survived an impeachment trial by just one vote.

His impeachment was initiated over the unlikely issue of the Tenure of Office Act, when he attempted to replace Secretary of War Edwin Stanton with Gen. Ulysses S. Grant, in itself an ill-advised idea because Grant undermined him and returned the office to Stanton, falsely claiming he had never agreed to accept it. So Andrew Johnson did not have a forlorn first year; he had a disastrous four years, though he made a valiant effort, and historian Clinton Rossiter wrote of him: "He was a man of few talents but much courage, whose protests against the ravages of the Radical Republicans in Congress were a high rather than a low point in the progress of the presidency."

CHAPTER 6

PROFESSIONAL GENERALS OF THE NINETEENTH CENTURY: COUNTERWEIGHTS OF THE WEST

ANDREW JACKSON (1829), WILLIAM HENRY HARRISON (1841), ULYSSES S. GRANT (1869) (SEE ALSO ZACHARY TAYLOR, CHAPTER 5)

The rise of the West, that is west of the Appalachian Mountains, altered the demography of the United States and, accordingly, the balance of power—at least for a time—and confirmed James Madison's sage prediction about expansion as the key to success for a large democracy. Democratic city-states such as Rome and Athens had succeeded, but no nation had ever attempted to replicate self-government on a large scale. Britain was moving in that direction, but it was certainly not a democracy of the common man in the early 1800s, and there was much skepticism that such a democracy was even possible. The Father of the Constitution, James Madison, disagreed and wrote in *The Federalist Papers* No. 10 (boldface by the author):

> *The smaller the society, the fewer probably will be the distinct parties and interests composing it; the fewer the distinct parties and interests, the more frequently will a majority be found of the same party; and the smaller the number of individuals composing a majority, and the*

*smaller the compass within which they are placed, the more easily will they concert and execute their plans of oppression. **Extend the sphere**, and you take in a greater variety of parties and interests; you make it less probable that a majority of the whole will have a common motive to invade the rights of other citizens; or if such a common motive exists, it will be more difficult for all who feel it to discover their own strength, and to act in unison with each other.*

The nation was split along North-South lines even before the American Revolution, and it continued that way until a glimmer of Madison's prediction offered the specter of hope. In the early 1800s, the frontier extended from the Appalachian Mountains to the Mississippi River, and until California's admission in 1850, every state west of the Mississippi, except Texas, bordered that river. These new states bred a new kind of politician. Whether born there or transplanted, they viewed themselves as westerners, even frontiersmen in the cases of Jackson, Harrison, and Taylor. By any standard, they were not cut from the cloth of the East Coast aristocracy. Although all of them (including Grant) were slaveholders at one time, true to Madison's prediction, they proved to be independent voices in the North-South issues of the times and, in the case of Taylor, a strong voice that nearly settled the slavery issue.

Eventually, their West would be absorbed into the mainstream of the North-South divide, leaving it for the rise of the Far West to finally provide the Madisonian balance they unknowingly had brought to the national scales. Yet, when they served, they were the true counterweights of the West.

ANDREW JACKSON—TRAIL OF TEARS
1829–1837

Born/Died: 1767 Waxhaws area on NC/SC border–1845 Nashville, TN
Education: Studied law as an apprentice in North Carolina, which culminated in the practice of law

Occupation: Planter, lawyer
Political Party: Democratic
Government Service: Military Governor (FL) 1821, Senator (TN) 1797–1798, 1823–1825, Representative (TN) 1796–1797
Military Service: Major General; War of 1812, Creek War, First Seminole War, American Revolution
Preceded by: John Quincy Adams (Jackson claims "Corrupt Bargain" gives contested 1824 election to Adams; Jackson forces in Congress thwart Adams's agenda; Tariff of Abominations passed harming agrarian South; strong anti-slavery stance)

Andrew Jackson embodied almost everything opponents of democracy had feared. Unlike his distinguished predecessors, Jackson was from humble origins, a rough-hewn, bad-tempered, poorly educated, self-made frontiersman, and brutal authoritarian—the scourge of Native Americans, one of whom, inexplicably, became his adopted son. Outgoing President John Quincy Adams so despised him that he refused to attend the inauguration because he could not bring himself to shake the new president's hand, or perhaps because he was unsure if Jackson would offer it or do so in a peaceful manner. The campaign of 1828 had been nasty, and Jackson's wife died shortly before he took office, a tragedy he attributed to the resurrected attack on her character, claiming she had married him while still married to her first husband, which was true, but accidental. Jackson had already killed one man in a duel over the issue, and his hatred for Adams was no less intense.

Following the inauguration, the mixed crowd of gentry and drunken ruffians accompanied the new president into the White House and quickly tore it apart, Jackson escaping out the back. This was America's new common-man democracy in action, perhaps evoking images of the Paris mobs storming the Bastille in 1789. To Europeans and sophisticated, educated Americans alike, the nation's experiment with democracy had taken a wrong, regressive turn.

Jackson had gained fame as a general who marched into Spanish-held Florida without authorization—an action which then–Secretary of State Adams retroactively supported—subdued the Creek Indians, and

President Andrew Jackson as major general during the War of 1812

LIBRARY OF CONGRESS

won the last battle of the War of 1812 at New Orleans. By 1829, the frontier spirit was alive, embodied in the westward-expanding nation with embellished tales of backwoodsmen such as Davy Crockett, and that spirit was now flooding the government, from the White House to Congress.

President John Quincy Adams, impervious to that trend and contemptuous of Jackson, left behind a minefield in the form of the 1828 Tariff of Abominations, and he was soon in Congress as a representative from Massachusetts authoring the Tariff of 1832. It was a weak attempt to lower the impact of the hated tariff, and it was too little too late. John C. Calhoun, who had served as Adams's vice president and was now serving Jackson in the same capacity, formed the Nullification Party in his home state of South Carolina, asserting a state's right to nullify the tariff. Jackson threatened military action, South Carolina backed down, and Calhoun resigned. A new tariff, the Compromise Tariff of 1833, was passed, and the crises subsided.

Still, all this was just background noise in 1829. Jackson had his own agenda, and it would not be pleasant for Native Americans or the economy. On March 23, 1829, less than three weeks after the inaugural, President Jackson—with ominous overtones of worse to come—ordered the Creek Indians to obey Alabama laws or move across the Mississippi. Then, on December 8 in his annual message to Congress, he made his intent unmistakably clear:

A portion, however, of the Southern tribes, having mingled much with the whites and made some progress in the arts of civilized life, have lately attempted to erect an independent government within the limits of Georgia and Alabama. These States, claiming to be the only sovereigns within their territories, extended their laws over the Indians, which induced the latter to call upon the United States for protection.

. . . I informed the Indians inhabiting parts of Georgia and Alabama that their attempt to establish an independent government would not be countenanced by the Executive of the United States, and advised them to emigrate beyond the Mississippi or submit to the laws of those States. . . . As a means of effecting this end I suggest for your consideration the propriety of setting apart an ample district west of the Mississippi, and without the limits of any State or Territory now formed, to be guaranteed to the Indian tribes as long as they shall occupy it, each tribe having a distinct control over the portion designated for its use. There they may be secured in the enjoyment of governments of their own choice, subject to no other control from the United States than such as may be necessary to preserve peace on the frontier and between the several tribes. There the benevolent may endeavor to teach them the arts of civilization, and, by promoting union and harmony among them, to raise up an interesting commonwealth, destined to perpetuate the race and to attest the humanity and justice of this Government.

Here it was, delivered in benevolent and bigoted language, the justification for the infamous Trail of Tears. The new president asked an accommodating Congress to authorize the removal of Indians from their ancestral lands, regardless of their state of civilization or peaceful existence. Congress passed the legislation in May, and the "removals" commenced, continuing throughout Jackson's two terms and on into the succeeding Van Buren Administration.

Not only were the Indians peaceful, but some sought redress through the courts, and in 1832 Chief Justice John Marshall's Supreme Court ruled in *Worcester v. Georgia*: The Cherokee Indians constituted a sovereign nation, and what Congress passed and the president signed was unconstitutional. It was a decision Jackson famously ignored, writing to former business partner and military subordinate Brig. Gen. John Coffee, who along with Secretary of War John Eaton was empowered to carry out Jackson's removal orders: "the decision of the Supreme Court has fell still born, and they find that they cannot coerce Georgia to yield to its mandate."

Three-term member of the House of Representatives from Tennessee and famed frontiersman David Crockett (he never signed his name "Davy") of Tennessee, who had served under Jackson in his Indian campaigns, broke with the president over the Indian Removal Act, and lost his seat in Congress to Jacksonian retaliation. He was joined in protest by, among others, Speaker of the House Henry Clay of Kentucky, Sen. Daniel Webster of Massachusetts, and Sen. Theodore Frelinghuysen of New Jersey, three men who would shortly also break with Jackson and form the Whig Party. Frelinghuysen captured their sentiments: "Do the obligations of justice change with the color of the skin? Is it one of the prerogatives of the white man, that he may disregard the dictates of moral principles, when an Indian shall be concerned? No."

Choctaws, Cherokees, Chickasaws, Creeks, and Seminoles made the trek west, and an estimated quarter of them perished in a sordid episode without precedence in American history. Europeans who may have been repelled by what appeared to be the coarsening of American democracy when Jackson entered the White House must have been revolted by the racist and brutal treatment he meted out to the Indians, with one European observer, Alexis de Tocqueville (see Chapter 5), describing Jackson as "a man of violent character and middling capacaties."

In that same first-year message to Congress, Jackson also delivered his promised economic disruption:

The charter of the Bank of the United States expires in 1836, and its stock holders will most probably apply for a renewal of their privileges. In order to avoid the evils resulting from precipitancy in a measure involving such important principles and such deep pecuniary interests, I feel that I can not, in justice to the parties interested, too soon present it to the deliberate consideration of the Legislature and the people. Both the constitutionality and the expediency of the law creating this bank are well questioned by a large portion of our fellow citizens, and it must be admitted by all that it has failed in the great end of establishing an uniform and sound currency.

His antipathy for a central bank is difficult to fathom. A man of strong likes and dislikes, he decided to remove the bank as well as the Indians, and not waiting until the bank's charter was up, he transferred federal funds from the bank on September 10, 1833, distributing the money to various state banks in what was known as the Bank War. The state banks then issued paper money at will. National monetary policy had devolved to the states with disastrous results. Jackson was censured by Congress, and, worse, by the marketplace when the Panic of 1837 struck.

Andrew Jackson did not just have a bad first year; he had a mean first year. It was an inauspicious start, and he seemed to care less. However, history has been kind to this rough-cut westerner who rained down death and privation on Native Americans and crippled the economy, because his egalitarianism changed the nature of the American body politic. He was hailed as a man of the people—adult white male people, almost all of whom were becoming enfranchised, state by state, as property ownership and other impediments to suffrage were disappearing.

WILLIAM HENRY HARRISON—HEALTH OF THE PRESIDENT
1841

Born/Died: 1773 Charles City, VA–1841 Washington, DC
Education: Hampden-Sydney College (withdrew), University of Pennsylvania School of Medicine (withdrew)
Occupation: Professional Army officer; professional politician
Political Party: Whig
Government Service: Ambassador (Colombia) 1828–1829, Senator (OH) 1825–1828, Representative (OH) 1816–1819, Governor (IN Terr.) 1801–1812, Representative (NW Terr.) 1799–1800, Secretary (NW Terr.) 1798–1799
Military Service: Major General; War of 1812, Indian Wars

President William Henry Harrison
LIBRARY OF CONGRESS

Preceded by: Martin Van Buren (continues Trail of Tears under Jackson's Indian Removal Act; Panic of 1837 caused in part by Jackson's termination of the national bank and disbursement of federal funds to state banks; views slavery as a state issue)

The first Whig Party president's great mistake was dying, which he accomplished thirty days after taking office.

He was a genteel Virginian who gravitated to what is now Indiana and Ohio in the Northwest Territory, becoming its governor, and a general who gained fame for his victory over the Shawnee at the Battle of Tippecanoe. Like Jackson, he was an Indian fighter.

With the 1828 election of Andrew Jackson, the advent of near-universal white male suffrage had turned elections into egalitarian events. Presidential candidates would thereafter need to find a way to connect with the common man, and Jackson, a successful planter and general, wrote the script Harrison would follow. Like Jackson, he portrayed himself as a frontiersman. In this he was aided by the *Baltimore Republican*, which took a sarcastic swipe at Harrison's age: "Give him a barrel of hard [alcohol] cider and settle a pension of two thousand a year on him, and take my word for it, he will sit the remainder of his days in his log cabin." Harrison embraced the image and latched onto the symbols of log cabin and hard cider to accompany the catchiest slogan in American political history: "Tippecanoe and Tyler too." John Tyler, whose father's plantation was just down the road from the Harrison plantation (which upon inheriting he sold to his brother) in Virginia, was his running mate.

The issue of age was not misplaced. Harrison was sixty-eight in 1841, the oldest man to become president until Ronald Reagan took the oath of office just before his seventieth birthday in 1981. The state of nutrition and medical science in 1841 was such that, unlike Reagan 140 years later, Harrison was considered an old man. It was a reality, not a perception, and his health was a significant concern.

The president died from pneumonia, not the result of giving a coatless, hatless two-hour Inaugural Address in cold, wet weather as legend would have it. A walk in the rain a few weeks later as well as medical ineptitude caused his demise. He had not taken proper care of himself in inclement weather or control of his own house, the White House, which he allowed to be overrun by an incessant stream of office seekers who deprived him of a place to recuperate. On March 10, 1841, he wrote: "The fact is that I am so much harassed by the multitude that call upon me that I can give no proper attention to any business of my own [including health]." Meanwhile, doctors administered curatives bearing little scientific grounding.

As a former general, Harrison had witnessed doctors caring for numerous battlefield casualties and camp diseases, and he should have been able to discern the difference between science and quackery. In this and in his reckless disregard for personal care, he erred in a fundamental presidential obligation: to properly care for the president's health.

This fundamental failing left the country with a constitutional crisis over succession (see Chapter 9, Tyler).

ULYSSES S. GRANT—TRUST AND DISTRUST
1869–1877

Born/Died: 1822 Point Pleasant, OH–1885 Mount McGregor, NY
Education: US Military Academy (West Point)
Occupation: Professional Army officer
Political Party: Republican
Government Service: Secretary of War 1867

Military Service: Federal Lieutenant General; Civil War, Mexican-American War

Preceded by: Andrew Johnson (attempts to employ Lincoln's post–Civil War conciliatory Reconstruction policy in the South; thwarted by Radical Republicans; survives trial after impeachment)

Ulysses S. Grant excelled against mediocrity. How else to explain his phenomenal successes and equally phenomenal failures?

Grant graduated from West Point in 1843, rendered gallant service in the Mexican-American War (which he opposed), and went on to dreary peacetime duties. According to Capt. Rufus Ingalls, his friend and classmate, Grant "fell into dissipated habits, and was one day too much under the influence of liquor to properly perform his duties. For this offence Col. Buchanan demanded that he should resign or stand trial." Grant resigned from the Army in 1854, when future Confederate President Jefferson Davis was secretary of War. A substantial body of evidence indicates he suffered from alcoholism and at one point joined the Sons of Temperance. Albert D. Richardson, a Grant advocate, wrote: "[W]hiskey-drinking was well-nigh universal, and Captain Grant was exposed to constant temptation. His wife and children helped him in his fight against his appetite. His safety lay in absolutely abstaining from its use, and for the most part he kept clear of blame."

His father-in-law provided a farm and slaves; the farm failed, and he went on to equally unsuccessful business endeavors in St. Louis and southern Illinois. When the Civil War began, he like most West Pointers with combat experience was offered a position in the US volunteer Army and was soon commanding a regiment, then a brigade after being promoted to brigadier general of volunteers, all before seeing action.

A brief discussion of his Civil War military career is pertinent as it goes to the heart of unraveling the enigma that was General Grant. He and his fellow cadets had studied under Professor Dennis Hart Mahan, '24, father of famed naval theorist Alfred Thayer Mahan (see Chapter 15, Wilson), who until 1871 infused cadets with the strategies and tactics of the great captains of history, especially the relatively recent campaigns of Napoleon, emphasizing mobility, mass, economy of force, large flanking moves, the offensive over the defensive, and, above all, single-minded aggressiveness.

Started by politicians, the Civil War was fought by West Point generals, 220 of the 560 Federal generals, 140 of the 400 Confederate generals. No other source came close to providing such cadres, and of the senior generals on both sides, almost all were West Point graduates. Not a single major battle was fought where West Pointers were not in command of one or both sides. However, friendships knew no boundaries, and these same men of West Point came together at the end of hos-

President Ulysses S. Grant as lieutenant general during the Civil War
LIBRARY OF CONGRESS

tilities and probably did more than any other single set of people to heal the wounds of war and ensure the peace. Grant and his friends were a case in point. Three officers, James Longstreet, Cadmus Wilcox, and Bernard Pratt, West Pointers all, who served as attendants at Grant's wedding, would later join the Confederate Army. Following the war, they renewed their friendships. Longstreet became a Republican, and Grant appointed him minister to Turkey. When Wilcox died in 1880, four of his pallbearers were former Federal generals and four were former Confederate generals.

At the Battles of Fort Henry and Fort Donelson in 1862, Grant cooperated with the river Navy and gained impressive victories. Then he moved his army south to Shiloh only to be surprised by Gen. Albert Sydney Johnston, '26 (two years ahead of Jefferson Davis and three years ahead of Robert E. Lee) and Gen. P. G. T. Beauregard, '32, his second in command. In a classic example of two principles of war, mass and economy of force, Beauregard concentrated troops from all across the Western Theater, and had not Johnston died in the battle, it is unlikely Grant's army would have survived until Maj. Gen. Don Carlos Buell, '41, arrived with another army to save it.

The subsequent Vicksburg Campaign, waged against the Confederate Army of Lt. Gen. John C. Pemberton, '37, was Grant at his best. The campaign was as brilliant as Pemberton was inept. Next came Chattanooga, where his greatly superior forces defeated the greatly disrespected Gen. Braxton Bragg, '37, after which President Lincoln called Grant east, where officers from the Federal Army of the Potomac cautioned him, "You have not faced Bobby Lee yet." Indeed, he had not. In the Overland Campaign of 1864, the Army of the Potomac lost more men than Lee's entire Army of Northern Virginia had under arms. The casualties were so great, the gains so meager, and the public outcry so strong as to convince Lincoln he would lose the coming election. The president's fortunes abruptly changed when Maj. Gen. William T. Sherman, '40, took Atlanta in September.

Having learned Lee was no Pemberton, Grant employed overwhelming numbers to bludgeon his way to Richmond and on to Appomattox, where he offered Lee compassionate terms of surrender in 1865. It was Grant's last military battle; his political battles were about to begin.

By 1868, the tide of northern sentiment was running against black suffrage, and Republicans lost at the polls in Connecticut, Maine, and California, causing the party to back away from the issue. Historian Lewis Gould wrote: "The earlier generation that had opposed slavery and fought the Civil War was giving way to professional politicians. . . . Economic issues such as the currency and the protective tariff meant more to these men than did the fate of African Americans in the South." Instead, candidate Grant's supporters waved the "bloody shirt," a symbol provided by a wounded Federal soldier as a reminder of the war and the general's part in it. Even so, black votes gave Grant the edge.

Once in office, Grant's demons returned, and to what degree alcoholism played a role will never be known. There is no question that his behavior was inconsistent. Away from the unrelenting, unforgiving demands of the battlefield, he "found politicians intimidating," according to William Gienapp in *Origins of the Republican Party*, "and so surrounded himself with army buddies and nobodies whom he thought he could control." No longer amid high-ranking military professionals of proven courage and integrity, he was instead mired in a swamp teeming with some of the worst politicians of the age—an era of machine politics that brought a variety of dishonest, manipulating, and devious characters into the political forefront. Once again Grant was confronted with mediocrity and competence, except many of the competents were dishonest.

Enter Jay Gould and James Fisk, two intelligent, successful, devious crooks who tried to corner the gold market in the fall of 1869. Grant countered by selling government-held gold, only to soon discover his own family members and longtime aide Orville Babcock had been in on the scheme.

Meanwhile, the originally apolitical Grant aligned himself with the Radical Republicans who were intent on inflicting a harsh Reconstruction policy upon the South. Liberal Republicans became disillusioned with Grant and the party over the issue, and Grant dug deeper, allying himself with New York machine boss Sen. Roscoe Conkling.

Brig. Gen. Orville Babcock, '61, became Grant's aide-de-camp in 1864 and, later, his private secretary in the White House. In this position, he exerted significant influence on the president. One of his first missions in 1869 was to annex the Dominican Republic, an island nation where Grant, harking back to the American Colonization Society ideas of Lincoln and Monroe, believed former slaves could go. The gambit collapsed amid suspicions of corrupt dealings and motives. Former abolitionists were dumbfounded, and long-serving Republican Sen. Charles Sumner of Massachusetts broke with Grant over the issue, splitting the party. Sumner, along with Carl Schurz and Horace Greeley, left the president and the Radical wing to form the Liberal Republicans, leaving Grant to face two opposition parties in Congress.

Babcock would go on to involvement in the Whiskey Ring Scandal and the Safe Burglary Conspiracy, be indicted for both, and somehow be acquitted. Even so, Grant would not dismiss him from White House duties until public outcries demanded it in 1876. Why Babcock was not involved in the Crédit Mobilier Scandal (see Chapter 12, Garfield) is unknown.

Although Grant was not implicated in these and other scandals, the man who had been in overall command of the Federal armies during the Civil War, failed as a president because he failed as a leader, unable to fathom the depth of depravity in the political swamp of postwar America. He admitted as much, but in gentler terms: "It was my fortune, or misfortune, to be called to the office of Chief Executive without any previous political training."

None of the Twelve General/Presidents Took the Country into a Major War

Of the twelve generals who became presidents, George Washington, Andrew Jackson, William Henry Harrison, Zachary Taylor, Ulysses S. Grant, and Dwight D. Eisenhower commanded armies in combat. The others, non-professional wartime volunteers, included Franklin Pierce, who commanded a brigade in the Mexican-American War, and Andrew Johnson, Rutherford B. Hayes, James Garfield, and Benjamin Harrison, who led brigades or divisions in the Civil War. Chester A. Arthur, a political appointee, served in non-combat positions during that war, witnessing firsthand the aftermath of battle.

Of these, only one (Washington) served in the eighteenth century, only one (Eisenhower) served in the twentieth century, and, of the others, four served in a twenty-eight-year period before the Civil War and six served in a twenty-eight-year period following the Civil War. Together, all ten of the nineteenth-century generals served in the sixty-four years from 1829 to 1893, an era of White House generals.

Of note is the fact, whether military professionals or wartime volunteers, all of them came to know the hell on earth that is war. A year after the end of World War II, Eisenhower said: "I hate war as only a soldier who has lived it can, only as one who has seen its brutality, its stupidity." Ike and his one-time boss, General of the Army Douglas MacArthur, disagreed on much: not on this. MacArthur echoed the sentiment in his famous "Duty, Honor, Country" final farewell speech to the cadets and faculty of West Point in 1962:

The long gray line has never failed us. Were you to do so, a million ghosts in olive drab, in brown khaki, in blue and gray, would rise from their white crosses, thundering those magic words: Duty, Honor, Country.

This does not mean that you are warmongers. On the contrary, the soldier above all other people prays for peace, for he must suffer and bear the deepest wounds and scars of war. But always in our ears ring the ominous words of Plato, that wisest of all philosophers: "Only the dead have seen the end of war."

Indeed, none of the generals-turned-presidents could be described as warmongers. Even Grant, who was criticized for his costly tactics in 1864 and the campaigns he later waged against Native Americans, said, "Although a soldier by education and profession, I have never felt any sort of fondness for war and I have never advocated it, except as a means of peace."

It is reasonably certain that all of these former generals would have concurred with these views of war, and despite the fact that they, like most presidents, had occasions to use military force, not one of them ever brought the nation into a major war.

CHAPTER 7

TAXATION WITH REPRESENTATION: TARIFFS TO INCOME TAXES

JOHN QUINCY ADAMS (1825), BENJAMIN HARRISON (1889), WILLIAM HOWARD TAFT (1913), RONALD REAGAN (1981), AND GEORGE H. W. BUSH (1989)

It is said death and taxes are life's only certainties. Neither is particularly appealing, and like death, taxes are not and never have been fair. In the beginning, America's primary sources of revenue were land sales and tariffs (see Chapter 8, Chart: Significant US Tariffs). The land ran out; tariffs did not. By the time Andrew Jackson became president in 1829, the nation had clearly split along northern industrial and southern agrarian lines. Cotton had become king in the South, and it was sold to northern and European buyers alike, which resulted in reciprocal trade, forcing northern factories to compete with foreign—especially British—factories. After all, ships carrying cotton to Europe could not afford to return empty. This trade, far more than slavery, created sectional divisions because northerners had a vested interest in keeping foreign goods expensive, and southerners had the opposite incentive lest they lose their foreign trading partners.

The northern solution was to impose high tariffs on foreign goods, and these tariffs created an unequal burden on the South. The boiling point came when Jackson's vice president, John C. Calhoun of South Carolina, resigned over high tariffs and asserted a policy of nullification for his state (see Chapter 6, Jackson). A compromise was reached, but the North-South divide was now an open sore waiting to become toxic three decades later. The Republican Party, formed in 1854, took up the cause of high protective tariffs from the remnants of the Whig Party, and this discriminatory tax remained a Republican tenet from Abraham Lincoln to Herbert Hoover. The despised tax reached a crescendo under McKinley.

Further, when Theodore Roosevelt, a progressive Republican, became president upon McKinley's assassination in 1901, the Robber Barons were in full swing, creating a yawning income gap between workers and industrialists. The Roosevelt solution was an income tax, and it was enacted under his successor, William Howard Taft. Like the tariff, it was terribly flawed and led to one of the most incomprehensible burdens a free people ever imposed upon itself. Initially only a tax on millionaires, it laid the groundwork for inequity. The constitutional question raised over prior income taxes was overcome by passage of the Sixteenth Amendment, and abuses quickly came. Woodrow Wilson during World War I and Franklin Roosevelt during World War II turned the millionaire's tax into everyman's tax to finance those epic military struggles, even as special interest lobbying created increasingly beneficial loopholes for the wealthy.

President Herbert Hoover, one of the most admired humanitarians in the world due to his Belgian relief efforts during World War I, came into office in 1933 and promptly brought the country the worst of both taxes, lowering income taxes on the wealthy while increasing tariffs in the infamous Smoot-Hawley Tariff Act (see Chapter 8, Hoover), and all at a time after the stock market crashed. The Great Depression was the result. Somehow his ideology had not allowed him to do for his countrymen what he had done for the Belgians.

Following World War II, free trade became the watchword as the global economy proved the folly and mutual harm of protective tariffs.

Meanwhile, income taxes spiraled into the stratosphere, prompting the famous Kennedy tax cut of 1963 that lowered the top rate of 91 percent (a carryover from World War II) to 70 percent, and to the surprise of many, the rate reduction actually increased revenue. Upon becoming president in 1981, Ronald Reagan claimed he was following the Kennedy blueprint by lowering the top rate to 28 percent. The outcome was quite different. Revenue fell and budgets ballooned. Neither he nor President George W. Bush in 2001, who also slashed taxes for the wealthy, understood there was a point of diminishing returns.

JOHN QUINCY ADAMS—TARIFF OF ABOMINATIONS
1825–1829

Born/Died: 1767 Braintree (now Quincy) MA–1848 Washington, DC
Education: Harvard College (later Harvard University)
Occupation: Lawyer, professional politician
Political Party: Whig, Anti-Masonic, National Republican, Democratic-Republican, Federalist
Government Service: Representative (MA) 1831–1848, Secretary of State 1817–1825, Ambassador (Britain) 1814–1817, (Russia) 1809–1814, and (Prussia) 1797–1801, Senator (MA) 1803–1808, Ambassador (The Netherlands) 1794–1797
Military Service: None
Preceded by: James Monroe (first pro-North protective tariff; Panic of 1819 caused by "Mr. Madison's" War of 1812; Missouri Compromise establishes north-south line perpetuating slavery; Era of Good Feelings; runs unopposed for reelection after Federalist Party collapses; fails to recognize impact of inventions on demographics and economy; Monroe Doctrine)

As obdurate as his father, President John Adams, John Quincy Adams was neither fish nor fowl, becoming a member of more political parties than any other president. He began his party switching, if not philosophies, in 1808,

changing from his father's Federalist Party to the Democratic-
Republican opposition after voting
for President Jefferson's ill-advised
Embargo Act. He switched again
in 1824, running for president as a
self-proclaimed National Republican, then having been declared
a Quasi-Federalist, he joined the
Anti-Masonic Party once out of
office until finally becoming a
member of the new Whig Party
while serving as a member of
Congress.

President John Quincy Adams
T. SULLY, LIBRARY OF CONGRESS

From an early age he was a
traveler in training for the presidency, witnessing firsthand some
of the great events and influential people of the times. He knew
everyone from the kings, queens, and emperors of Europe to every American president and president-to-be from George Washington to Abraham Lincoln. As President Madison's ambassador to Russia, he was in
Moscow when Napoleon occupied the city in 1812. Two years later, he
was called upon to negotiate the Treaty of Ghent, ending the War of 1812
(see Chapter 4, Madison) and happened to be in Paris when Napoleon
returned from exile en route to Waterloo in 1815. Returning to America,
he became President James Monroe's secretary of State in 1817, and it
was Adams who drafted the Monroe Doctrine.

Of even greater moment and more revealing was his view of the just-
enacted Missouri Compromise (see Chapter 5, Monroe). His diary entry
of February 24, 1820:

> *I told [South Carolina Sen. John C.] Calhoun I could not see things
> in the same light. It is, in truth, all perverted sentiment—mistak-
> ing labor for slavery and dominion for freedom. The discussion of this*

Missouri question has betrayed the secret of their souls. In the abstract they admit that slavery is an evil, they disclaim all participation in the introduction of it, and cast it all upon the shoulders of our old Grandam Britain. But when probed to the quick upon it, they show at the bottom of their souls pride and vainglory in their condition of masterdom. They fancy themselves more generous and noble-hearted than the plain freemen who labor for subsistence. They look down upon the simplicity of a Yankee's manners, because he has no habits of over-bearing like theirs and cannot treat negroes like dogs. It is among the evils of slavery that it taints the very sources of moral principle. It establishes false estimates of virtue and vice: for what can be more false and heartless than this doctrine which makes the first and holiest rights of humanity to depend upon the color of the skin? . . .

I have favored this Missouri compromise, believing it to be all that could be effected under the present Constitution, and from extreme unwillingness to put the Union at hazard. But perhaps it would have been a wiser as well as a bolder course to have persisted in the restriction upon Missouri, till it should have terminated in a convention of the States to revise and amend the Constitution. This would have produced a new Union of thirteen or fourteen States unpolluted with slavery, with a great and glorious object to effect, namely, that of rallying to their standard the other States by the universal emancipation of their slaves. If the Union must be dissolved, slavery is precisely the question upon which it ought to break. For the present, however, this contest it laid asleep.

This was a quill pen–full. Adams was at once an abolitionist, a pragmatist, and a Hartford Convention secessionist (see Chapter 4, Madison), making him the only abolitionist and the last Federalist (his father was the only other) to hold the office when he succeeded Monroe as president in 1825. These facts are disputed because he placed preservation of the Union above slavery, and he did not favor the immediate, uncompensated end of the "peculiar institution." Still, he was among the foremost outspoken foes of the institution, who, unlike Lincoln, did not carefully couch his words. Out of belief or expediency, he had become a Democratic-Republican in 1808, but his Federalist views remained, including advocacy of high protective tariffs, a national bank, strong central government, and infrastructure improvements from roads to canals and eventually rails. Arthur Schlesinger Jr. dubbed this "rebaptized Federalism," and wrote that Adams was "a Federalist in sheep's clothing."

John Kennedy wrote in *Profiles in Courage* that Adams was "out of tune with the party intrigues and political passions of his day . . . [and he had] an integrity unsurpassed among the major political figures of our history. . . . His [and his father's] failures, if they can be called failures, were the result of their own undeviating devotion to what they considered to be the public interest and the result of the inability of their contemporaries to match the high standards of honor and rectitude that they brought to public life."

Although Gen. Andrew Jackson outpolled Adams in both the popular and electoral votes, neither of them gained a majority in 1824, leaving it up to the House of Representatives to decide the issue. Speaker of the House Henry Clay, an opponent of Jackson, used his influence to elect Adams, after which Adams named him secretary of State, prompting Jackson to declare a "corrupt bargain" had been struck. From that moment, Adams, not dissimilarly from his father's situation with Jefferson, was stymied by the Jackson forces in Congress. Facing a hostile Congress, he refused to employ the diplomatic and political skills he had so assiduously acquired over a lifetime of preparation. Call it pride, stiff-necked stubbornness, or out and out disdain. Whatever the motivation, he refused to court Congress, and the Jacksonian-controlled Congress returned the favor.

He did manage to show the Federalist colors so well concealed during the election and sign the 1828 Tariff of Abominations, so called because unlike previous tariffs, it went too far and was manifestly unfair to southern and western farmers and was correspondingly beneficial to northern manufacturers. This set the stage for what Madison earlier feared: the tyranny of the majority. If one region of the country could impose an unfair tax burden on another region, it would be the equivalent of taxation without representation, the primary complaint registered by colonists leading up to the American Revolution and later by farmers in the Whiskey Rebellion.

Alexander Hamilton wrote of this concern in *The Federalist Papers* No. 35:

> *BEFORE we proceed to examine any other objections to an indefinite power of taxation in the Union, I shall make one general remark; which is, that if the jurisdiction of the national government, in the article of revenue, should be restricted to particular objects, it would naturally occasion an undue proportion of the public burdens to fall upon those objects. Two evils would spring from this source: the oppression of particular branches of industry; and an unequal distribution of the taxes, as well among the several States as among the citizens of the same State.*
>
> *Suppose, as has been contended for, the federal power of taxation were to be confined to duties on imports, it is evident that the government, for want of being able to command other resources, would frequently be tempted to extend these duties to an injurious excess.*

This inequitable form of taxation would plague the nation for the next century, and join slavery as a primary issue dividing the agrarian South from the industrial North. From 1828, the protective tariff would also become the opposing tenet of opposing parties, first between Jacksonian Democrats who opposed it and disaffected Democratic-Republicans and former Federalists who favored it. Later, Whigs, followed by Republicans, would take up the pro–protective tariff mantle (see Chapter 8, Chart: Significant US Tariffs).

On the positive side, Adams did further some of his internal improvement projects such as the Cumberland Road and the C&O Canal, though woefully little else. He was simply too out of step with his adopted party. More than any other president, he had been groomed for the office, and had superbly performed his duties as an ambassador and secretary of State. Then, following in his father's footsteps, those diplomatic skills were shunted aside once he became the chief executive, just when it would have taken a master diplomat to navigate the Jackson-infested waters of his day.

Still, it is difficult to relegate him to the list of failures, though fail he certainly did—spectacularly with the Tariff of Abominations—and right from his first day in office. But his prescience lived on. The nation did need roads, bridges, and canals. He was almost a century ahead of his time in advocating what would later be known as the Federal Reserve, while his unabashed opposition to slavery provided a voice that needed to be heard, and never was it more eloquent than while a member of the House of Representatives in 1841; he mounted a successful defense before the US Supreme Court for slaves who had revolted on the ship *Amistad*. It was a voice he used over and over, opposing Texas entry as a slave state in 1845 and voting against the bill authorizing war with Mexico in 1846 because he believed it was a war of conquest and would end up encouraging the spread of slavery. In 1847, a new Whig congressman from Illinois, Abraham Lincoln, joined him in opposition to the war, albeit on the abuse of executive powers—powers which he himself would employ fourteen years later.

BENJAMIN HARRISON—1890 MCKINLEY TARIFF AND THE PANIC OF 1893 1889–1893

Born/Died: 1833 North Bend, OH–1901 Indianapolis, IN
Education: Miami University (OH)
Occupation: Lawyer
Political Party: Whig, Republican
Government Service: Senator (IN) 1881–1887
Military Service: Federal Brigadier General; Civil War
Preceded by: Grover Cleveland (honest government; merit-based hiring in lieu of Jackson-era spoils system; only Democratic president between 1861 and 1913; stymied by Republican Congress; two terms separated by Benjamin Harrison's one term)

The grandson of William Henry Harrison, Benjamin Harrison was the transitional president, the man who split Grover Cleveland's two terms, and more importantly the Republican who paved the way away from the

machine politics of his predecessors to the reform agenda of Theodore Roosevelt.

It was Harrison who pressed
for what could be dubbed pre-
Progressive legislation such as
the Sherman Anti-Trust Act,
though he was less vigorous in
its enforcement. He continued to
adhere to the dominant underpinning of the Republican Party:
the protective tariff, never understanding how the protective tariff
was harming the farmers of the
South, Midwest, and West. At
the same time, he was advocating
policies intended to aid those sec-
tions such as a bimetallist mon-

President Benjamin Harrison
LIBRARY OF CONGRESS

etary policy in the 1890 Sherman Silver Purchase Act, making both silver
and gold legal tender as advocated by those regions.

In the end, both policies were disastrous and led to the Panic of 1893.
Foreign countries would only accept gold as payment, which diminished
US gold reserves and led to deflation. (Not until 1934 would US economists convince successive administrations that the total output of goods
and services, not gold or silver, was the true support of paper currency.)
Worse, the McKinley Tariff Act of 1890, named for Ohio Republican
and future President Sen. William McKinley, raised tariffs by as much as
50 percent on most imports, creating the highest protective tariff in US
history, and at a time when the federal budget was in surplus! Clearly, the
advocates of a tariff for revenue only were overruled by the advocates of
protective tariffs, and once again it increased hardships for Americans
who relied upon reciprocal trade and/or the purchase of imported goods.
Signing this act was the great mistake of his first year, and it would undermine his efforts at reform. Ironically, Harrison's predecessor, Cleveland,
who also became his successor, was blamed for the Panic of 1893.

Harrison's first year, steeped in the Republican orthodoxy of the times, was in contrast with his later efforts to rebuild the Navy, improve civil rights, and achieve the peaceful annexation of Hawaii, which his successor, Grover Cleveland, revoked.

WILLIAM HOWARD TAFT—INCOME TAX AND SUFFRAGE
1909–1913

Born/Died: 1857 Cincinnati, OH–1930 Washington, DC
Education: Yale College (later Yale University)
Occupation: Lawyer
Political Party: Republican
Government Service: Chief Justice of the United States 1921–1930, Secretary of War 1904–1908, Governor-General (The Philippines) 1901–1903, Judge US 6th Circuit Court of Appeals 1892–1900, Solicitor General 1890–1892
Military Service: Connecticut Home Guard, no active service
Preceded by: Theodore Roosevelt (first true Progressive; Meat Inspection Act, Pure Food and Drug Act, etc.; trust buster; Panama Canal; supports income tax amendment; advocates defense preparedness; embraces technology from automobiles to airplanes; supports women's suffrage; supports civil rights)

Theodore Roosevelt's designated successor, William Howard Taft, disappointed his mentor for not being sufficiently progressive, a break that led to Roosevelt's opposition on the Progressive (Bull Moose) Party ticket in 1912, which split the Republican vote and catapulted Woodrow Wilson and the Democrats into the White House. The problem began in 1909, Taft's freshman year in the presidency. His progressivism had not progressed much beyond that of Roosevelt in 1901, whereas Roosevelt had moved on, embracing one liberal concept after another, including women's suffrage.

President William Howard Taft
LIBRARY OF CONGRESS

On the other hand, while both Roosevelt and Taft had a hand in passage of the Sixteenth Amendment, the responsibility must lie at the feet of the president who proposed it to Congress, which Taft did shortly after his inauguration, clearly not comprehending how lobbying from the amendment's moneyed-interest targets would eventually turn the income tax it authorized into an unfathomable burden on average citizens.

The public's primary problem in a presidential campaign is to determine who a candidate really is and where the candidate really stands on the issues, a near impossible task with Taft, because he seemed not to know himself. A lawyer by profession, he took a legalistic view of the Constitution akin to that of Franklin Pierce rather than the expansionist view practiced by Jefferson or espoused and practiced by Jackson and Theodore Roosevelt. He may have even flirted with the Lincoln interpretation, which swung from hardline strict constructionism to broad expansionism as it suited the situation. Whatever this future chief justice of the United States had in mind, it alienated his friend and mentor, Roosevelt.

An example of his tenuous convictions came at the end of his first year as president, when the National American Woman Suffrage Association (NAWSA) invited him to speak at their April 14, 1910, convention. His intent in speaking was not clear. He had no hope of dissuading his listeners; conversely, if his intent was to insult them, he was entirely successful: "If I could be sure that women as a class, including all the intelligent women . . . would exercise the franchise, I should be in favor of it. At present there is considerable doubt." In case anyone missed the insult, he went on: "The theory that Hottentots or any other uneducated, altogether unintelligent class is fitted for self-government at once or to take part in government is a theory that I wholly dissent from."

The women's suffrage movement had been active since before the Civil War and gained momentum following the conflict when the Fifteenth Amendment granted the vote to newly freed adult male slaves, most of whom, through no fault of their own, were illiterate. This was just one more injustice simmering in the postwar period, waiting for progressive leaders to come to the fore. By 1910, the Progressive Era had been going on since Theodore Roosevelt took the oath of office in 1901. The tide of history was with the women, but Taft did not see it, and managed to insult a group that was on the verge of making up more than half of the electorate.

There were other issues, of course, including a slackening of antitrust cases and a bungled attempt to lower tariffs, which he had promised in the campaign. Then there was his firing of popular Cabinet secretaries and others such as Chief of the Forest Service Gifford Pinchot, which further angered Roosevelt, especially since Taft had specifically promised not to do so.

It could be argued that his primary error was the slowing of reform, and it would be left to his successor, Woodrow Wilson, to pick up where Roosevelt had left off, making Taft nothing more than a bump in the reformist road. However, what he wrought with the income tax and what he failed to right with women's suffrage proved to be more than mere bumps. Certainly, any reading of history's pendulum should have told even the thickest of politicians the time for national women's suffrage was at hand. Then again, Taft was one of the more thick-minded politicians of the era.

RONALD REAGAN—FLAT TAX
1981–1989

Born/Died: 1911 Tampico, IL–2004 Simi Valley, CA
Education: Eureka College
Occupation: Actor

Political Party: Republican, Democratic
Government Service: Governor (CA) 1967–1975
Military Service: Captain; stateside service during World War II, Army Reserve 1937–1942
Preceded by: Jimmy Carter (misjudges oil reserves; stagflation; Panama Canal Treaty; Camp David Accords; advocates women's rights; Iranian Hostage Crisis; poor relations with Congress; maintains outsider status)

In 1956, Soviet Premier Nikita Khrushchev announced to the West, "We will bury you," by which his interpreter later explained "he meant historical evolution. If one society dies off, somebody's got to be there to bury it." It was this idea that a country burdened by an inept political and economic system would collapse of its own weight that Ronald Reagan grasped—about Khrushchev's Soviet Union, not the United States.

Reagan was an ideologue, not an academic; an actor more comfortable with a script than ad-libbing; a thorough delegator, not a hands-on executive. His ideologically driven presidency took him down three conflicting paths. He had promised to cut taxes, dramatically increase defense spending to "bury" the Soviet Union, and balance the budget. He succeeded on the first, received mixed reviews on the second, and flunked the third.

In 2008, the CIA (the agency refers to itself simply as "the CIA") released this assessment: "A review of CIA's estimates of Soviet defense spending in 1982 [and thereafter] found that while outlays for military procurement had leveled-off in the USSR since 1975 and the growth in total defense spending had slowed in real terms, the Agency's assessments continued to maintain that defense spending was rising at the historic rates of 4 to 5 percent per year."

This was in line with the view that the US military buildup in the 1980s did not cause an increase in Soviet military spending; however, such US spending clearly dispelled the Kremlin-held illusion of military supremacy or parity, and this undoubtedly had political implications. In any event, a new kind of Soviet leader, Mikhail Gorbachev, rose to power in 1985. His policies of perestroika (openness) and glasnost (restructuring) overturned communist dogma, eventually freed Eastern European nations to follow their own courses, and finally brought about the collapse of the Soviet Union. Could all this have been achieved with less US defense spending? Possibly, but credit is due nonetheless, if for no other reason than that it caused the Politburo to change course and place a Soviet liberal in charge. It is the sort of pressure that caused communist China to later introduce capitalism as the only means of keeping pace with the West.

It was the third item of the Reagan agenda, balancing the budget, that missed the mark. His economic wizard, David Stockman, the director of the Office of Management and Budget, broke the bad news: The three goals were economically incompatible.

President Ronald Reagan at Rancho Del Cielo, California
WHITE HOUSE PHOTOGRAPHS

In just four years, the Reagan-Stockman team doubled the national debt. Not accepting the idea of diminishing returns, Reagan had expected his tax cut to increase revenues just as the Kennedy tax cut had. JFK, in one of the final acts before his assassination in 1963, had pressed for a change in tax rates beginning with a reduction in the World War II and Korean War confiscatory 91 percent taxes levied against the highest income bracket down to 70 percent. It was a classic x-y chart seeking the intersection of decreased taxes with increased revenue, revenue spurred by consumer spending and job growth. Of course, such a chart was based upon theoretical assumptions and predictions. One misbegotten idea should have been clear: A top rate of 28 percent was well beyond the intersection where revenue could offset expenditures, yet that was the figure Reagan put in place, starting with 50 percent in 1981 and working down to 28 percent in 1986, when the president finally achieved his goal of a flat tax. Only two brackets then remained, the first at 15 percent for incomes up to $29,750 and 28 percent thereafter.

Arthur Laffer, an economics professor and strong advocate of supply-side economics (John Maynard Keynes said Say's Law, the basis of supply-side economics, postulated that supply creates demand, whereas Keynes wrote in his 1936 seminal treatise *The General Theory of Employment, Interest, and Money* that demand creates supply), created the famous Laffer Curve showing the critical intersection, but with a caveat: It was a curve devoid of figures, leaving Reagan and Stockman free to plug in whatever they chose. What they chose undermined the original primary purpose of the tax when the Sixteenth Amendment was ratified in 1913, which was to address the out-of-control income inequality prevalent during the age of the Robber Barons. The potential for just such an occurrence should have been obvious to President Taft and the other Sixteenth Amendment advocates. A subsequent objective was to replace the regionally biased protective tariff with an income tax as the nation's primary source of revenue.

Following the Great Recession of 2007-08, the issue of income inequality surfaced once again; it had begun simmering with Reagan's Kemp-Roth tax cut of 1981, even though it was only much later, especially after the Great Recession, that middle-income earners realized the wealth of the wealthiest Americans had been accelerating while their wages were stagnating. The middle class was shrinking. The chart below, Income Tax as a Percentage of Gross Income 1913–2013, provides graphic evidence of the reason why. By 1988, a family of four earning inflation-adjusted earnings of $100,000 a year was, for the first time since the inception of the modern income tax in 1913, taxed at a higher rate (32 percent) than families earning inflation-adjusted incomes of $1,000,000 a year (24 percent). Subsequent administrations and Congresses tweaked the tax code, yet by 2013 the middle-income family was paying 24 percent to the $1,000,000 family's 35 percent, not a sufficient difference to unflatten the flat tax.

By December 1981, even David Stockman had enough: "I mean, Kemp-Roth was always a Trojan horse to bring down the top rate. . . . It's kind of hard to sell 'trickle down.' So the supply-side formula was the only way to get a tax policy that was really 'trickle down.' Supply-side is 'trickle-down' theory." And "None of us really understands what's going on with all these numbers."

Even so, his name was on it. Hillary Clinton called it "Stockman's Revenge—which I think was [New York Sen.] Daniel Patrick Moynihan's term for the massive deficits that the Reagan tax cuts and defense buildup had created."

Together, Reagan and Stockman tried to close the budget gap by slashing non-defense spending with a vengeance. Here, once again, ideology played a role as the president brought to the White House policies he had pushed as governor of California: cutting back on subsidized housing and deinstitutionalizing the mentally ill, which, in fairness, had been an ongoing trend, a trend Reagan accelerated. While these cuts were only an infinitesimal segment of the budget cuts, they had a lasting impact on society as seen in an explosion of the homeless population.

Peter Dreier, the E. P. Clapp Distinguished Professor of Politics and director of the Urban and Environmental Policy program at Occidental College in Los Angeles, wrote, "In his first year in office Reagan halved the budget for public housing and Section 8 to about $17.5 billion. . . . In 1970 there were 300,000 more low-cost rental units (6.5 million) than low-income renter households (6.2 million). By 1985 the number of low-cost units had fallen to 5.6 million, and the number of low-income renter households had grown to 8.9 million, a disparity of 3.3 million units. . . . Homeless people . . . by the late 1980s had swollen to 600,000 on any given night—and 1.2 million over the course of a year. . . . In early 1984 on *Good Morning America*, Reagan defended himself . . . saying that 'people who are sleeping on the grates . . . the homeless . . . are homeless, you might say, by choice.'"

Reagan, like Hoover before him, was personally compassionate, though philosophically entrenched in the idea that government's primary function is to safeguard the nation against threats, foreign and domestic, and should otherwise stand aside if possible, adhering to the concept of least government is best government. Like Lincoln, he came into office with inflexible ideas. Unlike Lincoln, he failed to moderate them as the complexities of the office confirmed man's—and his—fallibility. In one respect that inflexibility caused him to steadfastly remain the most ardent opponent of communism ever to sit in the Oval Office, which led if not to single-handed victory, to victory in the Cold War all the same.

Income Tax as a Percentage of Gross Income 1913–2013

(Income for a family of four adjusted for inflation to 2013 dollars)

Notes:
1. OASDIHI = Social Security, Disability Insurance, and Medicare
   (Employer plus Employee shares; see explanation in essay below)
2. Taxable Income up to $100,000 = Gross Income – Standard Deduction – OASDIHI
   (Taxpayers with large or high-interest mortgages would itemize at levels above the standard deduction.)
3. Taxable Income for $1,000,000 and $500,000 = Gross Income – 20%
   (20% = Mortgage interest, property taxes, reduced rates on investment income and dividends, etc.)
4. Tax law changes usually are phased in or lag (Kennedy's proposed law in 1963; passed in 1964; implemented in 1965)
5. Calculations explained in the Sample Calculation below and in Appendix A.

		$1,000,000 Gross Income	TAX % of Gross	$500,000 Gross Income	TAX % of Gross	$100,000 Gross Income	TAX % of Gross	$50,000 Gross Income	TAX % of Gross
1st Income Tax after Passage of the 16th Amendment	1913	40,000	2%	20,000	1%	4,000	0%	2,000	0%
World War I	1918	60,000	27%	30,000	18%	6,000	4%	3,000	1%
Harding-Coolidge Tax Cut	1925	80,000	17%	40,000	10%	8,000	1%	4,000	0%
Depression/Deflation	1932	60,000	23%	30,000	14%	6,000	2%	3,000	0%
Depression/Deflation	1936	60,000	25%	30,000	17%	6,000	2%	3,000	0%
World War II	1944	80,000	65%	40,000	52%	8,000	28%	4,000	21%
Postwar Boom	1955	120,000	58%	60,000	47%	12,000	20%	6,000	13%
JFK Tax Cut Implemented	1965	140,000	50%	70,000	43%	14,000	19%	7,000	14%
Vietnam War	1972	180,000	53%	90,000	45%	18,000	24%	9,000	19%
Oil Shock/Inflation	1975	230,000	56%	115,000	49%	23,000	28%	11,500	21%

SOURCES: CREATED BY THE AUTHOR FROM IRS, TAX FOUNDATION, AND BUREAU OF LABOR STATISTICS

Oil Shock/Inflation	1980	350,000	57%	175,000	53%	35,000	33%	17,500	21%
Reagan Flat Tax Initiated 1981–1986	1988	510,000	24%	255,000	25%	51,000	32%	25,500	21%
Era of the Flat Tax	1993	620,000	33%	310,000	32%	62,000	33%	31,000	21%
Era of the Flat Tax	2003	790,000	32%	395,000	35%	79,000	31%	39,500	20%
Era of the Flat Tax	2013	1,000,000	35%	500,000	39%	100,000	24%	50,000	20%

Sample Calculation for $100,000 Income in 1980

Definitions:

Inflation Adjuster: 35% x 100,000 = $35,000 in 2013 dollars

Standard Deduction: $3,400

Four Exemptions: $4,000

Tax Rate: 32%

OAS (Social Security, Employee share): 4.52%

DI (Disability Insurance, Employee share): 0.56%

OASDI limit (maximum amount subject to the tax): $25,900

HI (Medicare, Employee share): 1.05%

HI limit (maximum amount subject to the tax): $25,900 (unlimited after 1993)

Calculations:

Gross Income − Standard Deduction − Four Exemptions = Taxable Income

$35,000 − $3,400 − $4,000 = $27,600

OASDHI Tax = $25,900 x (4.52% + 0.56% + 1.05%) = $1,587.67

Employee + Employer OASDIHI = 2 x $1,587.67 = $3,175.34 (See explanation in the essay below)

Income Tax = 32% x Taxable Income of $27,600 = $8,832

Total Taxes = OASDIHI of $3,175.34 + Income Tax of $8,832 = $12,007.34

Total Taxes as a percentage of Gross Income = $12,007.34/($35,000 + $1,587.67) = 32.8% rounded to 33%

(Note: Because the Employer share of OASDIHI is treated as income—see essay below—it is both included in the Total Taxes of $12,007.34 and added to the Gross Income of $35,000 in the final calculation.)

Why Social Security Benefits Should Be Paid Out of General Revenue and Not from a Regressive Social Security Tax

1. When an employer pays into Social Security on behalf of an employee, it is equivalent to paying it to the employee, which is why self-employed people pay the full amount of Social Security (employee and employer shares) taxes.

2. According to the Social Security Administration, in 1990 a total of 27.7 percent of men and 16.4 percent of women who reached age twenty-one would not reach age sixty-five and, therefore, would not receive any Social Security benefits unless they chose to retire at sixty-two with benefits reduced by 30 percent or their surviving spouse was sixty or older at the time of their death. The retirement age is increasing to sixty-seven for people born after 1959. As a result, a substantial number of people who pay the Social Security tax will never receive any benefits from the program.

3. Workers began paying the Social Security tax in 1937, but retirees also began receiving lump sum benefits that year and monthly checks beginning in 1940, confirming that workers were paying for the prior generation's retirements, not their own.

4. According to the official Social Security site: "Since the assets in the Social Security trust funds consists of Treasury securities, this means that the taxes collected under the Social Security payroll tax are in effect being lent to the federal government to be expended for whatever present purposes the government requires. In this indirect sense, one could say that the Social Security trust funds are being spent for non–Social Security purposes." Clearly, there is no Trust Fund because it has already been loaned to the government and spent, and the government's only means of repaying it is either from general tax revenues or borrowings.

5. In 1969, Social Security Trust Funds were included in the Unified Budget. The funds were later taken "off budget," but current budget reporting of the Trust Fund is presented two ways: on budget and off budget. The on-budget method treats the Trust Funds as revenue and accordingly reduces the federal deficit by the Trust Fund amounts.

6. The tax is regressive because it is only assessed on income up to a specific level ($118,500 for 2015) and is not assessed against investment income. Further, it is assessed against gross income, not taxable income, and as a result, it is the largest single tax most middle- and lower-income Americans pay.

7. Currently, the Social Security tax is 10.6 percent and the Disability Insurance tax is 1.8 percent for a total of 12.4 percent, half paid by employees and half paid by employers on behalf of the employee. Another 2.9 percent for Medicare, which is paid in like manner, is assessed on income without limit, certainly a fairer form of taxation, if not a graduated one. Here is the startling calculation: A person earning $70,000 pays $5,355 directly and the employer pays a like amount for the employee. Adding the employer's half to the wages means the employee is actually earning $75,355 and paying $10,710 in these targeted taxes for a total of 14.21 percent of gross wages ($10,710/$75,355). Meanwhile, an individual earning $500,000 pays 12.4 percent on $118,500 or $14,694 plus 2.9 percent on $500,000 or $14,500 for a total of $29,194. Once again, the half paid by the employer must be added to the wages bringing the total compensation to $514,597. Dividing this amount into $29,194 yields only 5.67 percent compared with the 14.21 percent paid by the lower earning individual. If the $500,000 earner receives say $200,000 from investments and $300,000 in wages, the percentage drops to 4.57 percent because investment income is not taxed for Social Security, Disability Insurance, or Medicare. Investors who receive all of their income from non-wage sources pay none of these taxes.

8. Because Social Security taxes are paid by working generations for the benefit of retired generations, the tax should be a general obligation of the government and benefits should be paid out of general revenue, not from regressive targeted taxes.

GEORGE H. W. BUSH—"NO NEW TAXES"
1989–1993

Born/Died: 1924 Milton, MA
Education: Yale University
Occupation: Oilman
Political Party: Republican
Government Service: Vice President 1981–1989, CIA Director 1976–1977, US Representative to China 1974–1975, Republican National Committee Chairman 1973–1974, UN Ambassador 1971–1973, Representative (TX) 1967–1971
Military Service: Navy Lieutenant (JG); World War II (youngest naval aviator)
Preceded by: Ronald Reagan (near fatal assassination attempt; reduces taxes to flat tax; major Defense budget increase; cuts social spending; homeless population increases; doubles national debt; supports Mujahedeen against Soviets in Afghanistan; given primary credit for ending Cold War)

Next to Herbert Hoover and John Quincy Adams, no one was more prepared for the presidency than George H. W. Bush, who, unlike them, was also a war hero. As the youngest US Navy flyer in World War II, he was shot down in the Pacific. The son of US Sen. Prescott Bush of Connecticut, he was educated at Yale and went on to make a fortune in Texas oil before becoming a US representative from that state. Later, he became the US ambassador to the United Nations, chairman of the Republican National Committee, the first US ambassador (called chief of liaison) to communist China, Central Intelligence Agency director, and Ronald Reagan's two-term vice president. Despite this abundance of political, managerial, diplomatic, and military experience, Bush was unprepared for the presidency. Economics were his downfall.

His campaign pledge, "Read my lips; no new taxes," gave way to a different statement once he was in office: "It is clear to me that both

President George H. W. Bush and Gen. H. Norman Schwarzkopf Jr., in Kuwait, 1990
DAVID VALDEZ, NATIONAL ARCHIVES AND RECORDS ADMINISTRATION

the size of the deficit problem and the need for a package that can be enacted require all of the following: entitlement and mandatory program reform, tax revenue increases, growth incentives, discretionary spending reductions, orderly reductions in defense expenditures, and budget process reform."

Like Coolidge and Hoover, Bush never acknowledged the difference between personal, state, and federal finances, and admitted as much, stating in a press conference he was more comfortable with foreign policy issues.

The odd part about the recanted pledge was that it failed in its purpose (see chart above). The luxury tax, in particular, undermined the yacht and plane industries, putting people out of work, while collecting only a fraction of the promised revenue. Further, his increases did not reverse the real problem by correcting the regressive Reagan flat taxes. With the luxury tax, he had moved in the right direction in the wrong way. The problem was the 28 percent top income tax rate. For such an experienced hand, the blame can only be leveled on a lack of understanding of economics, the bane of so many presidents.

Even so, his tax pledge and retraction are certain to be forgotten by posterity, overshadowed by the spectacular success of Desert Storm, the campaign led by Gen. H. Norman Schwarzkopf to evict Saddam Hussein's Iraqi Army from Kuwait in 1991. The Pentagon and Secretary of Defense Dick Cheney, a man who avoided the Vietnam era draft with five deferments, rejected Schwarzkopf's initial plan as "High diddle, diddle, right up the middle."

Wild estimates of US casualties of thirty thousand or more were being discussed, but the author wrote in his weekly column (later incorporated into America's longest-running syndicated column, *Washington Merry-Go-Round*): "The war will last as long as it takes a tank to drive to Baghdad and American casualties will be under 500," noting that US armed forces were technologically superior to and better trained than any force on Earth, and when properly deployed could overwhelm any enemy in a conventional battle in days. In fact, our forces did not go to Baghdad—and, as later events proved, should not have. American casualties were under three hundred. Schwarzkopf performed to perfection. Unlike LBJ in 1964 (see Chapter 4, Johnson), Bush and his administration had taken care to select the right general for the job.

When then-Major Schwarzkopf was an instructor at West Point, teaching one of the typically small classes of fewer than twenty cadets, he refuted the current orthodoxy that they were being trained as commanders more than leaders. Using a World War I analogy, he said, "If you're not the first or second up and over, no one else is going to go." Having already served his first tour in Vietnam, he knew what he was saying. Known as "The Bear," Gen. H. Norman Schwarzkopf went on to defend Saudi Arabia, liberate Kuwait, and save thousands of lives through a combination of compassion and military brilliance. He nearly saved George H. W. Bush's reelection prospects.

Ex-Presidents

One advantage modern ex-presidents have over their nineteenth-century predecessors is a larger population base, which converts to a sufficiently large consumer base to turn memoirs and speech making into money machines. While this is generally a post–World War II phenomenon, the nineteenth-century exception was Grant, who, with the aid of former Confederate soldier Mark Twain, completed his best-selling autobiography while succumbing to cancer.

Several other ex-presidents struggled to remain solvent, a time-consuming ordeal that deprived the nation of the benefit of their experience and advice. This was particularly true for Founding Fathers James Madison and James Monroe, while Thomas Jefferson barely survived economic disaster.

Neither Jefferson nor John Adams were contented presidents, but they did spend their long post-presidential years as renewed friends and elder statesmen helping to guide the nation in its infancy with an enriching philosophical dialogue that included James Madison and others in an age of bountiful correspondence.

John Quincy Adams made his mark not in the White House, but as an ardent foe of slavery in the House of Representatives, where he served eighteen years after serving one term as president. In this, he became the beacon not followed.

Rutherford B. Hayes, who declined to run for a second term, proved to be an outstanding ex-president. Correctly recognizing education as the key to personal and national success—and essential to bringing freed slaves into the mainstream—Hayes became a strong advocate of aid to education, and also a foe of the concentration of wealth in the era of the Robber Barons.

Theodore Roosevelt was undoubtedly the highest-profile former president in history, writing, lecturing, exploring, and openly weighing in on the issues of the day, particularly pressing for military preparedness and pushing for involvement in World War I. He remained a force until his death.

Conversely, Herbert Hoover was perhaps the lowest-profile ex-president of those who continued to make a difference. Independently wealthy, Hoover was able to devote his time whenever called, which President Truman did, making use of his valuable advice and experience, their party differences, as with most former presidents, being irrelevant.

Jimmy Carter was unpopular when he left office after one term, though not as unpopular as Harry Truman was when he left. Truman found no post-presidential niche, having fallen out with his successor, Dwight D. Eisenhower, and opposing John Kennedy's run for the office in 1960. Yet, over time his presidency has, at least in part, been reevaluated in a positive way. Carter's presidency has not. Instead, he went on to make his mark as the most acclaimed ex-president since Theodore Roosevelt, devoting himself to causes such as Habitat for Humanity and serving—some say interfering with—the cause of peace around the world.

(See The Freshman President's Epilogue: The World's Most Exclusive University)

CHAPTER 8

PANIC, LAISSEZ FAIRE, AND DEPRESSION

MARTIN VAN BUREN (1837), CALVIN COOLIDGE (1923), AND HERBERT HOOVER (1929)

President Herbert Hoover, a self-made millionaire, may have admired another self-made man, President Martin Van Buren. If not, he certainly emulated him as well as the man he did not admire, Calvin Coolidge. Within weeks of taking office in 1837, Van Buren stood by as the nation suffered its worst financial depression up to that time. Within months of taking office in 1929, Hoover stood by as the stock market crashed, then turned the Crash into the Great Depression through rigid adherence to a self-defeating ideology.

The pendulum of needed knowledge has occasionally swung in concert with a president's area of expertise, and so it seemed when these two millionaires, Van Buren and Hoover, brought their financial acumen to the office. It was not so. The great financial convulsions occurring on their watches were doctrinaire downturns, although in both cases the doctrines they followed were more intuitive than educated. They would too late discover that the skill inherent in accumulating individual wealth did not translate into the management of a national economy.

An individual cannot print money, impose taxes, or direct and control any of the other economic functions peculiar to national governments.

Indeed, an attempt to run a national budget as if it were a personal budget is nothing more than an exercise in hubris-laden folly. This was more the case with Van Buren than Hoover. The partially self-educated Van Buren created a powerful political machine in New York and made his fortune as an attorney and speculator, neither of which endeavors qualified him as an economist. Hoover, on the other hand, had run an international mining business, a war-time relief effort, and served as the US secretary of Commerce, all of which brought him nearer to being an economist than any other president. Clearly, if there was a president to deal with an economic crisis, Herbert Hoover should have been that person.

Coolidge was not wealthy, a fact Hoover viewed as a failing, and his reliance upon Andrew Mellon, one of the wealthiest men in the country, aligned his views with those of Van Buren and Hoover, all to the financial detriment of the nation.

What Van Buren, Coolidge, and Hoover needed was an Alexander Hamilton (see Chapter 1), not an Andrew Mellon.

MARTIN VAN BUREN—PANIC OF 1837
1837–1841

Born/Died: 1782 Kinderhook, NY–1862 Kinderhook, NY
Education: No formal education
Occupation: Lawyer, professional politician
Political Party: Democratic
Government Service: Vice President 1833–1837, Ambassador (Britain) 1831–1832, Secretary of State 1829–1831, Governor (NY) 1829, Senator (NY) 1821–1828, Attorney General (NY) 1815–1819
Military Service: None
Preceded by: Andrew Jackson (spoils system replaces merit-based government hiring; threatens military action against South Carolina over tariff issue in Nullification Crisis; Indian Removal Act forces Native Americans off their southeastern lands and a quarter of them die on the Trail

of Tears; closes Bank of the United States and places federal funds in state banks; state banks print money and Panic of 1837 ensues; introduces common-man democracy)

Van Buren had been President Andrew Jackson's vice president, and he shared Jackson's aversion to a national bank, but on what financial principle? This bias led to the dispersion of monetary policy to the states, and when the Bank of England's money tightening reverberated across the ocean, there was no Federal Reserve (which would not come about until 1913) to fill the void. The Panic of 1837—one of those recurring financial jolts to the economy during the nineteenth and early twentieth centuries—was the result. Van Buren was simply not equipped to handle the situation, and the Panic-caused depression lasted throughout his one-term presidency. For four years he remained a virtual spectator of economic chaos.

President Martin Van Buren
LIBRARY OF CONGRESS

The diminutive Van Buren sported side whiskers and was attentive to attire and speech alike. Ebullient in social settings, he was a man of measured words when donning his legal or political personas, a technique that allowed him to draw out others while implying agreement. It also served to conceal his shortcomings of knowledge, experience, and education, leaving his listeners mesmerized by the knowing nod of feigned comprehension—at least until they departed and realized he had neither agreed nor disagreed, or even elucidated.

David (Davy) Crockett, along with or through fellow legislator Augustin Smith Clayton, wrote a political screed denouncing Van Buren, primarily because President Andrew Jackson had selected him as his successor. To Crockett, this anointing smacked of royalty, and in 1835, the year before Van Buren was elected, the venomous book was released. Despite its partisanship, it contained elements of truth well known to those who knew Van Buren and his inclination to pretend adherence to both sides of an issue.

He is "secret, sly, selfish, cold, calculating, distrustful . . . [and] how artful his practices may be to keep on both sides and all sides of a question," Crockett and Clayton wrote. "I have almost given up the Ship as lost. I have gone So far as to declare that if he martin vanburen is elected that I will leave the united States for I never will live under his kingdom. before I will Submit to his Government I will go to the wildes of Texas" (spelling and punctuation as written).

True to his word Crockett departed for Texas and immortality at the Alamo even before the ballots of 1836 were cast. Van Buren went on to the White House, where despite his best efforts, his vacillating nature accentuated an inability to come to grips with the overwhelming weight of the office.

On September 5, 1837, just months after his inauguration, Van Buren wrote his own political epitaph: "The less Government interferes with private pursuits, the better for the general prosperity." The Panic of 1837 proved him wrong. He waffled on slavery, saying it was constitutional and up to the states; demurred on Texas statehood; continued the Jacksonian anti-national bank policy; and, worst of all, pressed on with the Indian Removal Act. It was actually during his administration that the despicable ordeal became known as the Trail of Tears.

Physical Traits and Whether They Matter

Left-Handers

Garfield, Hoover, Truman, Ford, Reagan, G. H. W. Bush, Clinton, and Obama
Approximately 10 percent of people are left-handed, yet five (more than 70 percent) of the last seven presidents are among them. There have been

attempts to attach scientific significance to this phenomenon, one of which is the need for left-handers to be more mentally flexible in a world made for right-handers.

Redheads

Washington, Jefferson, Jackson, Van Buren, Grant, Coolidge, Eisenhower, and Kennedy (reddish brown)

More than 8 percent of our presidents were redheads compared to approximately 4 percent of the general population.

Short and Tall

Twenty presidents were six feet tall or taller, with Lincoln at 6'4" the tallest. All five presidents since Carter have been six feet or taller. Eleven were less than 5'9", Madison the shortest at 5'4", and all of them served before the twentieth century. Over the years, nutrition has impacted average heights both positively and negatively, though this does not explain why modern male presidents have been above today's average American male adult height of 5'10".

Do Physical Traits Matter?

Washington, Jefferson, Jackson, and Kennedy were tall redheads, but America has never had a tall, left-handed, redheaded president, though statistically, such a person would have an electoral advantage.

In a 2013 issue of the *Telegraph*, Dr. James Le Fanu wrote: "Height should not matter—but it does. Tallness, particularly in men, has always been a valuable biological characteristic, where those fortunate enough to be at least 6ft benefit from a pervasive positive discrimination. Employers consistently prefer the taller of equally qualified candidates, to whom they pay more generous starting salaries.

"Historically, too, tallness distinguished the ruler from the ruled, the rich from the poor—hence we 'look up' to our betters, and 'down' on our inferiors."

Like life, the presidential selection process is unfair.

CALVIN COOLIDGE—THE ROAD
TO DEPRESSION
1923–1929

Born/Died: 1872 Plymouth Notch, VT–1933 Northampton, MA
Education: Amherst College
Occupation: Lawyer
Political Party: Republican
Government Service: Vice President 1921–1923, Governor (MA) 1919–1921, Lieutenant Governor (MA) 1916–1919, State Senator (MA) 1912–1915, Mayor (Northampton, MA) 1910–1911, State Representative (MA) 1907–1908
Military Service: None
Preceded by: Warren G. Harding (lowers income taxes and increases tariffs; scandal-plagued administration with Teapot Dome, other scandals; accurately admits, "I am not fit for this office"; dies while serving)

Upon arriving in Washington, the Social Register described him as "a politician who does not, who will not, who seemingly cannot talk."

Upon becoming Warren G. Harding's vice president, Calvin Coolidge received a telegram from Wilson's outgoing Vice President Thomas Marshall: "Please accept my sincerest sympathy." Neither of them dreamed Coolidge would soon be president due to the death of Harding.

Coolidge, a former governor, jumped into the budget business from day one on the job, not fully understanding the gulf of differences between state and federal finances or even personal finances. In addressing one group, he admitted, "I believe in budgets. . . . I have had a small one to run my own home; and besides that, I am the head of the organization that makes the greatest of all budgets, that of the United States government." To him, debt was anathema, and he certainly did not make a distinction between short-term debt to fund operations and long-term debt to fund infrastructure or military needs. Indeed, a balanced budget was his holy grail, even at the expense of national defense or humanitarian endeavors.

He turned down Brig. Gen. Billy Mitchell's plea for more naval aviation funding. He turned down requests to rebuild after Mississippi flooding extracted a terrible toll of lives and property. He reveled in the word, "No."

Secretary of the Treasury Andrew Mellon had been appointed by President Harding and would also serve both Coolidge and Hoover, causing Nebraska's Republican Sen. George Norris to later quip, "Three presidents served under Mellon." As one of the wealthiest men in America, Mellon was also one of the largest taxpayers, and while his integrity was beyond reproach, it is fair to note the obvious conflict of interest in

President Calvin Coolidge
LIBRARY OF CONGRESS

his role reducing the top tax rate, albeit a wartime rate, from 77 percent to 24 percent by 1929 (see Chart, Chapter 7). This was part of the Mellon Plan that became the Revenue Act of 1924, one of the first bills President Coolidge signed into law. Taxes and regulations were reduced, the rich got richer, speculation became rampant, and the national economy was set on a course for 1929 and a crash. Between 1920 and 1927, spending was cut by 50 percent, and Mellon practically invented what the Reagan Administration would later call "trickle down" economics.

Coolidge's economic world view was seen through the prism of his father's farm and his own struggling law practice, a personal budget dilemma only resolved by a plea to his father for funds to fill the shortfalls, even while serving as vice president.

He had voted for women's suffrage, a state income tax, and other progressive programs, though none of that ideology seemed to carry over to his presidency, where he took the stance of a strict constitutional constructionist. Instead of looking at what the Constitution prevented him from doing, he refused to act unless the Constitution specifically authorized him to do it. Hence, his refusal to offer flood relief.

It is difficult to determine what Coolidge believed to be the proper role of the federal government because it is equally difficult to find a president who took a lower view of that role. With a disdain for regulations, he was a true believer in laissez faire. Cutting the budget was more important than maintaining a credible Army and Navy. Disaster relief was the job of the affected states. Debt was almost immoral. Yet, despite all this, his successor has taken most of the blame for the Great Depression. In fact Mellon was the culprit, and Harding, Coolidge, and Hoover were his gullible students. Later, for all of the Treasury secretary's budget and tax-slashing errors in the 1920s, Mellon would crown his career by urging the worst possible medicine to cure the Great Depression. Just as the Depression was worsening, and to the utter surprise of fiscally conservative Republicans, he would recommend a sizeable tax increase and endorse the Federal Reserve's counterproductive contraction of the money supply.

Even though history has been gentle with Coolidge, he finally began to see the truth of the yawning financial cliff he had helped create: "Well, they're going to elect that superman Hoover, and he's going to have some trouble. He's going to have to spend money. But he won't spend enough. Then the Democrats will come in and they'll spend money like water. But they don't know anything about money."

Coolidge, by then watching from the sidelines and writing a newspaper column, remained unrepentant, criticizing his successor: "The expenditure of money has been too large." Considering it would finally take the massive deficit spending of World War II to end the Great Depression, Coolidge could not have been more mistaken, even more mistaken than Herbert Hoover (see Chapter 15, Chart), the "superman" he disdained.

HERBERT HOOVER—THE GREAT DEPRESSION
1929–1933

Born/Died: 1874 West Branch, IA–1964 New York, NY
Education: Stanford University
Occupation: Mining engineer
Political Party: Republican
Government Service: Secretary of Commerce 1921–1928
Military Service: None
Preceded by: Calvin Coolidge (laissez faire anti-regulatory advocate; lowers taxes and spending, which adversely affects military and critical civilian programs; balanced-budget adherent, not comprehending the difference between state and federal budgets; Wall Street speculation runs unabated leading to Crash of 1929)

Herbert Hoover was what we now call a "Whiz Kid." He and his wife, Lou, both Stanford graduates, married on February 10, 1899, and sailed for China the following day, he as a mining engineer. The Boxer Rebellion broke out the following year, and the couple was embroiled in the conflict at Tientsin where both proved to be cool under fire. With support from the Dowager Empress, the Boxers were attempting to put an end to the foreign spheres of influence then carving up their country. This forced the foreign legations to become allies of necessity, and the shared danger brought Hoover into direct contact with several future European and Japanese leaders.

From China, Hoover went on to financial success, operating mining operations around the globe, and revealing in his memoirs an odd elitism: "If a man has not made a fortune by 40 he is not worth much." So much for his predecessor, the indebted Calvin Coolidge.

Despite that ill-stated view, when World War I broke out in 1914, Hoover revealed a humanitarian side, heading a relief organization bringing aid to German-occupied Belgium and northern France nearly three

President Herbert Hoover and First Lady Lou Hoover
LIBRARY OF CONGRESS

years before America's entrance into the conflict. Dubbed the "Napoleon of mercy," George H. Nash wrote in "An American Epic," he may have been "responsible for saving more lives than any other person in history." He literally saved a nation, and in the process became familiar with many of Europe's leading politicians, statesmen, and generals on both sides of the conflict.

Selfless, thoroughly honest, and indefatigable, he was the obvious choice of President Woodrow Wilson to lead the American Relief Administration responsible for feeding European friends and former foes alike at the end of the war. Headlined as one of the "Twelve Greatest American Men," by the *New York Times* on July 23, 1922, Hoover was admired by both Wilson and future President Franklin D. Roosevelt, Democrats who urged him to run for the presidency on their party's ticket. Instead, he became Commerce secretary under Republican Presidents Warren G. Harding and Calvin Coolidge.

By 1928, despite never having run for elective office, he was the first-ballot Republican presidential candidate. Bright, courageous, highly educated, ambitious, efficient, trustworthy, a proven manager, and renowned humanitarian, Herbert Hoover was arguably among the best prepared of all the unprepared men ever to win the presidency, which Hoover handily did that November. He was sworn in on March 4, 1929, a year ever after to be synonymous with financial collapse.

There had been other financial panics, but nothing like what struck in October 1929. The Dow Jones Industrial Average, which stood at 381.17 in September, was down to 41.22 by July 1932, an unprecedented 89 percent drop. The statistic fails to tell the story. The Dow actually recovered to 294.07 in April 1930 before taking its true dive, the dive that fell at the feet of President Hoover. He was the man to handle a food problem, even a famine, and no president was better qualified to address an engineering situation, but, like Van Buren, he was not the president to handle a financial panic even though he was closer to the economic profession than any of his predecessors—certainly closer than Coolidge whose laissez faire policies were so responsible for the initial Crash. The problem was that economics had become more complex in the twentieth century, prompted in part by the increased economic globalization resulting from World War I.

Hjalmar Schacht first met Hoover in Berlin in 1915 to discuss Belgian relief while World War I was raging. They would meet again in October 1930 when Schacht, then between terms as Germany's finance minister, traveled to the United States. By then Hoover was president of the United States. They discussed a reduction in Germany's World War I reparations payments (Hoover did place a one-year moratorium on them in 1931) and presumably the Great Depression, which was just inflicting the first of ten years of unparalleled financial agony.

Two years earlier, Schacht had discussed global economic problems with renowned British economist John Maynard Keynes and embraced his ideas. The essence of Keynesian philosophy was counter-cyclical spending, the idea that a nation could spend its way out of a recession or depression, which is precisely what Schacht did for Germany from

1933 onward. Under the pall of financial disaster, this view of economic philosophy must have entered into the Hoover-Schacht discussion. (Several alternate theories about the Depression's causes and recovery have been promulgated, but the fact remains that raising taxes and tariffs while cutting budgets drained money from the economy, whereas the massive deficit spending of World War II did the opposite, and the Depression ended.) Hoover, who had also met Keynes, wasn't listening to either the philosopher or to Schacht. Like his successor, Franklin Roosevelt, who met with Keynes in 1934, they seemed not to fully comprehend the economist's concepts, with Roosevelt saying, "He left a whole rigamarole of figures." Keynes left unimpressed.

Hoover's heart was in the right place; his pocketbook was not. A humanitarian, he was a Theodore Roosevelt Republican, a progressive who advocated a pension for citizens over sixty-five, which was not enacted, but served as the embryonic idea for Franklin Roosevelt's Social Security system. The Reconstruction Finance Corporation was created to help small banks, and the Federal Home Loan Banking Act was proposed and passed to help homeowners. This was all offset by Hoover's fiscal conservatism and adherence to balanced budgets, an adherence that led to spending cuts and revenue-raising programs such as the Smoot-Hawley Tariff Act. Proposed at the end of his first year in office, this ill-conceived legislation undermined US exports by initiating a trade war with Europe. With convoluted ideology, he refused to do for his countrymen what he had so nobly done for the Belgians.

So Hoover's first year was a disaster, and the next three years only got worse. With the Revenue Act of 1932, he imposed as much as a three-fold increase on some income tax brackets. Ironically, all this created large budget deficits as a vicious downward spiral saw budget cutbacks overwhelmed by falling revenues. According to Department of Commerce data, increased taxes and tariffs clearly backfired. Total government income fell from $3.862 billion in 1929 to $1.997 billion in 1933, Hoover's last year in office. His policies deflated the economy and increased unemployment.

Hoover's devotion to balanced-budget orthodoxy clouded his judgment and exposed a strange inability to learn and adapt. Both in business and in relief efforts, he had displayed a remarkable flexibility. Once in the White House, he seemed frozen by dogma. He believed in volunteerism, an altruistic dependence upon uncompensated work, to contend with the suffering graphically depicted in John Steinbeck's *Grapes of Wrath*, but charity could not take the place of government action. As a result, Hoover's inaction and ill-advised policies nearly wrecked the US economy and eroded faith in the American political system, all at a time when Germany was on the verge of spending its way to prosperity and rearmament.

With unemployment nearing 25 percent, some Americans began to flirt with alternate political systems, including communism and fascism. Meanwhile, American military power continued to ebb, reaching dangerously low levels, low enough to encourage potential enemies. Actual spending on military defense (which does not include pensions and other retiree benefits) grew slightly from 1929 to 1932, then dropped precipitously just as Hitler's German war machine was gearing up.

Financial crises are not kind to presidents, and like Van Buren, Hoover was a one-term president, because as with Van Buren, he refused to deviate from dogma even when it crippled his freshman year.

Hoover was a man of irony. He had delivered relief aid to the starving people of occupied Belgium in World War I and to a destitute Germany afterward, but refused to offer direct aid to hungry, humbled Americans during the Great Depression, claiming, "A huge work relief program might be as demoralizing as a dole." This apparently contradictory behavior can only be explained by a mental bifurcation in which he viewed aid to war-torn Europeans as an act of charitable necessity and aid to destitute Americans as an economic act to undermine incentive.

American Financial Crises

Panic of 1797	Panic of 1907
Depression of 1807	Depression of 1920–1921
Panic of 1819	The Great Depression 1929–1940
Panic of 1837	1973–1975 Recession (OPEC Oil Crisis)
Panic of 1857	1982 Recession
Panic of 1873 (The Long Depression)	The Great Recession 2008–2009
Panic of 1893	

Significant US Tariffs

Date	Tariff Title	Increase/ Decrease	Decription
1789	Hamilton Tariffs	▲	Protective and revenue
1790	"		
1792	"		
1816	Dallas Tariff of 1816	▲	Protective
1824	Tariff of 1824	▲	Protective (Britain targeted)
1828	1828 Tariff of Abominations	▲	Protective; nullification threatened
1828	Reciprocity Act	▼	
1832	Tariff of 1832	▲	Protective; Nullification Crisis: President Jackson threatens military action
1833	Compromise Tariff of 1833	▼	New England opposes
1842	Black Tariff of 1842	▲	Protective response to Panic of 1837; reverses 1833 tariff; imports halved
1846	Walker Tariff	▼	Toward revenue only; Britain repeals Corn Laws
1857	Tariff of 1857	▼	Toward free trade
1861	Morrill Tariff	▲	Begins protectionist era (1861–1913); in 1860 Republican Platform; alienates northern Democrats, southerners, and British; Republicans pass after southern senators resign during secession; Buchanan signs first act (benefits his home state of Pennsylvania); Lincoln signs second act
1872	Tariff of 1872	▼	
1875	Tariff of 1875	▲	Repealed 1872 reductions
1883	Mongrel Tariff	▼/▲	Complex and satisfied no one
1890	McKinley Tariff	▲	Protective, largest to date; "radical extension of the protective system"
1894	Wilson-Gorman Tariff Act	▼	Republicans who had "espoused the extreme protective policy suffered a crushing defeat"
1897	Dingley Tariff	▲	Reaction to Panic of 1893

Year	Act		Description
1909	Payne-Aldrich Tariff	▶	Progressive Era response to trusts
1913	Underwood Tariff	▶	Then increased in World War I
1921	Emergency Tariff of 1921	◀	Targeted for farmers
1922	Fordney-McCumber Tariff	◀	Large increase
1930	Smoot-Hawley Tariff	◀	Largest to date; foreign retaliation; contributed to the Great Depression
1934	Reciprocal Tariff Act	▶	Response to Great Depression
Moving toward free trade:			
1947	General Agreement on Tariffs and Trade	▶	UN-sponsored reductions
1962	Trade Expansion Act	▶	Presidential discretion to lower 50%
1963–1967	Kennedy Round	▶	Significant decreases
1973–1979	Tokyo Round		Addresses non-tariff trade barriers
1974	Trade Act of 1974		Presidential discretion for developing nations
1979	Trade Agreements Act of 1979		
1984	Trade and Tariff Act of 1984		
1988	Omnibus Foreign Trade and Competitiveness Act		
1993	NAFTA (North American Free Trade Agreement)	▶	United States, Canada, and Mexico free trade
1994	World Trade Organization		
2002	United States Steel Tariff		
2002	Trade Act of 2002		

SOURCES: PUBLIC RECORDS AND THE TARIFF HISTORY OF THE UNITED STATES BY FRANK WILLIAM TAUSSIG (SEE ENDNOTES)

CHAPTER 9

IN DEFIANCE OF PARTY

JOHN TYLER (1841), RUTHERFORD B. HAYES (1877), AND WILLIAM J. CLINTON (1993)

JOHN TYLER—THE MAN WITHOUT A PARTY 1841–1845

Born/Died: 1790 Charles City, VA–1862 Richmond, VA
Education: The College of William & Mary
Occupation: Planter, lawyer, professional politician
Political Party: Democratic, Whig
Government Service: Confederate Representative (VA) 1862, Vice President 1841, Governor (VA) 1825–1827, Senator (VA) 1827–1836, Representative (VA) 1816–1821
Military Service: Militia Captain; no active service
Preceded by: William Henry Harrison (oldest president before Reagan; does not take care of health; dies soon after inauguration)

Wittily referring to himself in the third person, John Tyler wrote, "He is the creature of accidents being an accident himself." Dubbed "His Accidency" by less friendly wits, Tyler was the first vice president to accede to the presidency under Article II, Section 1 of the Constitution: "In Case of the Removal of the President from Office, or of his Death, Resignation, or Inability to discharge the Powers and Duties of the said Office, the Same shall devolve on the Vice President." The problem came from the word "devolve," which was not altered until ratification of the Twenty-Fifth Amendment in 1967: "In case of the removal of the President from office or of his death or resignation, the Vice President shall *become President.*"

President John Tyler
LIBRARY OF CONGRESS

In the intervening 126 years, seven more vice presidents would follow this path to the presidency, and they would do so not through law, but upon the precedent established by Tyler in 1841.

A frail child and gaunt adult, Tyler was educated at the College of William & Mary, where his father had been Thomas Jefferson's roommate. He was the last of the long line of Virginia's plantation aristocrats (Washington, Jefferson, Madison, Monroe, and Harrison) who dominated the presidency for thirty-six of the nation's fifty-six formative years.

A lifelong politician, Tyler became anything other than a politic president. Originally a Democrat, he became a Whig, and was elected vice president on the Whig ticket. Throughout his career as a Virginia legislator and governor (like his father before him) and as a member of the US House of Representatives and Senate, he consistently followed principled lines over party lines and had somehow managed to maintain harmonious relations with enough colleagues to ensure a continuous career. This changed with his presidency. Apparently viewing the highest office as above politics in the tradition of George Washington, he alienated Whigs and Democrats alike, vetoing an unprecedented number of bills. In exasperation, the Whigs finally expelled him from their ranks. Tyler became a president without a party, unable to do more than assert a negative, veto-pen agenda.

His primary mistake was neither use of the veto nor his adherence to principles. As a freshman president, he forgot he was a politician, and he failed to engage, court, and woo the members of Congress, who not only expected it, but needed it, often as cover for them to also break ranks and follow principled paths.

Most of his Cabinet resigned, and he later wrote, "I was forced to make a cabinet upon the resignation of five members in a few hours." Not until the last year of his presidency did he awaken to reality. A strong advocate of expansion, he favored annexation of Texas, which had won its independence from Mexico in 1836. Opposition was intense. Northern Whigs and northern Democrats opposed admission of another slave state into the Union, and Mexico threatened war if annexation proceeded. Facing failure of his signature policy, Tyler suddenly realized that a statesman cannot succeed without simultaneously succeeding as a politician. The revelation came too late to secure him a second term or even a nomination. It did come in time to secure congressional approval for the annexation of Texas.

Unlike the President Tyler of 1841, President Tyler of 1844–1845 distributed political favors and employed the press, political appointments, secret negotiations, a national tour, and old-fashioned arm-twisting to achieve his end and set in motion the concept of Manifest Destiny that would turn the United States into a continental nation.

Tyler had misinterpreted the lessons from fellow Virginian George Washington, who was able to play the statesman only because his highly politicized surrogates performed the necessary work in the political trenches. The lesson would not be revisited until Eisenhower made the same mistake in 1953.

Tyler's terrible start was more than redeemed by his superb finish.

RUTHERFORD B. HAYES—THE GREAT SWAP
1877–1881

Born/Died: 1822 Delaware, OH–1893 Fremont, OH
Education: Kenyon College, Harvard Law School
Occupation: Lawyer
Political Party: Whig, Republican
Government Service: Governor (OH) 1876–1877, 1868–1872, Representative (OH) 1865–1867
Military Service: Federal Major General; Civil War
Preceded by: Ulysses S. Grant (numerous scandals such as Crédit Mobilier affecting Cabinet, associates, friends, and relations; allied with Radical Republicans and machine politicians; reverses Andrew Johnson's conciliatory Reconstruction policy in the South; attempts program to ship former slaves to the Dominican Republic)

Rutherford B. Hayes, a former Federal general, paid a high ethical price for the presidency. Democrat Samuel J. Tilden had won the popular vote in the 1876 election, but the electoral votes of Oregon, South Carolina, Louisiana, and Florida were disputed. A commission was appointed to determine the winner, and on a straight party-line vote of eight Republicans to seven Democrats, Hayes was declared the president. Democrats were livid and threatened to stall the election outcome in Congress with a filibuster, and were forestalled only after a compromise known as the Great Swap was engineered. Hayes could have the presidency if federal troops were pulled out of the South and home rule was restored, effectively ending the harsh Reconstruction imposed by Radical Republicans following the Civil War. However, this left four million freed slaves in limbo, unwelcome in the North, disenfranchised in the South.

"My task was to wipe out the color line, to abolish sectionalism, to end the war and bring peace," he wrote. "To do this, I was ready to resort to unusual measures and to risk my own standing and reputation within my party and the country." Here was a president committed to doing right and naively believing in the perpetuation of good deeds. Ending

President Rutherford B. Hayes
LIBRARY OF CONGRESS

a pointless military occupation was right. Educating freed slaves to become informed voters and ensuring their safety with federal marshals would have been right, but Congress did not agree. And no one spoke out against northern and western state laws restricting minority residency and property rights. In short, the election of 1876 enshrined the advance of bigotry.

The Thirteenth, Fourteenth, and Fifteenth Amendments, the Reconstruction Amendments, were construed, respectively, as freeing the slaves, providing equal rights including citizenship, and granting the right to vote. Although these laws of the land would be accepted and enforced in time, reality was otherwise in 1876.

The Thirteenth Amendment, passed in 1865 at the end of the Civil War, provided freedom without rights. The Fourteenth Amendment, ratified in 1868, sought to remedy this, but failed to include the vote. In theory, the Fifteenth Amendment, ratified in 1870, was the culmination of the journey from slavery to full citizenship through enfranchisement of the freedmen. But it wasn't, and most Americans knew it. Susan B. Anthony, Elizabeth Cady Stanton, and the National Woman Suffrage Association opposed the amendment because it granted the vote to former male slaves, who were generally illiterate, while denying the vote to women, who generally were not. In this respect, the amendment was an inexcusable statement of gender bigotry. Indeed, southern states were required to ratify the amendment as a condition for readmittance to the Union, and it could not have become law without their votes.

There was a flaw. The Fifteenth Amendment specifically failed to exclude literacy tests and poll taxes, which the US Supreme Court confirmed with convoluted language in the 1876 *Reese* case: "If citizens of one race having certain qualifications are permitted by law to vote, those of another having the same qualifications must be." The operative word was "qualifications." As a result, as late as 1940, only 5 percent of African Americans were registered to vote. It would take the Voting Rights Act of 1965 to finally rectify most of the omissions of the ninety-five-year-old Fifteenth Amendment. Gerrymandering—the use of convoluted congressional district boundaries to concentrate African Americans in electoral ghettos—continues to this day.

Meanwhile, by granting citizenship to freedmen, the constitutional provision counting a slave as three-fifths of a person was eliminated, which resulted in an immediate increase in the "legal" population and concurrent political power of states with large numbers of former slaves. This was the unintended consequence. Republicans who had expected to attract the votes of freed slaves soon discovered they had only managed to increase Democratic power, though at the time of ratification, they were elated. They had won the war, occupied the South, freed the slaves, and granted them citizenship. Their work was done.

Assimilation was another matter. Several northern state constitutions prohibited freed slaves from residing in their territory. To them, slaves and freed slaves were southern issues. The 1851 Indiana Constitution clause read: "No Negro or Mulatto shall come into, or settle in, the State, after the adoption of this Constitution." The 1847 Illinois Constitution prohibited immigration of freed black slaves. Laws prohibiting interracial marriage were prevalent throughout the South until the post–World War II period from 1945 to 1967, but also in West Virginia, Indiana, Oklahoma, Nebraska, North Dakota, South Dakota, Montana, Wyoming, Colorado, Utah, Arizona, Nevada, Idaho, Oregon, and California. Such laws had also existed in Maine, Rhode Island, Ohio, Michigan, Illinois, and New Mexico in the 1865–1900 post–Civil War period. In short, bigotry was a national pastime and often targeted Catholic, Jewish, and Chinese citizens as well.

This is what faced Rutherford B. Hayes in the election of 1876, when he naively helped undermine the cause of freedom for nearly a century. African Americans would not come north in large numbers until the

Great Migration, when World War I created a labor shortage in northern factories. Whereas black and white people had interacted for centuries in the South, this influx was a jolt to white northerners, and the reception proved to be highly inhospitable and gave rise to a new Ku Klux Klan, initially formed in Georgia, then becoming strongest in midwestern and western urban centers during the first two decades of the twentieth century, electing governors in Indiana, Colorado, Oregon, Alabama, and Georgia as well as members of Congress, mayors, and other government officials. This is what Alexis de Tocqueville anticipated (see Chapter 5) and what Rutherford B. Hayes wrought.

Hayes eventually realized electoral, social, and economic assimilation was impossible without education, and he spent the remainder of his life as one of the nation's foremost advocates of universal literacy.

WILLIAM J. CLINTON—A PRESIDENT FOR ALL REASONS
1993–2001

Born: 1946 Hope, AR
Education: Georgetown University, Oxford Rhodes Scholar, Yale Law School
Occupation: Lawyer, professional politician
Political Party: Democratic
Government Service: Governor (AR) 1979–1981, 1983–1992, Attorney General (AR) 1977–1979
Military Service: None
Preceded by: George H. W. Bush (famously says "read my lips, no new taxes," then imposes new taxes in face of Reagan budget deficits; ousts Iraqis from Kuwait in highly successful Operation Desert Storm)

President Bill Clinton never said, "The chief business of the American people is business." President Calvin Coolidge did. Clinton, a founder

President Bill Clinton
LIBRARY OF CONGRESS

of the Democratic Leadership Council, sought to move the party to the center, which after the debacle of his failed attempt to have universal health care enacted, often meant right of center, prompting Stephen Hess of the Brookings Institution to say: "I'm not sure how different this presidency is going to look than Calvin Coolidge's." In the process Clinton, like President John Tyler, often found himself in opposition to his own party.

On the September 23, 2007, airing of *Meet the Press*, moderator Tim Russert displayed a statement from Connecticut Sen. Chris Dodd: "The mismanagement in 1993 and 1994 has set back our ability to move toward universal health care immeasurably," to which Sen. Hillary Clinton of New York responded, "We made a lot of mistakes. . . . I learned a lot of lessons."

Those lessons were not learned in 1993, Bill Clinton's first chaotic year in the presidency. He entered the office announcing the country was getting a "two-fer," two for the price of one, and, true to the claim, placed his wife, Hillary Rodham Clinton, in charge of his proposed universal health care plan. While she would later find her footing as a US senator and as President Obama's first secretary of State, in 1993 she was not ready for congressional prime time. Her secretive and uncompromising approach to the health care legislation alienated enough senators and representatives to sink the bill. The president had delegated the job to the wrong person.

His first-year problems did not end there. Excluding most social issues, he joined Republicans on several key issues, becoming in the process a DINO (Democrat in Name Only). He even devised balanced and surplus budgets, although the end of the Cold War impacted those as much as ideological dogma, a dogma that included income tax increases too modest to unflatten the Reagan-era flat tax.

In 1993, he championed the North American Free Trade Agreement (NAFTA), which had more Republican than Democratic support (in a twist of history, a majority of Republicans abandoned their long-held adherence to high-tariff business protectionism, while many Democrats came to view tariffs as job protectionism). To this day, the jury on this agreement remains out, with complaints about Canada's Byzantine bureaucracy and the AFL-CIO claiming massive job losses to Mexico, while, on the other hand, agricultural exporters experienced significant gains. Did this battle result from a political metamorphosis following his failed attempt to obtain passage of universal health care? Or was he motivated by ongoing attempts to mollify Republicans who continually raised accusations of wrongdoing and immorality that culminated in the 1998 impeachment and trial—in which he was acquitted—over perjury and obstruction of justice accusations?

Whatever the motivation, he continued on the same path of accommodation, signing the Republican-sponsored Personal Responsibility and Work Opportunity Reconciliation Act of 1996 (PRWORA), which limited welfare benefits to five years, and, just months after his impeachment trial, signing the Republican-sponsored Gramm-Leach-Bliley Act revoking the portions of the Depression-era Glass-Steagall Act that prevented banks from engaging in brokerage activities. This led to later banking abuses that contributed to the Great Recession of 2007–2009.

Clinton remains an enigma. Even he admitted his first-year amazement: "Part of it is growing pains, learning pains. . . . I felt like the dog that chased the pickup truck. I got it, now what am I going to do?" Perhaps the writers and producers anticipated Clinton when in 1972 they released *The Candidate*, a film about a young idealist whose political managers got him elected through image making. Starring Robert Redford, the last line was: "What do we do now?"

Clinton was low on the scale of the unready, and his first-year universal health care fiasco provided the proof. White House disarray confirmed it. Joe Klein explained: "The internal mayhem at the White House was soon legendary. The public image was of callow, arrogant aides wandering about in dungarees, pulling unnecessary all-nighters. . . . And it was true that the atmosphere was, well, rather loose. Meetings were interminable, often inconclusive, and open to anyone on staff who happened to walk in."

The enigma that is Clinton runs the gamut: the warm, winning, you're-the-only-person-in-the-room personality of a Kennedy or Reagan combined with the purely Clintonian ability to laugh or cry on cue; the Rhodes Scholar studiousness reminiscent of Madison; the accommodative and disingenuous façade of Van Buren; the altruism of Carter; and the pragmatism of FDR. He was a president for all reasons.

They Lost the Popular Vote and Won
(including those who won with less than 40% of the popular vote)

Date	Winning Losers	Lost by	Losing Winners
1824	John Quincy Adams	38,149	Andrew Jackson
1876	Rutherford B. Hayes	254,235	Samuel J. Tilden
1888	Benjamin Harrison	90,596	Grover Cleveland
2000	George W. Bush	543,895	Al Gore
1860	Abraham Lincoln	Received less than 40%	Stephen Douglas, John C. Breckinridge, and John Bell
1992	William J. Clinton	Received less than 40%	George H. W. Bush and H. Ross Perot

COURTESY: US ELECTORAL COLLEGE

An Argument for Run-Off Elections

The public believes presidents are not elected by the popular vote. In fact, they are. It is just that it is a state-by-state popular vote. According to the US Electoral College, "Generally, the political parties nominate Electors at their State party conventions or by a vote of the party's central committee in each State. Each candidate will have their own unique slate of potential Electors as a result of this part of the selection process. . . . The winning candidate in each State—except in Nebraska and Maine, which have proportional distribution of the Electors—is awarded all of the State's Electors. In Nebraska and Maine, the state winner receives two Electors and the winner of each congressional district receives one Elector."

The idea of eliminating the Electoral College tends to arise when a candidate is elected president after failing to garner more than 50 percent of the popular vote as has happened in nineteen of forty-four elections: 1824, 1844, 1848, 1856, 1860, 1876, 1880, 1884, 1888, 1892, 1912, 1916, 1948, 1960, 1968, 1992, 1996, 2000, and 2004. Of these, the successful candidate was actually outpolled by the runner-up in 1824, 1876, 1888, and 2000. Further, John Quincy Adams only received 30.92 percent of the 1824 popular vote and Abraham Lincoln received 39.65 percent in 1860.

Despite these figures, the argument against replacing the Electoral College with the popular vote is that the popular margin of victory might be confined to one state or region. On the other hand, there is an argument for run-off elections.

Several states conduct run-off elections between the two candidates receiving the most votes in a general election, not including electors for the president and vice president. The obvious benefit is that run-off elections add legitimacy to the process by actually electing governors, senators, et al. with 50+ percent margins. This would hold equally true for national elections, but with a twist. A run-off for the president and vice president should be held if one ticket simultaneously fails to reach 50 percent of the popular vote and if the electoral vote could be sufficiently altered to change the outcome.

Historically, this method would have triggered run-offs in 1824, 1860, 1876, 1912, 1916, 1948, 1960, 1968, 1992, 1996, and 2000. Of these, only the elections of 1824 and 1876 went to the House of Representatives after neither candidate received a majority of the electoral votes, events that would have been precluded had there been run-off elections. Congress also decided between Thomas Jefferson and Aaron Burr in 1800, only because a quirk in the Constitution made the runner-up the vice president. Burr was supposed to be Jefferson's vice president. Unexpectedly, they tied. This was resolved with ratification of the Twelfth Amendment.

CHAPTER 10

EMPIRE WARS: MEXICO AND SPAIN

JAMES K. POLK (1845) AND WILLIAM MCKINLEY (1897)

Both wars were precipitated by aggressive US diplomatic and military actions. Both were wars of choice. Both were rooted in the concept of Manifest Destiny, a mystical, semi-religious idea that it was America's destiny to become a sea-to-sea nation in the case of President James K. Polk's Mexican-American War and a global empire in the case of President William McKinley's Spanish-American War, which prompted British writer Rudyard Kipling to pen his racist poem, "The White Man's Burden." There was one advantage. Both wars were the only wars America was prepared to fight at the outset with sufficient troops, training, equipment, and attainable objectives (wars in Vietnam, Iraq, and Afghanistan had ill-defined objectives). Eventually, the American public turned against wars of conquest, and the nation's flirtation with empire building came to a close with the dawn of the twentieth century.

JAMES K. POLK—THE MEXICAN-AMERICAN WAR
1845–1849

Born/Died: 1795 Mecklenburg County, NC–1849 Nashville, TN
Education: University of North Carolina
Occupation: Planter, lawyer
Political Party: Democratic
Government Service: Governor (TN) 1839–1841, Representative (TN) 1825–1833, 1835–1839
Military Service: Militia Colonel; no active duty
Preceded by: John Tyler (first vice president to succeed to office upon the death of a president; establishes succession precedent; vetoes numerous bills; Whigs expel him from party; secures congressional vote to annex Texas)

In the realm of American euphemisms, "Manifest Destiny" has earned a place on the mantel next to "Strategic Bombing" (see Chapter 15, Truman) and "Popular Sovereignty" (see Chapter 5). Professor Donald M. Scott wrote of "an unsigned [1845] article in . . . the *Democratic Review* . . . declared that expansion represented 'the fulfillment of our manifest destiny to overspread the continent allotted by Providence for the free development of our yearly multiplying millions.' . . . 'Manifest Destiny' was also a racial doctrine of white supremacy that granted no native or nonwhite American claims to any permanent possession of the lands on the North American continent and justified white American expropriation of Indian lands."

Polk promised to only serve one term, which gave him a degree of political freedom to pursue his agenda, including a reduced tariff and reversing the Jackson-era decision to deposit federal funds in state banks, placing them instead with the US Treasury, but it was in the area of land acquisitions where Polk made his mark (see Chapter 3, Map: Louisiana Purchase, Mexican Cession, and Oregon Territory).

President James K. Polk

There was nothing subtle in this. It was militaristic from the outset. The United States and Britain co-occupied the Oregon Territory. Polk demanded sole rights up to the 49th Parallel; Britain refused, and Polk upped the stakes to 54°40', evoking the famous war cry: "Fifty-four forty or fight." Negotiations with Mexico were equally unsuccessful. The Mexican government snubbed his emissary, not even listening to Polk's offer to purchase the land from west of Texas to California.

The game board was set. In the tradition of European expansionists, having created diplomatic disarray, he was ready with force. Simultaneously, Polk sent Maj. Gen. Zachary Taylor and a small army into the disputed territory between Mexico and Texas and a small expedition under Capt. John C. Fremont to foment rebellion in California. These provocative acts resulted in the desired Mexican provocations. A Mexican force skirmished with Taylor's army, providing Polk his excuse, and the puzzle pieces moved into place. Britain, recognizing this was no Madison-like bluff, quickly changed course and settled the Oregon issue at the 49th Parallel. Americans in California declared the Bear Republic, and a US naval squadron soon appeared in support. General Taylor fought two small battles and proceeded across the Rio Grande. This was followed up with a full-scale invasion of Mexico when Maj. Gen. Winfield Scott's army landed at Vera Cruz and fought its way to Mexico City.

More than thirteen thousand American soldiers and probably three times as many Mexican soldiers died in the war. An array of diverse voices was raised in opposition, from South Carolina's Sen. John C. Calhoun to Rep. John Quincy Adams of Massachusetts to a new representative from Illinois, Abraham Lincoln. In December 1845, Polk had announced in his first annual message to Congress, "We have not sought to extend our territorial possessions by conquest, or our republican institutions over a reluctant people." The unfolding events of 1846 proved otherwise. To opponents, it was naked aggression; to supporters, it was "Manifest Destiny." Either way, it was a war of choice.

After achieving victory in the Mexican-American War, Polk paid cash for what was called the Mexican Cession, followed by the Gadsden Purchase. In total, these lands acquired by war and money from Mexico would eventually add the states of New Mexico, Arizona, California, Nevada, and parts of Utah and Colorado to the Union.

As always, future generations would find ways to rationalize and justify, but they could hardly claim it was America's finest hour, and the concept of Manifest Destiny would be resurrected as justification for naked aggression by various countries and their unrestrained leaders in the twentieth and twenty-first centuries.

WILLIAM MCKINLEY—THE SPANISH-AMERICAN WAR
1897–1901

Born/Died: 1843 Niles, OH–1901 Buffalo, NY
Education: Allegheny College (withdrew), Albany Law School (did not graduate)
Occupation: Lawyer
Political Party: Republican
Government Service: Governor (OH) 1892–1896
Military Service: Federal Major; Civil War
Preceded by: Grover Cleveland (Panic of 1893 comes at beginning of his term; 1894 Wilson-Gorman Tariff Act slightly reduces the largest-in-US-history 1890 McKinley Tariff passed under President Benjamin Harrison when McKinley was a senator; 2 percent income tax is passed to offset it, but is struck down by Supreme Court in 1895)

President William McKinley
LIBRARY OF CONGRESS

American expansionists had been eyeing Cuba for most of the century, and filibuster (unofficial war making, not to be confused with the filibuster of senatorial debates) expeditions had taken place, occasionally with quasi-covert encouragement from the White House, never with success. Prior to the Civil War, northern opposition to annexation of the Spanish-held island was strong, since it would come into the Union as a slave territory or state. Later, after Spain lost most of its holdings in the Western Hemisphere, Cuba stood out as an exception. Meanwhile, the new steel and steam navies of European powers were leading the way in another round of imperialism, especially in Africa and Asia. This imperialist fever also infected a segment of the American public, driven in part by the yellow journalism of William Randolph Hearst, and Cuba looked like an easy and obvious place to continue (Hawaii had already been acquired). The anti-imperialists were nearly as vocal.

This is what confronted William McKinley on Inauguration Day in 1897. By fall of that year, he began positioning a fleet in Florida, preparatory to hostilities if diplomatic talks broke down. Those talks with the weak Spanish government centered on the ongoing insurgent war in Cuba and American interests in the sugar industry. Spain agreed to grant autonomy to the island, beginning on January 1, 1898, and McKinley sent the battleship USS *Maine* into Havana Harbor to protect US interests there. On February 15, the battleship blew up and sank. No one claimed blame; no one has ever conclusively proven it was an accident or an act of war. It did not matter. The event was so startling and the loss of life so great—75 percent of the ship's crew—that it set off a psychological explosion in the American psyche. American doves were silenced. Hawks would have what the newspapers called their "splendid little war," and

"Remember the *Maine*" became as potent as "Remember the Alamo" had been for Texans in 1836. America was being sloganeered into war.

One high-ranking dove remained, President McKinley. He and a few allies in Congress were being overwhelmed by an incited and enraged public as well as by congressional and administration hawks, such as Assistant Secretary of the Navy Theodore Roosevelt. All this made war inevitable—or did it? Civil War veteran McKinley, like most combatants who have seen the mangled bodies and heard the screams of the wounded and dying, knew what the civilian drumbeaters did not know. Even Theodore Roosevelt, who would be awarded the Medal of Honor in the war, would lament two decades later during World War I, "Just because they are my sons, they feel they must be extra brave. They take chances they wouldn't perhaps otherwise take." Then horrible reality came with a telegram informing him of his son's death, and he wrote Edith Wharton, "There is no use of my writing about Quentin; for I should break down if I tried." In 1898, the Spanish-American War would claim 2,446 sons of other American parents and even more Spanish sons.

McKinley, new to office, either did not believe he could or should stem the public's clarion call for war, or in the recesses of his mind, the thoughts of reelection motivated a need for public acclaim. This is a damning possibility, possibly less so when placed in context. The rationalization that a president, having learned his trade, is prepared to make significant second-term contributions can justify any number of policy decisions, and the thought may be even more subconscious than conscious. Did it also affect Woodrow Wilson on the eve of World War I?

Whatever the motivation, on April 20, 1898, McKinley took the nation to war, a war he opposed, but refused to forcefully speak out against. On the previous day, as if to undermine nearly a century of Cuban land lust, Congress passed the Teller Amendment, disavowing any intention to annex the island. The forces of imperialism had their war; the anti-imperialists had their amendment; and what was gained? Cuba was not annexed. The Philippines were taken, and a nasty guerilla war ensued. Guam and Puerto Rico became and remain US territories. There was nothing splendid about the "splendid little war."

McKinley did win reelection, only to be shot and killed five months into his second term.

CHAPTER 11

INVADE OR BLOCKADE: FORT SUMTER, THE BAY OF PIGS, AND THE CUBAN MISSILE CRISIS

ABRAHAM LINCOLN (1861) AND JOHN F. KENNEDY (1961)

Abraham Lincoln and John F. Kennedy entered office in 1861 and 1961, respectively, the first in the midst of a sectional crisis with secession a fact and civil war a possibility, the other at the height of the Cold War when nuclear war was about to become a probability. Both made serious mistakes; Kennedy would receive a second chance.

Following the bloodless bombardment of Fort Sumter, Lincoln called for an invasion of the seven seceding southern states with the result that four Upper South states reversed their anti-secession votes, joined the secession, and doubled the size of the Confederate armies.

Shortly after taking office, Kennedy authorized an American-trained Cuban exile invasion of communist Cuba at the Bay of Pigs. The plan was poor, the invasion force insufficient, air support nearly nonexistent, and Cuban dissatisfaction with Fidel Castro overestimated. The invasion was a fiasco, and Kennedy was obliged to accept his and America's responsibility.

The following year, urged on by Che Guevera, Castro allowed Soviet nuclear missiles to be stationed in Cuba. This time, Kennedy opted for a blockade instead of invasion and met with complete success. Without the learning curve at the Bay of Pigs, it is unlikely the Cuban Missile Crisis—the closest the superpowers ever came to nuclear war—would have played out as it did.

ABRAHAM LINCOLN—FORT SUMTER AND THE CIVIL WAR 1861–1865

Born/Died: 1809 Hardin (now Larue) County, KY–1865 Washington, DC
Education: Self-educated and intermittently tutored
Occupation: Lawyer
Political Party: National Union, Republican, Whig
Government Service: Representative (IL) 1847–1849, State Representative (IL) 1834–1842
Military Service: Militia Captain; Black Hawk War (non-combat)
Preceded by: James Buchanan (Democratic Party, the only national party, splits into North and South wings, while Republicans are primarily a northern-only party; Supreme Court issues Dred Scott decision allowing slaves to be brought into free states; persists in divisive popular sovereignty concept; as strict constitutional constructionist refuses to interfere with states' rights; states secede following Lincoln election in November; no military action taken before Lincoln assumes office in March)

The evil of slavery needed to be extinguished. The question was how. Unlike all previous presidents who struggled with the issue and often devised various compromises, Lincoln did not. He opposed the spread of slavery and was among those who advocated colonization of freed slaves, but he also opposed abolition because the Constitution did not ban slavery. He reiterated his position during the midst of Civil War:

Executive Mansion,
Washington, August 22, 1862.
Hon. Horace Greeley [editor of the New York Tribune*]:*

My paramount object in this struggle is *to save the Union, and is* not *either to save or to destroy slavery. If I could save the Union without freeing* any *slave I would do it, and if I could save it by freeing* all *the slaves I would do it; and if I could save it by freeing some and leaving others alone I would also do that. What I do about slavery, and the colored race, I do because I believe it helps to save the Union; and what I forbear, I forbear because I do* not *believe it would help to save the Union. (See Appendix C for the complete text)*

Therefore, Lincoln's freshman-year problems were only indirectly related to slavery. His missteps dealt with the politics of preserving the Union. A brief review of the issues raised in earlier chapters is warranted.

Liberia had been established as a home for freed slaves, and from the time Lincoln briefly served as a congressman, he pressed for a similar colony in Central America. Meanwhile, states such as Indiana and Lincoln's home state of Illinois altered their constitutions in the 1850s to deny residency for freed slaves (see Chapter 9, Hayes). Abolitionists made up only a small minority of the electorate as a whole and a minority in the new Republican Party as well, because few people believed assimilation would work or were willing to have it work. This was the dilemma. Those advocating emancipation had to either convince white people to accept black people into society or convince black people to emigrate to Liberia or elsewhere. By 1860, neither option was succeeding.

Instead, moderate Republicans and many northern Democrats sought a continuation of the method employed throughout the previous forty years: limit or end the expansion of slavery. Beginning with the 1820 Missouri Compromise, a north-south slave-no-slave line was drawn. This was followed by several other limits, including popular sovereignty advocated by Sen. Stephen Douglas, Lincoln's opponent, first for the Senate, then for the presidency. This concept only exacerbated the situation and led to a small civil war dubbed Bleeding Kansas after pro-slave and anti-slave advocates moved into the territory in an attempt to swell the votes for their respective positions.

Meanwhile, the rise of the Republican Party in 1854 and its platform planks advocating high tariffs and forbidding slavery in new territories mirrored Lincoln's view, famously expressed in his February 27, 1860, Cooper Union Speech, when he repeatedly stated he would not interfere with slavery where it already existed. The party also included a vocal minority of abolitionists and, in sum, was viewed as an anti-southern party.

President Abraham Lincoln as a candidate in 1860
LIBRARY OF CONGRESS

By 1860, the expansion of slavery had become a political power issue. After all, most of the land newly acquired from victory in the Mexican-American War was not suitable for slave-based agriculture (except California, which had been admitted as a free state by the Compromise of 1850). Non-slave states tended to vote with the high-tariff advocates of the North whose protectionist policies drove up the price of imports, disproportionately affecting slave states, which were dependent upon foreign trade to market cotton and other products.

Also, by 1860, most European nations as well as Mexico had already abolished slavery, providing a beacon and trend for the civilized world. Nearly 90 percent of white southerners, mostly yeoman farmers, were not slaveholders. On the other hand, twelve of the first eighteen presidents, including Ulysses S. Grant, were. Like his Civil War opponent, Gen. Robert E. Lee, Grant became a slaveholder through his wife's inheritance.

The election of 1860 was inherently divisive. The new Republican Party was a strictly northern party, and its candidates were not on the ballots in most southern states. The Democratic Party split into northern and southern wings, each with its own presidential candidates, Stephen

Douglas of Illinois and sitting Vice President John C. Breckinridge of Kentucky, respectively. Additionally, the neutral Constitutional Union Party and its candidate John Bell (see Chapter 9, Chart) emerged in the border states. This supplanting of the two national parties, Democrats and Whigs, with regional parties allowed Lincoln to garner an electoral majority with only 39 percent of the popular vote. Regionalism had replaced nationalism. It was only a small step for each region to complete the descent into distrust, and the election of Lincoln was followed by the secession of South Carolina, to be followed over the next two months by the secession of six other southern states and the formation of the Confederate States of America.

Into this morass stepped President-Elect Lincoln, a self-educated attorney with no managerial experience and whose national political career had consisted of one two-year term in the House of Representatives in 1847, where he gained notoriety opposing the Mexican-American War.

Like Monroe, Abraham Lincoln supported colonization and attempted to duplicate Liberia in Central America. His racial views were made clear during the famous Lincoln-Douglas debates of 1858, when he was vying with Stephen Douglas for a US Senate seat from Illinois. In the first debate, he said, "My first impulse would be to free all the slaves, and send them to Liberia," and in the fourth debate, he emphatically rejected any thought of assimilation:

> *I will say then that I am not, nor ever have been, in favor of bringing about in any way the social and political equality of the white and black races, [applause] that I am not nor ever have been in favor of making voters or jurors of negroes, nor of qualifying them to hold office, nor to intermarry with white people; and I will say in addition to this that there is a physical difference between the white and black races which I believe will forever forbid the two races living together on terms of social and political equality. And inasmuch as they cannot so live, while they do remain together there must be the position of superior and inferior, and I as much as any other man am in favor of having the superior position assigned to the white race.*

Lincoln lost to Douglas in 1858, but went on to win the presidency in 1860, and the period between the November election and March inauguration were to prove critical.

Ignoring the distinction between plurality and majority, President-Elect Lincoln wrote Pennsylvania's Rep. James Hale in January 1861, explaining his aversion to compromise:

> *We have just carried an election on principles fairly stated to the people. Now we are told in advance the Government shall be broken up unless we surrender to those we have beaten, before we take the offices. In this they are either attempting to play upon us or they are in dead earnest. Either way, if we surrender, it is the end of us and of the Government. They will repeat the experiment upon us ad libitum. A year will not pass till we shall have to take Cuba as a condition upon which they will stay in the Union.*

This lawyerly leap of adversarial logic equating compromise with "surrender" assumed a majority mandate, and ignored more than seventy years of give-and-take history, dramatically contrasting with the politically astute words of a seasoned President Lincoln in subsequent years. This, his first great mistake, left the pro-Union Upper South in an untenable position (see Jonathan Worth's letter below).

By the time of his inauguration on March 4, 1861, nothing was more critical than to ensure no additional states seceded, which is why the new president's first actions as president are difficult to comprehend. The Upper South states of North Carolina, Virginia, Tennessee, and Arkansas had voted against secession, and the other Border slave states of Delaware, Maryland, Kentucky, and Missouri had also held with the Union. Former President John Tyler wrote, "So all is over and Lincoln elected. S. Carolina will secede. What other States will do, remains to be seen. Virginia will abide developments." It was time for the lawyer to become president, but the lawyer persisted, and he persisted in silence, ignoring his secretary of State–designate, William Seward, who repeatedly urged him to speak to the concerns of the pro-Union southern citizens and leaders who had rejected secession.

Fort Sumter sitting in the middle of South Carolina's Charleston Harbor remained in Federal hands, making it a potential flashpoint, and Confederate authorities expected it to be peaceably evacuated as had almost all other federal forts and arsenals in the seceded states.

In January, President James Buchanan had sent an unarmed resupply ship to Charleston, which was turned back by southern warning shots. By early April, supplies were running low at the fort, and the new president made the fateful decision that would catapult the nation into war while Congress was out of session. From the fort, Maj. Robert Anderson, himself a Kentucky slaveholder, advised his one-time West Point artillery student, now Confederate Gen. P. G. T. Beauregard, he would vacate the place if he was not resupplied by April 15. However, Lincoln had already ordered an armed fleet with supplies and reinforcements to sail for Charleston and so informed South Carolina's governor. This was mistake number two, though it was intentional, not accidental, and almost certain to lead to war, a war that would force the Upper South out of the Union.

In 1848, while serving in Congress, Lincoln had written to his law partner, William H. Herndon—a proponent of the president's right to declare war without congressional approval—about the war with Mexico and presidential limitations:

> *The provision of the Constitution giving the war-making power to Congress was dictated, as I understand it, by the following reasons. Kings had always been involving and impoverishing their people in wars, pretending generally, if not always, that the good of the people was the object. This, our convention understood to be the most oppressive of all Kingly oppressions; and they resolved to so frame the Constitution that no one man should hold the power of bringing this oppression upon us. But your view destroys the whole matter, and places our President where Kings have always stood.*

As president, he took a different view, though it is difficult to assess his thoughts. Did he intend to force a war and blame the South for firing the first shot? If so, Confederate authorities foolishly fell into his trap. Or was he simply playing the attorney, an adversary rigidly standing by legal conclusions instead of the statesman, diplomat, and politician invoking pragmatism to avoid war? Or, in the event of war, had he unrealistically convinced himself that the Upper South would remain in the Union and provide troops and free passage for Federal forces to attack their fellow southerners?

President John F. Kennedy, who greatly admired Lincoln, chose not to emulate him 101 years later when faced with the prospect of nuclear war over Soviet missiles in Cuba. Kennedy chose a naval blockade over invasion. Did Lincoln consider that possibility? In the end, Lincoln opted for both an invasion and a full naval blockade against the advice of General-in-Chief Winfield Scott, whose Anaconda Plan called for a blockade and a limited invasion down the Mississippi (see Appendix B).

Scott was the only American officer to have served as a general in three major wars (like Napoleon, he became a general at the age of twenty-seven), the War of 1812, the Mexican-American War, and the Civil War, and he had been successful in each, spectacularly so in Mexico. He was among those—including Robert E. Lee and Jefferson Davis in the South—who understood it would not be a quick, low-casualty war. The forces arrayed against one another and the sheer expanse of territory were too great. The South would be fighting a defensive war and had no major offensive strategic plan at the outset. The North, on the other hand, was attempting to subdue the South, but Scott advised against a full-scale invasion. It would be too bloody and make reconciliation too difficult. On March 3, 1861, the day before Lincoln's inauguration, he wrote incoming Secretary of State William Seward, offering four options, to which Lincoln took offense:

> I. Throw off the old, & assume a new designation — the Union party [which Lincoln would do in 1864];—adopt the conciliatory measures proposed by Mr. Crittenden, or the Peace convention. . . .
>
> II. Collect the duties on foreign goods outside the ports of which this Government has lost the command, or close such ports by acts of congress, & blockade them.
>
> III. Conquer the seceded States by invading Armies. No doubt this might be done in two or three years. . . . The destruction of life and property, on the other side, would be frightful. . . . The conquest

completed at that enormous waste of human life,—Fifteen devastated provinces—not to be brought into harmony with their conquerors. . . .

IV. Say to the seceded—States—wayward sisters, depart in peace!

Confederate Lt. Gen. Thomas "Stonewall" Jackson's 1846 West Point classmate Federal Maj. Gen. George B. McClellan, considered one of the most brilliant generals in the army, disagreed with Scott and maneuvered to have him removed. That Lincoln and his corrupt Secretary of War Simon Cameron concurred proved to be Lincoln's third freshman-year mistake.

Whatever his reasoning, Lincoln chose the path most likely to lead to war, and he was ready with his proclamation. After enduring a thirty-four-hour bloodless artillery duel, Fort Sumter ceased fire on April 13, 1861, and its garrison was allowed to sail for New York the following day. On the 15th, in a reversal of his 1848 opinion, Lincoln, without consulting Congress then out of session and which he chose not to call into emergency session until July 4, issued a proclamation to all states calling for seventy-five thousand volunteers to put down the rebellion. Just as quickly, four Upper South states, North Carolina, Virginia, Tennessee, and Arkansas, reversed their previous decisions and seceded with the concurrence of statewide votes, eventually providing more than 50 percent of the Confederate Army's manpower and suffering more than 50 percent of the Confederacy's casualties (see chart on page 186).

Future North Carolina governor Jonathan Worth, a strong unionist, wrote on May 17, 1861:

I have always regarded the dissolution of the Union as the greatest misfortune which could befall the whole nation. . . . If he [Lincoln] had withdrawn the garrison of Fort Sumter on the principle of military necessity and in obedience in what seemed the will of Congress in refusing to pass the force bill [in March 1861], this state and Tennessee and the other slave states which had not passed an ordinance of Secession, would have stood up for the Union. . . . [H]e knew he would crush the Union men in the Slave States by the policy he adopted. All of us who had stood by the Union, felt that he had abandoned us. . . . I am still a Union man, but for military resistance to Lincoln.

Losing those states proved to be one of the great political miscalculations in American history, and the president knew he could lose no more, writing to Orville Browning in September, "I think to lose Kentucky is nearly the same as to lose the whole game. Kentucky gone, we cannot hold Missouri, nor, as I think, Maryland." It is of note that Lincoln and his wife as well as Confederate President Jefferson Davis were from Kentucky, and all of Mrs. Lincoln's brothers would fight for the Confederacy. Lincoln's favorite brother-in-law, Confederate Brig. Gen. Ben Hardin Helm, would be killed leading his Kentuckians of the Orphan Brigade against Federal Kentuckians at the Battle of Chickamauga in 1863, after which his widow, Mary Todd Lincoln's sister, would move into the White House. It was indeed a strange war, and Lincoln did hold onto Kentucky, if not all of its citizens.

No president had faced such a maelstrom, and no president was less prepared to cope with it. It is nearly certain that Lincoln the canny politician of 1865 would not have made the same decisions as the untested Lincoln of 1861. Once the war began, his first-year errors mounted. Unlike Confederate President Jefferson Davis, a West Point graduate who had served with distinction in the Mexican-American War and went on to become President Franklin Pierce's secretary of War, Lincoln had only briefly served in the Black Hawk War as a junior militia officer who never saw action. This adversely impacted his initial selection of army commanders, which in turn adversely impacted battlefield performances.

In the spring of 1862, Gen. George B. McClellan received the president's authorization to approach Richmond from the southeast between the York and James Rivers in the Virginia region known as the Peninsula. As a result of McClellan's departure from Washington, Lincoln and his new secretary of War, Edwin Stanton, took over direction of the other Federal armies with disastrous consequences. Those armies lost ten battles in quick succession, most notably against Maj. Gen. (later Lt. Gen.) Thomas "Stonewall" Jackson in Virginia's Shenandoah Valley. With never more than seventeen thousand men, Jackson defeated or tied up more than sixty thousand Federals, finally prompting Lincoln to relinquish his role as general-in-chief to Henry Halleck. He later lamented, "You and I, Mr. Stanton, have been trying to boss this job, and we have not succeeded very well with it."

It had been the steepest learning curve in presidential history. Lincoln did eventually learn how to select military as well as civilian subordinates and how to delegate. When he realized his generals could not out-general Robert E. Lee, he brought in U. S. Grant, who would employ the North's overwhelming numbers to defeat him through attrition (see Chapter 6, Grant).

In August 1862, the hardened and pragmatic Lincoln was emerging, for while he was writing to Greeley that only saving the Union mattered, a draft of the Emancipation Proclamation sat in his desk waiting for a Union victory. It was all quite Machiavellian, a pragmatism very much at odds with the inflexible sentiments expressed in his January 1861 letter. Britain and France were on the verge of recognizing the Confederacy, but slavery had long since been banned by those countries, and emancipation could turn the war into a crusade that would dim affections for the South. On the other hand, there was the problem of loyal slave states, which Lincoln solved by only emancipating "all persons held as slaves within any State or designated part of a State the people whereof shall then be in rebellion against the United States."

Secretary of State Seward was exasperated: "We show our sympathy with slavery by emancipating slaves where we cannot reach them and holding them in bondage where we can set them free."

An often overlooked passage of the proclamation read, "And I further declare and make known that such persons of suitable condition will be received into the armed service of the United States." This was the third leg of a masterful political document. After satisfying loyal slave states and even exempting occupied cities such as New Orleans and striking a sympathetic chord with Europeans, he, in this passage, offered runaway slaves a job in the Federal Army, albeit at reduced wages, this at a time when northern morale and consequent enlistments were running low.

The president had learned his trade. The Emancipation Proclamation was clearly a war measure. At the end of the war, he supported passage of the Thirteenth Amendment, which did free the slaves. He never proposed more. The Fourteenth and Fifteenth Amendments offering, respectively, equal rights and the vote, came in the years following his death. He had never proposed or supported such actions, and he had made this clear in the midst of the war on August 14, 1862, just as he was drafting the

Emancipation Proclamation. In his Address on "Colonization to a Committee of Colored Men, Washington, D.C.," he delivered this revealing
statement:

> *Perhaps you have long been free, or all your lives. Your race are suffer-
> ing, in my judgment, the greatest wrong inflicted on any people. But
> even when you cease to be slaves, you are yet far removed from being
> placed on an equality with the white race. You are cut off from many
> of the advantages which the other race enjoy. The aspiration of men is
> to enjoy equality with the best when free, but on this broad continent,
> not a single man of your race is made the equal of a single man of ours.
> Go where you are treated the best, and the ban is still upon you.*
>
> *I do not propose to discuss this, but to present it as a fact with
> which we have to deal. I cannot alter it if I would. It is a fact, about
> which we all think and feel alike, I and you. We look to our condition,
> owing to the existence of the two races on this continent. I need not
> recount to you the effects upon white men, growing out of the institu-
> tion of Slavery. I believe in its general evil effects on the white race.
> See our present condition—the country engaged in war!—our white
> men cutting one another's throats, none knowing how far it will
> extend; and then consider what we know to be the truth. But for your
> race among us there could not be war, although many men engaged
> on either side do not care for you one way or the other. Nevertheless,
> I repeat, without the institution of Slavery and the colored race as a
> basis, the war could not have an existence.*
>
> *It is better for us both, therefore, to be separated. I know that there
> are free men among you, who even if they could better their condition
> are not as much inclined to go out of the country as those, who being
> slaves could obtain their freedom on this condition. I suppose one of the
> principal difficulties in the way of colonization is that the free colored
> man cannot see that his comfort would be advanced by it. You may
> believe you can live in Washington or elsewhere in the United States
> the remainder of your life [as easily], perhaps more so than you can in
> any foreign country, and hence you may come to the conclusion that you
> have nothing to do with the idea of going to a foreign country. This is
> (I speak in no unkind sense) an extremely selfish view of the case. . . .*

If the Upper South Had Not Seceded

Notes:

1. The Upper South made up more than 52% of the Confederacy's population, and at least a like percentage of armed forces and casualties. North Carolina alone "sustained about one fourth of the Confederate losses."

2. A portion of southern soldiers came from the North as did a portion of northern soldiers come from the South, and both sides drew on the Border States. Further, freed slaves began filling northern ranks as the war wore on.

3. "Federal [soldiers and sailors] . . . outnumbered the Confederates about three to one," and it would have been six to one if the Upper South had not seceded.

	White	Free African American	Combined Total
7 Original Seceding States			
South Carolina	291,388	9,914	301,302
Mississippi	353,901	773	354,674
Florida	77,747	932	78,679
Alabama	526,431	2,690	529,121
Georgia	591,588	3,500	595,088
Louisiana	357,629	18,647	376,276
Texas	421,294	355	421,649
Total	**2,619,978**	**36,811**	**2,656,789**
4 Seceding Upper South States			
Virginia	1,047,411	58,042	1,105,453
Arkansas	324,191	144	324,335
North Carolina	631,100	30,463	661,563
Tennessee	826,782	7,300	834,082
Total	**2,829,484**	**95,949**	**2,925,433**
Free Population	**5,449,462**	**132,760**	**5,582,222**
Upper South % of Free Southern Population	**52%**	**72%**	**52%**
Border State Popoulation	**2,743,728**	**120,243**	**2,863,971**
Northern State Population	**18,810,123**	**225,973**	**19,036,096**

(CREATED BY THE AUTHOR FROM THE US CENSUS BUREAU AND SOURCES LISTED IN ENDNOTES)

The place I am thinking about having for a colony is in Central America.

Lincoln's last speech, referencing the new anti-slavery government in Louisiana, delivered April 11, 1865, spoke to the issue of the African-American franchise: "It is also unsatisfactory to some that the elective franchise is not given to the colored man. I would myself prefer that it were now conferred on the very intelligent, and on those who serve our cause as soldiers."

Today, the argument is often heard that the Civil War preserved the Union, but at what cost. More than 623,000 soldiers, Americans all, and untold numbers of civilians, mostly southern, died in the war, and debilitating wounds shortened the lives of many others. In total, the human cost of the war must have exceeded one million lives, the percentage equivalent in modern times of ten million people. It was a terrible price to pay, especially when political solutions and/or a naval blockade might have prevented it. Everything hinged on the four Upper South states, yet Lincoln, playing the officious and victorious attorney more than the president-elect, made no effort to hold them in the Union. His silence was his first great error. His machinations that virtually enticed the bombardment of Fort Sumter was the second. His call for a military invasion rather than first trying a blockade of the seven seceded states was the third. And by his own admission, his personal direction of the Federal armies in the spring of 1862 was the fourth.

He did propose a conciliatory Reconstruction policy, and his successor attempted to implement it, only to receive a near revolt among Radical Republicans in Congress. Had Lincoln lived, it is fair to assume he would have been more successful in reconciling the nation and lessening the hardships and antagonisms that ran for decades.

Secessions

America was founded on secession from Britain, but the term has ever since been an incendiary concept for the nation, beginning with the derision vented toward secessionist New Englanders whose 1814-15 Hartford Convention proposed separation during the War of 1812, to Andrew Jackson's threat of force against South Carolina during the Nullification Crisis of 1832, to Zachary Taylor's promise to "hang" advocates of secession in 1850.

On the other hand, secessionists who broke away from Mexico were welcomed into the Union as Texans and Californians, and America went to war in 1898 to aid secessionists in Cuba.

The twentieth century brought a complete reversal, with President Woodrow Wilson's 1918 address to Congress: "'Self determination' is not a mere phrase; it is an imperative principle of action which statesmen will henceforth ignore at their peril." This statement was not in his famous Fourteen Points, the blueprint for peace in World War I, but it was put into practice with the breakup of the Austro-Hungarian Empire following the war, which included the creation of Yugoslavia and Czechoslovakia. In an apparent retraction, the man behind the phrase, Walter Lippmann, later wrote: "To invoke the general principle of self-determination, and to make it a supreme law of international life is to invite sheer anarchy. For the principle can be used to promote the dismemberment of practically every organized state."

Even so, the concept was embraced in 1945 by the victors of World War II and enshrined in Article I of the United Nations Charter: "Section 2: To develop friendly relations among nations based on respect for the principle of equal rights and self-determination of peoples, and to take other appropriate measures to strengthen universal peace."

Following the fall of the Soviet Union, fifteen new nations were peacefully created, and with its hold over Eastern Europe lost, both Czechoslovakia and Yugoslavia broke up, the first peacefully, the second through civil wars. In all, thirty-four new countries have been formed since 1990, mostly through peaceful secession.

Notable secessionist movements also arose in Spain, Belgium, Britain (Scotland), and Canada (Quebec), as well as various regions in Africa and Asia. Even in the United States, some residents of Alaska and Texas have floated the idea.

All this is context for the words of that most famous of secessionist enemies, Abraham Lincoln, who spoke at Gettysburg, Pennsylvania, on November 19, 1863, three months after the epic battle fought there: "It is for us the living, rather, to be dedicated here to the unfinished work [preservation of the Union] which they who fought here have thus far so nobly advanced. It is rather for us to be here dedicated to the great task remaining before us—that from these honored dead we take increased devotion to that cause for which they gave the last full measure of devotion—that we here highly resolve that these dead shall not have died in vain."

In the end, it turns on the tense: our rebellion or their rebellion.

JOHN F. KENNEDY—THE BAY OF PIGS AND THE CUBAN MISSILE CRISIS
1961–1963

Born/Died: 1917, Brookline, MA–1963 Dallas, TX
Education: Princeton University (withdrew), Harvard University
Occupation: Professional politician, writer
Political Party: Democratic
Government Service: Senator (MA) 1953–1960, Representative (MA) 1947–1953
Military Service: Decorated Navy Lieutenant; World War II
Preceded by: Dwight D. Eisenhower (Korean War ends; McCarthyism ends without presidential input; Interstate Highway System built; space race commences; Cold War turns into nuclear arms race and surrogate wars; military advisors sent to Vietnam; Cuba falls to communist rebels)

Former President Harry S. Truman famously said of John F. Kennedy, the first Catholic president, "It's not the Pope I'm afraid of, it's the Pop." And the Pop, Joseph P. Kennedy, was formidable. One of America's wealthiest men, he made a fortune in stocks and liquor, became the first head of the Securities and Exchange Commission, and was America's ambassador to the Court of St. James (Britain), where, after the outbreak of World War II, he predicted Britain's defeat.

The political mantle was passed to John Kennedy after his older brother was killed in the war and he was medically discharged due to injuries at least in part sustained when his PT boat was rammed and sunk in the Pacific. Joe Kennedy's overweening ambition was to place a son in the White House, and John Kennedy reluctantly gave up his preferred writing career, although, with the help of his wife, Jacqueline, and Ted Sorensen, he would later pen *Profiles in Courage,* placing him in the ranks of Theodore Roosevelt and Woodrow Wilson as a presidential author of note. He won the Pulitzer Prize in 1957.

Following the war and a brief stint as a writer, he was elected on the Democratic ticket to the US House of Representatives from Massachusetts, a member of the same class of 1947 as California Republican Rep. Richard M. Nixon, to whom he delivered a campaign donation on behalf of his father. Six years later, he became a US senator and married Jacqueline Bouvier in 1953, the same year Nixon became vice president. Seven years later he was running for president against Nixon.

Kennedy was young and charming, and while campaigning in Oregon, he stayed at Portland's grand dame Benson Hotel, where this author's parents happened to be dining. As they were leaving, Senator Kennedy eyed my mother, Henrietta (Hank) Cohn, as his elevator doors were closing. She was his age, and with her movie star good looks, she was as beautiful as he was handsome. Stopping the doors and leaving his entourage, he walked briskly over and warmly shook her hand with both of his, slowly and sensually asking in his sonorous Bostonian accent, "How do you do?" To my father's dismay, she swore she would never wash her hand again. Father never mentioned if the future president shook his hand. Mesmerized, she believed he could have won the presidency on charisma alone.

There were concerns about his age. There need not have been. Like most combat veterans, he was older than his age, and he was Harvard educated, a student of history, and independently wealthy to boot, a description identically applicable to the man who was actually nine months younger when he became president: Teddy Roosevelt.

Kennedy narrowly defeated Nixon and went on to disaster. With his background, he should have been better prepared, and his self-scolding lasted for months following the botched Bay of Pigs operation.

Fidel Castro and his communist insurgents overthrew Cuba's Batista government in 1959, and the Eisenhower Administration soon began

devising plans for a counter-rev-
olution. During the Cold War,
America and its allies from Japan
to Turkey to Iran to Pakistan to
Western Europe hemmed in the
Soviet Empire; the reverse could
not be allowed. For nearly 150
years, the Monroe Doctrine had
placed the nations of the world on
notice that the Western Hemisphere nations were going to
remain free from across-the-seas
domination. Further, the Soviet
Union had already demonstrated
expansionist intent, first by violating the Yalta agreement guar-
anteeing free and fair elections
in Eastern Europe, and next by

President John F. Kennedy
ABBIE ROWE, JFK LIBRARY

encouraging and supporting North Korea's invasion of South Korea, as
well as insurgencies in French Indochina and elsewhere. Further provocative actions included the Berlin blockade and the invasion of Hungary.

Under these circumstances, the idea of a Soviet puppet state ninety
miles south of Florida was simply unacceptable. Therefore, the CIA
helped organize a Cuban expatriate force, and training commenced in
South Florida and Central America. Kennedy was briefed on the operation, but not the plan until he was sworn into office, and he gave it the
go-ahead. In this he showed undue deference to the military, the CIA,
and to the former president who had been a five-star general when JFK
was a Navy lieutenant.

Meanwhile, the CIA failed to inform him that the operation had
been compromised. Castro and his Soviet patrons knew it was coming.
As a result, the fourteen hundred men of Brigade 2506, the invasion force,
landed on April 17, 1961, and were overwhelmed at the Bay of Pigs.
Kennedy, deeming the invasion a failure, refused to provide overt US air
support. Most of the brigade's soldiers were captured and would later be

exchanged for $53 million in food and medicine. On April 21, 1961, Kennedy accepted responsibility in a televised address: "There's an old saying that victory has a hundred fathers and defeat is an orphan. . . . Further statements, detailed discussions, are not to conceal responsibility because I'm the responsible officer of the Government." In private he was even harsher: "How could I have been so far off base? . . . All my life I've known better than to depend on the experts. How could I have been so stupid to let them go ahead?"

Here was a president's classic first-year failure, although it may be said the lessons it provided laid the groundwork for the far more important confrontation to come. Ted Sorensen, his friend, biographer, and special counsel, wrote about the causes: "In part they arose because of the newness of the president and his administration. He did not fully know the strengths and weaknesses of his various advisors. He did not yet feel he could trust his own instincts against the judgments of recognized experts. . . . Nor were his advisors as frank with him, or as free to criticize each other's work, as they would later become."

And "later" would come sooner and larger than anyone imagined. Just eighteen months later, in October 1962, irrefutable evidence was presented to the president of Soviet nuclear missiles being assembled in Cuba. It is not hyperbole to state that what would come to be known as the Cuban Missile Crisis posed the greatest threat to the United States not only in the Cold War, but in the history of the nation. The prospect, even the likelihood of thermonuclear war was at hand. Soviet Premier Nikita Khrushchev, sensing weakness and a lack of resolve, saw opportunity and took it. The logic was simple enough. If the United States and its allies could surround the Soviet Union with bombers, ships, troops, tanks, and missiles, why would a few Russian missiles in Cuba be considered provocative? They were, and Kennedy was urged to invade.

Instead, he convened the ExComm (Executive Committee of the National Security Council), with his brother Bobby, the attorney general, as the ramrod. The one absolute was that the missiles must go. Invasion looked like the only option, and preparations were commenced as the committee argued on. Finally, a majority began to coalesce around the possibility of a blockade, which would be called a quarantine, a "blockade" being an act of war. Here was the critical juncture. Would it be invade or blockade? It was up to the president, and had it not been for the harsh education provided at the Bay of Pigs, he might have gotten it wrong. He chose the blockade.

Warren Rogers's moment in history came in those most dangerous of Cold War days. He had served as a young Marine on Guadalcanal in World War II and was now a distinguished reporter for the *New York Herald Tribune*. He was also a friend to both John Kennedy and his brother Bobby, the attorney general. Warren would become my good friend years later. On October 24, 1962, he was at the National Press Club bar, and the Russian bartender overheard him tell another journalist he would be going in with the invasion of Cuba. The information was quickly reported to the Russian Embassy, and knowing that Warren and the Kennedys were close, a Russian agent named Boris, of course, was dispatched the next morning to catch up with him in a parking lot behind the Willard Hotel near the White House. He asked, "What do you think of the situation?"

Warren replied, "I think it is extremely grim."

Boris quickly moved to the crux: "Do you think Kennedy means what he says?"

Warren was unequivocal: "You're damn right, he does. He will do what he says he will do."

Boris reported the conversation to Moscow, including: "The Kennedy brothers have decided to risk all."

The Russian Embassy then sent Georgi Kornienko to meet Warren for lunch and was told, "The attack could begin at any moment."

Meanwhile, television reports were being parsed for direction. Would it be war or peace? Was the young president, who the previous year had taken responsibility for the bungled Bay of Pigs invasion, up to it? Films of military units being deployed to Florida were shown hour by hour, and Warren went with them. The Soviet ships had not stopped. Kennedy ordered the blockading fleet to contract its picket line and try again. War seemed inevitable.

The Kremlin received Kornienko's report Friday morning, October 26, and "Rogers was the star of Khrushchev's intelligence folder."

What we did not know at the time were the intricacies. We did not know what the bluffs were or if they were bluffs, but it turned out that Kennedy was precisely the right person in the right position to defuse the crisis, in no small part due to the lessons learned from his first calamitous year in the White House. He achieved victory without war because Khrushchev finally understood Kennedy would "do what he said he would do." Khrushchev turned his ships around, and the Cuban Missile Crisis ended the next day, October 27, 1962. Warren's comments had "reached the attention of Nikita Khrushchev and altered the course of the Cuban Missile Crisis." So wrote Russian Aleksandr Fursenko and American Yale Professor Timothy Naftali, who had been given access to Soviet archives following the demise of the Soviet Union when writing their 1997 book, *One Hell of a Gamble*. Only then did Warren and the world discover his role in the only nuclear confrontation of the Nuclear Age, a confrontation that for thirteen days in October 1962 seemed to make the Earth stop. The Soviets removed their missiles from Cuba, and as an unannounced side agreement, the US also agreed to remove its obsolete Jupiter missiles from Turkey and Italy at a later date because submarine-based Polaris missiles had already replaced them in US strategic planning.

When Warren passed away in 2003, his widow, Alla, asked me to deliver a memorial service eulogy at the National Press Club, where he had served as president, and as painful as such events are, the large gathering delighted in the concluding line: "With New Orleans drawl and Irish twinkle, Warren would tell his grandchildren, 'You know (long pause) I saved the world.'"

The Case for a National Election Law

The United States does not have a uniform election law; it has fifty election laws because each state chooses its own manner for casting and counting ballots, which has led to a variety of abuses, from ballot-box stuffing, waylaying of ballots, destroying ballots, counting ballots of deceased voters, vote buying, voting machine manipulations, and political interference. It is not that a federal election law would stop all misdeeds, but it would certainly reduce them. Election violations became endemic when machine politics took hold after the Civil War, New York's infamous Tammany Hall being especially notorious in its skewing of elections. Modern times have certainly not been immune. Chicago's Daley machine machinations affected the 1960 vote in Illinois. Florida politicians succeeded in delaying, then stopping the vote count in 2000. Ohio's voting machines came into question during the 2000 and 2004 elections. And these were just instances of abuses in presidential elections.

State elections, especially where one-party rule dominates, have come under less scrutiny, with some egregious exceptions making headlines and creating nicknames, such as the infamous "Landslide Lyndon" case, when Lyndon Johnson won a US Senate seat by the narrowest of margins in Texas after both sides overtly and covertly flaunted the state's election laws.

The argument could be made that federal laws should address federal elections, not state elections. But most elections include federal and local candidates, making it impossible to separate the reach of a federal law unless the states issued separate ballots for local candidates and issues, an occurrence that would signal an intent to manipulate. Further, the public believes most elections are fair, and they are because most elections aren't close, not because opposing factions are saints. When elections are close, the worst of political partisanship often emerges.

The Voting Rights Act of 1965 ensured the right to vote, not the right to have the vote counted, which is what a federal election law would do with one type of ballot, one type of voting machine, one set of voting hours, one method for issuing and counting absentee ballots, and one enforcement agency. The subject of federalism would surely be raised, and while there are many areas of law that are appropriately delegated to the states, the election of national leaders should not be among them.

CHAPTER 12

MACHINE MEN

JAMES GARFIELD (1881) AND CHESTER A. ARTHUR (1881)

JAMES GARFIELD — GENDER-BIASED SUFFRAGE
1881

Born/Died: 1831 Cuyahoga County, OH–1881 Elberon, NJ
Education: Western Reserve Eclectic Institute (later Hiram College, withdrew), Williams College
Occupation: Lawyer
Political Party: Republican
Government Service: Representative (OH) 1863–1881
Military Service: Federal Major General; Civil War
Preceded by: Rutherford B. Hayes (ends Reconstruction; federal troops withdrawn from South; confronted with nationwide bigotry over freed slaves; freedmen gained constitutional rights, which are undermined in practice; assimilation and education become key)

In 1880, former Brig. Gen. James Garfield defeated another general, Maj. Gen. Winfield Scott Hancock, and the nation lost. Hancock, a hero of the Civil War, was respected and admired on both sides of the Mason-Dixon Line. At Gettysburg, as commander of the II Corps, he held Cemetery Ridge against Pickett's Charge and fell wounded only yards away from his close friend Confederate Brig. Gen. Lewis Armistead, who died leading his men as depicted in the famous painting with hat atop sword.

President James Garfield
LIBRARY OF CONGRESS

By 1880, Hancock was the senior general in the Army, a Democrat, and favored in the South for his fair treatment of the region during Reconstruction. As such, he could have been instrumental in healing the wounds of war, except his party's platform included a plank calling for tariffs for revenue only, a clear renunciation of the protective tariffs so coveted by factory workers and corporations in the North and so despised by farmers in the South. It was this targeted tax that caused so much dissension throughout most of the nineteenth century and had been a leading factor in the North-South antipathy leading to civil war. The election of 1880 confirmed its continued divisive impact on the nation when Hancock won the Solid South and New Jersey and no other state. The Republican hold on the office would continue, and so would high, protective tariffs.

Garfield was a different sort. A volunteer officer in the Civil War, he had a disdain for West Pointers primarily because most of them refused to make war on civilians, including Hancock, West Point Class of 1844. Yet, in his inconsistent manner, he loyally served as chief of staff to Maj. Gen. William Rosecrans, West Point '42, until he disloyally undermined him. When

Maj. Gen. U. S. Grant, who graduated from the Academy in 1843, relieved Rosecrans, Garfield expected to be appointed in his stead. He was not, and remained disaffected with Grant thereafter. Garfield eventually resigned his commission and entered the House of Representatives where he remained until 1881, when he was sworn in as president after defeating Hancock.

Garfield had been involved in the Crédit Mobilier Scandal, a front company established by directors of the Union Pacific Railroad to build a portion of the transcontinental railroad; the company directors lined their pockets in the process. Bribes of stock were given to members of Congress, Garfield among them. Despite this sordid background, Garfield became a member of the "Half Breeds," a racist term used to describe Republican reformists in contrast with Radical Republican "Stalwarts" led by New York's Republican Sen. Roscoe Conkling and his machine.

A devout believer in the spoils system and avid opponent of reform, Conkling controlled appointments to the lucrative New York Customs House, headed by his underling, Chester A. Arthur, and together they padded their pockets as well as the rolls with excess people, all devotees of Conkling. In this, they ran afoul of President Hayes, who fired Arthur and many others. When Hayes chose not to run for reelection, and Conkling's choice of Grant for a third term failed, the Republican convention turned to Garfield. Conkling was furious. In response, the Half Breeds placed a Stalwart on the ticket, Chester A. Arthur. Certain the ticket would lose, Conkling ordered Arthur to reject the nomination, but Arthur refused, claiming he had never dreamed of receiving such an auspicious honor. The ticket did win, and Garfield set forth his agenda during the inauguration:

> *The free enjoyment of equal suffrage is still in question. . . . It should be said with the utmost emphasis that this question of the suffrage will never give repose or safety to the States or to the nation until each, within its own jurisdiction, makes and keeps the ballot free and pure by the strong sanctions of the law. . . .*
>
> *Grave doubts have been entertained whether Congress is authorized by the Constitution to make any form of paper money legal tender. . . . These notes are not money, but promises to pay money. If the holders demand it, the promise should be kept. . . .*

*The development of the world's commerce has led to an urgent
demand for shortening the great sea voyage around Cape Horn by
constructing ship canals or railways across the isthmus which unites
the continents. . . .*

*The civil service can never be placed on a satisfactory basis until
it is regulated by law.*

Like the Founding Fathers, who eloquently and forcefully spoke of
the rights of man, by which they meant adult white males, Garfield, without any apparent sense of hypocrisy, spoke of "free suffrage," by which
he meant adult white and black males. The women's suffrage movement,
then in full swing, could not have been more disillusioned.

The next issue, that of hard money, would lead to continued financial
turmoil and contrasted with the laudable advocacy of two other issues, the
not-yet selected or named Panama Canal and civil service reform. The last
of these turned Conkling apoplectic and led to Garfield's assassination at
the hand of a disgruntled office seeker, shouting, "I am a Stalwart of the
Stalwarts! I did it and I want to be arrested! Arthur is President now!"

Garfield's acceptance of Conkling's man on the ticket and acceptance
of Conkling's demands on several appointments undermined his reform
agenda, while his indirect denial of women's suffrage showed him to be
oblivious to the changing times, all freshman-year failings.

CHESTER A. ARTHUR—CONKLING'S MAN
1881–1885

Born/Died: 1829 Fairfield, VT–1886 New York, NY
Education: Union College
Occupation: Lawyer
Political Party: Republican, Whig
Government Service: Vice President 1881, Collector of the Port of New
York 1871–1878

Military Service: Federal Brigadier General; Civil War (non-combat)

Preceded by: James Garfield (assassinated as Republican Party's radical-liberal schism widens, fueled by machine politics and racial bigotry; Garfield and Arthur are from opposite wings; women's suffrage movement alienated when freed male slaves receive the vote and they do not)

In response to a query about the possibility of voting for Garfield and not Arthur in the 1880 election, the editor of *The Nation*, E. L. Godkin, wrote: "[T]here is no place in which his powers of mischief will be so small as in the Vice-Presidency, and it will remove him during a great part of the year from his own field of activity. It is true General Garfield, if elected, may die during his term of office, but this is too unlikely a contingency to be worth making extraordinary provision for." Not exactly prescient.

President Chester A. Arthur
LIBRARY OF CONGRESS

While vice president, Arthur, ever loyal to Conkling, fought with Garfield over additional appointments and, when rebuffed, went public, writing in the *New York Herald*: "Garfield has not been square, nor honorable, nor truthful with Conkling. It is hard to say of a President . . . but it is unfortunately only the truth."

Then, on July 2, 1881, Garfield was shot and obviously disabled and unable to perform the duties of office. Even so, Arthur refused to take the reins, leaving the nation leaderless until the president succumbed to the wound on September 19. There was no precedent for assumption of the office under such circumstances. Neither was there a prohibition, and Arthur should have acted. It may be that the public's low opinion of him and his own self-doubt prevented this. The issue would surface again when Woodrow Wilson became incapacitated in 1919 and after John Kennedy was shot in 1963, all of which would lead to the adoption of the Twenty-Fifth (Succession) Amendment in 1967.

When Arthur's checkered past was questioned, he responded, "Madam, I may be president of the United States, but my private life is nobody's damned business." And somehow, he got away with it. He is given credit for breaking with Conkling and signing the Pendleton Civil Service Law, but he also signed the racist Chinese Exclusion Act. True to Republican orthodoxy, he pressed for high tariffs, only to end up with a mishmash known as the Mongrel Tariff.

Why he acted as he did, inconsistently and often out of character, is unknown, and was probably unknown to him, a man who never dreamed he would be where he was. After all, he was regarded as a political machine hack, a view with which he undoubtedly concurred, and probably explains his first-year failure to assume the office or at least the presidential duties during Garfield's pre-death incapacitation. His self-doubt left the nation leaderless for two months.

CHAPTER 13

REFORM MEN

GROVER CLEVELAND (1885) AND THEODORE ROOSEVELT (1901)

GROVER CLEVELAND—THE VETO PRESIDENT
1885–1889, 1893–1897

Born/Died: 1837 Caldwell, NJ–1908 Princeton, NJ
Education: No college education
Occupation: Lawyer
Political Party: Democratic
Government Service: Governor (NY) 1883–1885, Mayor (Buffalo, NY) 1882, Sheriff (Erie County, NY) 1871–1873
Military Service: Paid a substitute to take his place during the Civil War (allowed by law)
Preceded by: Chester A. Arthur (machine politician; failed to assume office during Garfield's incapacitation; signed Pendleton Civil Service Law, but also the Chinese Exclusion Act)

The *New York Herald*: "We are told that [Cleveland's opponent] Mr. Blaine has been delinquent in office but blameless in private life, while Mr. Cleveland has been the model of official integrity, but culpable in his personal relations." And so he was, having accepted responsibility for fathering a child out of wedlock and buying his way out of Civil War service—a legal, though hardly admirable activity—Grover Cleveland was an early example of how the political pendulum swings from era to era, depending upon the mood of the public and the state of the nation. Not unlike

President Grover Cleveland and Frances Folsom wedding
LIBRARY OF CONGRESS

the 1945–1975 period following World War II, the final thirty-five years of the 1800s were dominated by war veterans, politicians who had served in the Civil War, with one exception, Grover Cleveland.

By the election of 1884, the Democratic Party had recovered, its northern and southern branches having reunited. Because the South viewed the Civil War as a Republican war, it became the Democratic Party's most reliable regional constituency, hence the moniker: Solid South. For the next century, Democratic issues would come and go, some pleasing, some displeasing southerners. All were trumped by the unacceptable idea of voting for Republicans who had brought devastation to their region. While they could vote for a Democratic northerner such as Major General Hancock, who had simply done his duty, voting for a Republican general like Ulysses S. Grant, who was tied to the Radical

Republicans and a harsh Reconstruction policy, was anathema. Interestingly, although he was thirty-one when the war began, GOP nominee James G. Blaine also had not served, but he was a Republican with ethical problems. Further, Cleveland's clean political record attracted breakaway reform-minded Republicans, known as Mugwumps, who proved just enough to defeat a scandal-tainted opponent.

True to expectations, Cleveland proved to be thoroughly honest. What surprised supporters was his inaction. He spoke the words of reform, and sought to implement them on a direct basis, generally hiring people and, to the dismay of Democrats, keeping Republicans in office on the basis of merit, reversing the spoils system introduced by Andrew Jackson fifty-one years earlier. Reform legislation was another matter. The nation would have to wait another sixteen years before an activist reformer, Theodore Roosevelt, would finally change the government's way of doing business.

In fairness, Cleveland did face a Republican-controlled Senate, which undoubtedly influenced his counter-approach to reform. Viewing himself as the guard rather than the advocate, he vetoed 414 bills, and only two were overridden by Congress. Many of the vetoed bills were for pensions and private relief bills for Union veterans of the Civil War, which, coming from one who had not served, was an interesting reversal of previous administrations' actions. He claimed: "Public money appropriated for pensions . . . should be devoted to the indemnification of those who in the defense of the Union and in the nation's service have worthily suffered, and who in the day of their dependence resulting from such suffering are entitled to the benefactions of their Government." This did not enhance his popularity with the veterans' organization, the Grand Army of the Republic.

The next highest veto totals by his predecessors were ninety-three from Grant, fifteen from Andrew Johnson, twelve from Jackson, ten from Tyler, and no more than seven by any others. And the total for Cleveland was only for his first term. When combined with his non-successive second term, the total came to 584 vetoes, a total not surpassed until Franklin Roosevelt vetoed 635 bills over three terms (he died at the beginning of his fourth term).

The problem was that he was stopping, but not promoting, legislation, and in this he was most criticized, "ineffective" being the most common term applied to him.

H. Paul wrote in *An Honest President: The Life and Presidencies of Grover Cleveland*, "The consensus of Cleveland biographers is that the president-elect was appalled to see how unprepared he was for the magnitude of the duties he had obligated himself to assume," and he wrote, "I cannot look upon the prospect of success in this campaign with any joy, but only with a very serious kind of awe." Such self-doubting may have been the cause of his poor relations with Congress. Whatever the cause, he displayed an inability or unwillingness to aggressively advance his programs.

THEODORE ROOSEVELT—PANIC OF 1907
1901–1909

Born/Died: 1858 New York, NY–1919 Oyster Bay, NY
Education: Harvard University, Columbia Law School (withdrew)
Occupation: Author, rancher, professional politician
Political Party: Republican
Government Service: Vice President 1901, Governor (NY) 1899–1900, Assistant Secretary of the Navy 1897–1898, President New York City Police Board 1895–1897, US Civil Service Commission 1889–1895, Deputy Sheriff Dakota Badlands 1884–1886, Assemblyman (NY) 1882–1884
Military Service: Colonel; Spanish-American War (awarded the Medal of Honor in 2001)
Preceded by: William McKinley (USS *Maine* blown up in Havana Harbor; reluctantly takes nation into Spanish-American War to free Cuba; imperialism rejected, however the Philippines, Guam, and Puerto Rico are annexed; Cuba is not; assassinated)

Theodore Roosevelt was what today would be referred to as a RINO, a Republican-in-name-only. The Republicans of his day persisted in their

President Theodore Roosevelt as colonel of the Rough Riders atop
Kettle Hill following the Battle of San Juan Hill during the Spanish-
American War, 1898
LIBRARY OF CONGRESS

adherence to high tariffs and pro-business policies. Roosevelt did not. He
came from the New York aristocracy, those upper-class folks memorial-
ized by writers such as Roosevelt's friend Edith Wharton in novels such
as *The House of Mirth*, published in 1905.

Roosevelt epitomized the Progressive Movement, opposing high tariffs that primarily benefited northeastern businessmen and opposing the
Robber Barons, whose monopolies he attacked with a zeal not seen before
despite the passage of the Sherman Anti-Trust Act in 1890. He sympathized with labor and refused to use troops to break strikes. He endorsed
women's suffrage. He would obtain passage of the Meat Inspection Act
and the Pure Food and Drug Act. He was also a staunch supporter of
military readiness, especially of the Navy. It was all too much for mainstream Republicans, and he would eventually break with them and form

a new Progressive Party, dubbed the Bull Moose Party, and run for president under its banner in 1912.

Yet, despite all this, he was not immune to a freshman-year mistake, and it was significant. His predecessor, William McKinley, had been the author of the highest tariff in US history (see Chapter 8 Chart: Significant US Tariffs) when he was a senator in the 1890s. Just before his assassination in 1901, he had come around to a new view, establishing reciprocal treaties with several other nations, promising to match tariff reductions with tariff reductions. It was not exactly a leap to free trade, but it was headed there, a policy perfectly coinciding with Roosevelt's views.

Under the circumstances, it was reasonable for voters to assume he would see the treaties through to ratification. He did not. It is said the issue bored him. It is also possible that he caved in to big business or party machine pressure. Or he was consumed by so much else, he simply did not recognize the magnitude of the tariff problem. He was especially preoccupied with gunboat diplomacy to aid rebels in Colombia who, having broken away from that country, formed the new nation of Panama and quickly signed a ninety-nine-year lease with the United States to build the Panama Canal. He won the Nobel Peace Prize after mediating an end to the Russo-Japanese War, and he negotiated an end to the Filipino Insurrection. Further, he was busting trusts like Carey Nation had been busting saloons in her drive for Prohibition. These things may have germinated in his first year, but they did not take place then. His abandonment of the reciprocal treaties did. Whether a result of boredom or coercion, it was a lapse completely out of character and is therefore unexplainable. So, the high tariffs continued throughout his two presidential terms and certainly contributed to the Panic of 1907.

His conditional support in 1910 for a constitutional amendment authorizing a federal income tax, which his successor would achieve, did eventually lead to a reduction in the tariff he had ignored in 1901. Of course, this was overshadowed by progressive initiatives—his initiatives—that changed the face of America, forever altering the political debates and paving the way for his cousin Franklin Delano Roosevelt, a Democrat, to create the regulations and safety nets of the 1930s.

Teddy Roosevelt took the best from the past and set the stage for the best of the future.

Why We Should Not Rank the Presidents

There is a tendency to rank the presidents, and Theodore Roosevelt certainly belongs on Mount Rushmore. Even so, it is a tendency to avoid just as all such rankings involving non-equivalent tests should be avoided. It is akin to the patently unfair ranking of students based upon grades even though they take different courses and different tests, all with different degrees of difficulty. The same holds true for presidents. None of them faced the same trials and tests.

Scope and scale increased as the nation increased in size, population, and the diversity of the population. Science made the world increasingly smaller, drawing the nation ever closer to the problems of the world, creating what Thomas Jefferson (not George Washington) warned against: "Entangling alliances." We can only imagine how he would have dealt with issues facing FDR, as the nation became the world's superpower in the midst of World War II.

Socio-economic issues also changed with the times. The great nineteenth-century issues of slavery, suffrage, and regionally discriminatory tariffs were not the primary issues of the twentieth century, except, perhaps, the Smoot-Hawley Tariff of the Hoover Administration.

We may surmise that any number of presidents would not have handled the Cuban Missile Crisis as adeptly as did John Kennedy—think John Adams, Andrew Jackson, James K. Polk, Abraham Lincoln, or William McKinley—or reacted as poorly to the 1929 Stock Market Crash as did Herbert Hoover—consider James Monroe, Martin Van Buren, Ulysses S. Grant, or Benjamin Harrison—then again we can never know.

CHAPTER 14

UNPARDONABLE SCANDALS: TEAPOT DOME, DIRTY TRICKS, AND AN UNPARDONABLE PARDON

WARREN G. HARDING (1921), RICHARD M. NIXON (1969), AND GERALD R. FORD JR. (1974)

One was a dupe, one was inherently flawed, and one was naïve.

Warren G. Harding looked the role, but was otherwise not presidential material, and his corruption-filled administration seemed to be the result of his devil-may-care, easygoing, can't say "No" approach to life that carried over to governing.

Politicians lie to win; statesmen lie to govern. It was a distinction Richard Nixon neglected to make, and he brought his infamous campaign dirty tricks into the Oval Office, employing government lying and covert actions—normally tenets of national security—for political sabotage.

This is the man Gerald Ford pardoned.

WARREN G. HARDING—TEAPOT DOME
1921–1923

Born/Died: 1865 Corsica (now Blooming Grove), OH–1923 San Francisco, CA
Education: Ohio Central College
Occupation: Newspaper editor
Political Party: Republican
Government Service: Senator (OH) 1915–1921, Lieutenant Governor (OH) 1904–1906
Military Service: None
Preceded by: Woodrow Wilson (Democratic reformer like Republican Theodore Roosevelt; Federal Reserve created; readiness advocates unable to convince Wilson to build up military; income tax begun; drawn into World War I unready; Versailles Peace Treaty rejected by US Senate; becomes incapacitated)

It is difficult to assess presidential intelligence. Presidents are not required to pass a test; they never reveal IQ scores; and their mental lapses are usually obscured by a coterie of protective aides and officials. They need only be native born and at least thirty-five years of age, and so Warren Gamaliel Harding was constitutionally qualified. Harding, himself, thought otherwise and said so to Nicholas Butler Murray, president of Columbia University: "I am not fit for this office and never should have been here," to which Murray added: "Harding was one of the kindest men who ever lived, but he was without any serious qualifications for the presidency. . . . He had no wide or accurate knowledge of public questions or of the foundations of history, economics and public law on which those questions rest. . . . He would not have consciously done a wrong act in his great office but he had neither the intellect nor the character to prevent himself from being made use of for unworthy purposes by unworthy men who loudly professed their personal and political friendship."

President Warren G. Harding at the White House
LIBRARY OF CONGRESS

Harding was the only newspaper publisher to reach the presidency, and he left no question about his job preference: "You see, White, what really interests me is my newspaper [the *Marion Star*]. There is nothing to this job here. As a matter of fact, I go to press at the White House every afternoon at three o'clock."

What Harding seemed to enjoy most in the White House was inviting pals over to play poker, and it was from among these pals he selected some of his Cabinet members, among them, Secretary of the Interior Albert Fall, Attorney General Harry Dougherty, and Director of the Veterans' Bureau Charles R. Forbes. These first-year appointments would haunt his presidency, and Theodore Roosevelt's outspoken daughter, Alice, described the scene as having "the general atmosphere of a convivial gambling saloon."

Fall eventually went to jail for accepting bribes to provide no-bid oil leases of Wyoming's Teapot Dome oil field and California's Elk Hills and Buena Vista oil fields to Harry F. Sinclair of Mammoth Oil and Edward I. Doheny of Pan American Petroleum and Transport Company, respectively.

Dougherty failed to act after discovering irregularities in Fall's actions, and he was later tried and acquitted by a single hold-out vote for illegally profiting from alien assets seized during World War I.

And when Harding discovered Forbes was selling Veterans' Bureau hospital supplies for personal gain, the president physically assaulted him in the White House.

There were others, but Harding suddenly died while traveling in the West. He had managed to reverse Teddy Roosevelt's progressive direction of the party, and returned it to the guardian of "low taxes, [high] tariffs, less central government."

The Constitution only allows impeachment for "high crimes and misdemeanors," not bad judgment, but had he lived, an exception might have been made in Harding's case.

RICHARD M. NIXON—DIRTY TRICKS
1969–1974

Born/Died: 1913 Yorba Linda, CA–1994 New York, NY
Education: Whittier College, Duke University Law School
Occupation: Lawyer
Political Party: Republican
Government Service: Vice President 1953–1961, Senator (CA) 1950–1953, Representative (CA) 1947–1950
Military Service: Navy Lieutenant Commander; World War II (non-combat)
Preceded by: Lyndon Johnson (a domestic issues president whose program includes civil rights, Medicare, War on Poverty; is drawn into Vietnam War, selects wrong general, war of attrition ensues; communist Tet Offensive unhinges US war effort; campus unrest)

Watergate wasn't an aberration; it was a culmination. Richard Nixon and dirty tricks went hand in hand. In 1950, he won election to the US Senate

President Richard M. Nixon
COURTESY OF THE NIXON PRESIDENTIAL LIBRARY & MUSEUM

from California, defeating Rep. Helen Gahagan Douglas, the Democratic nominee, whom he called the "Pink Lady," claiming she was "pink right down to her underwear." Nixon had not originated the line, but he ran with it fully aware his opponent was no more a communist than he was. She responded by attaching to him the moniker "Tricky Dick." It was then that Rep. John F. Kennedy delivered a $1,000 campaign donation from his father, former ambassador to Britain Joseph P. Kennedy. Before long, three men, all supported by the elder Kennedy, were serving together in the US Senate: Richard M. Nixon, John F. Kennedy, and Joe McCarthy, staunch anti-communists all, though the first two could see firsthand what Joe Kennedy could not: McCarthy was a personable fraud.

The exceptionally bright and inherently self-conscious Nixon saw in McCarthy (see Chapter 2, Eisenhower) what could happen when dirty tricks turn into demagoguery. Nixon belonged more to the Thomas Jefferson school. Like Jefferson, Nixon often used surrogates to slander opponents but otherwise remained quite objective, less doctrinaire. He was also insecure, socially awkward, and far from wealthy, the opposite of his handsome colleague, JFK, whom he would face ten years later in their competing bids for the presidency.

President Eisenhower had never been close to his vice president, Richard Nixon, a relationship Nixon's daughter Julie described as "delicate and tenuous." Dr. Albert Hutschnecker commented that "Eisenhower was always telling Nixon to straighten his tie or pull back his shoulders, or speak up or shut up." Then there was this, Eisenhower's most memorable line about Nixon's 1960 presidential campaign. On August 24, 1960, Charles Mohr of *Time* asked Eisenhower: "We understand that the power of decision is entirely yours, Mr. President. I just wondered if you could give us an example of a major idea of his [Nixon's] that you had adopted in that role, as the decider and final—" Eisenhower interrupted, "If you give me a week, I might think of one. I don't remember."

Here was a president who had led Allied forces in victory over Germany and Italy during World War II talking about the man who eight and a half years later would be commander-in-chief during the turning point of the Vietnam War. Not only had Nixon not played an integral role in the Eisenhower Administration, he apparently had not received the benefit of high-level military advice from someone so ably capable of dispensing it.

Nixon would lose in 1960, but go on to win in 1968 after Kennedy's successor, Lyndon Johnson, decided not to run following the shock of the North Vietnamese and Viet Cong Tet Offensive, an event that scrambled his Vietnam policy. The enemy lost heavily, and the South Vietnamese Viet Cong rebels were permanently crippled, though their tactical defeat proved to be a strategic victory when the American public realized, despite White House pronouncements to the contrary, the war was not winding down.

Nixon campaigned against the Democratic nominee, LBJ's Vice President Hubert Humphrey, with a promise: He had a secret plan to end the war.

On May 10, 1968, representatives from the United States, South Vietnam, North Vietnam, and the Viet Cong began the Paris Peace Talks. If they were successful, the Democratic ticket would probably win the presidential election in the fall; if not, Richard Nixon would be the odds-on favorite. Soon, suspicions arose that Nixon was undermining the talks. Johnson certainly believed it to be the case, telling Illinois Republican and Senate Minority Leader Everett Dirksen, "He oughtn't be doin' this—this is treason. . . . Nixon ought to play it just like he has all along, 'that I want to see peace come the first day we can, that it's not going to affect the election either one way or the other.' . . . Tell them that their people are messing around with this thing and if they don't want it on the front pages they'd better quit it."

Nixon, according to Jeffrey Frank in *Ike and Dick*, "was not, to put it charitably, eager for a pre-election breakthrough in Paris . . . and there is every reason to believe that his wishes were clear to [South Vietnamese] President Thieu." Thieu was unhappy about the peace talks, and he was probably led to believe he would get a better deal from a Nixon Administration. In the words of LBJ, this worst of all dirty tricks was "treason," and is raised here due to the evidence cited and President Thieu's behavior during the period. In any event, the peace talks stalled, and Nixon was elected.

If true, this allegation is far more serious than Watergate, the infamous break-in of the Democratic National Headquarters carried out by Nixon's dirty tricksters known as the "Plumbers." With classic "plausible deniability," Nixon attempted to distance himself from the crime and, in so doing, committed another crime, the cover-up, which is what led to his resignation.

With so much baggage and experience behind him, the stage for Richard Nixon's first year as president was set. From his bed at Walter Reed Army Hospital, Eisenhower said of the new president, "You know, I know Dick [Nixon] knows what to do. I just question whether he knows how to organize the government to get it done." Today, the pragmatic Nixon would be described as a progressive. He supported civil rights, the Equal Rights Amendment, and budget flexibility, but he was more complex than the sum of his platform positions because his pragmatism also extended to ethics. In place of a plan to end the war, he privately lamented it was already lost, and the only war aim left was to extricate with honor. During the 1969-70 period, Nixon ordered bombing and ground campaigns, including the May 1970 invasion of North Vietnamese sanctuaries in Cambodia's eastern region, which set the stage for an extrication that took more than twenty thousand additional American lives.

Before I was wounded on March 18, 1970, I would tell the new men joining my unit on the Cambodian border it did not matter why they were there; it only mattered that we did our duty, performed our missions, and took care of each other. In just a few months from the fall of '69 to the spring of '70, the attitudes of replacement troops had dramatically changed. Most of them were draftees; all of them knew the war was lost, and they realized the president's secret plan to end the war simply did not exist. As a result, they were more apprehensive, more tenuous than previous recruits, but only initially. Within days they were combat veterans, as courageous and caring as the "old-timers"—those mostly-teenagers who had been in combat for a month or more—because once the firing commences, the whys and wherefores disappear. Even so, no American president has ever asked so much from so many for such a forlorn hope. It was reminiscent of the last Confederate charge at Appomattox in 1865 when soldiers died without any expectation of success. For each of those fighting in Vietnam, it would be a year of last charges. This was Nixon's secret plan.

GERALD R. FORD JR.—PARDONING
THE UNPARDONABLE
1974–1977

Born/Died: 1913 Omaha, NE–2006 Rancho Mirage, CA
Education: University of Michigan, Yale Law School
Occupation: Lawyer, professional politician
Political Party: Republican
Government Service: Vice President 1973–1974, Representative (MI) 1949–1973
Military Service: Navy Lieutenant Commander; World War II
Preceded by: Richard M. Nixon (Supreme Court *Roe v. Wade* decision legalizes abortions; invasion of Cambodia; opening to communist China; Watergate; impeachment hearings; resignation)

President Gerald R. Ford

It is believed that a trial of Richard Nixon, if it became necessary, could not fairly begin until a year or more has elapsed. In the meantime, the tranquility to which this nation has been restored by the events of recent weeks could be irreparably lost by the prospects of bringing to trial a former President of the United States. . . .

Now, Therefore, I, Gerald R. Ford, *President of the United States, pursuant to the pardon power conferred upon me by Article II, Section 2, of the Constitution, have granted and by these presents do grant a full, free, and absolute pardon unto Richard Nixon for all offenses against the United States which he, Richard Nixon, has committed or may have committed or taken part in during the period from January 20, 1969 through August 9, 1974. (See Appendix D for the complete text)*

With these words, President Gerald Ford, having become president on August 9, 1974, proclaimed the president of the United States to indeed be above the law, or in the words of former President Richard Nixon himself in his 1977 David Frost interview, "Well, when the president does it that means that it is not illegal." He went on to quote Lincoln as justification: "Actions which otherwise would be unconstitutional, could become lawful if undertaken for the purpose of preserving the Constitution and the Nation."

This did not wash. Nixon, a lawyer by trade, was well aware of the famous 1866 Supreme Court decision in *ex parte Milligan*: Lincoln's use of military tribunals when civilian courts were operating was unconstitutional. He was also aware of Supreme Court Chief Justice Roger Taney's ruling at the time and the Supreme Court's later ruling in another case that only Congress could suspend habeas corpus, a direct rebuke of Lincoln's action to the contrary with John Merryman and many others during the Civil War.

Ford's action set an awful example and sent a worse message, although not a precedent, because the president of the United States has the constitutional authority to pardon, as President Bill Clinton did in the controversial pardon of financier Marc Rich on his last day in office.

Ford's political star never recovered from this ill-advised action, and the balance of his first year got worse. North Vietnam violated the 1973 Paris Peace Accords and launched a limited invasion of South Vietnam in December 1974 as a test, and Ford failed to honor the US commitment to South Vietnam. The full-scale invasion came in March. Ford responded by requesting $522 million in aid for South Vietnam, which Congress promptly refused. In fact, military options were available, including use of B-52 strikes, which would have been devastating to a conventional force in the open, but neither Ford nor the nation had any stomach left for the war. Repercussions were immediate. South Vietnam fell in April 1975 as the evacuation of US personnel turned into a desperate televised fiasco.

"He's the weakest president in U.S. history," said Pham Van Dong, prime minister of North Vietnam from 1955 to 1976 and of unified Vietnam from 1976 to 1987. North Vietnamese colonel Bui Tin explained: "We tested Ford's resolve by attacking Phuoc Long. When Ford kept American B-52s in their hangars, our leadership decided on a big offensive against South Vietnam."

In May, Cambodian Khmer Rouge soldiers captured the US merchant ship *Mayaguez* in international waters, and the botched American response cost the lives of forty-one Marines. The Khmer Rouge would go on to slaughter approximately two million Cambodians and ethnic minorities, a modern holocaust finally stopped by the North Vietnamese Army in 1979.

If the United States was not going to honor its promises to South Vietnam, their government should have been so informed. If US forces and civilian personnel were going to be withdrawn, an orderly plan should have been in place. The planners of US disengagements in Iraq and Afghanistan surely looked upon the retreat from Vietnam as a negative example, and the Obama Administration decision to reenter the region to counter ISIS in Syria and Iraq confirms that American public and political approval can be attained when the nation acts with professionalism and competence. That was not the case in 1975, when the nation was roiling from a domestic constitutional crisis and an untried hand was at the helm.

CHAPTER 15

AN ABSENCE OF DETERRENCE: WORLD WAR I AND WORLD WAR II

WOODROW WILSON (1913), FRANKLIN ROOSEVELT (1933), AND HARRY S. TRUMAN (1945)

President George Washington was an advocate of peace through strength, as he ably demonstrated when employing overwhelming force to put down the Whiskey Rebellion. The rebels quit without a fight. It was an example Presidents Woodrow Wilson and Franklin Roosevelt failed to follow.

Wilson entered office in 1913, and the following year, World War I broke out in Europe. Former President Theodore Roosevelt urged him to build up the Army and Navy. Wilson refused. After America entered the war in 1917, it took more than a year for US troops to be trained and shipped to France in sufficient strength to make a difference, and they were very nearly too late.

Franklin Roosevelt became president in 1933, the same year Adolf Hitler came to power in Germany. Hitler immediately commenced a military buildup and Japan did likewise, while Roosevelt, burdened by isolationists and the Great Depression, kept military budgets low. As a result, America was unprepared when the Japanese attack on Pearl Harbor forced the nation into the war.

Within a year of becoming president upon FDR's death in 1945, Harry Truman missed the opportunity to thwart the Soviets in Eastern Europe, dropped atomic bombs on Japan, and demobilized the US armed forces in the face of a communist threat. It was among the most inauspicious beginnings in the history of the presidency.

WOODROW WILSON—WORLD WAR I
1913–1921

Born/Died: 1856 Staunton, VA–1924 Washington, DC
Education: Davidson College (withdrew), College of New Jersey (later Princeton University), University of Virginia Law School (withdrew), PhD from Johns Hopkins University
Occupation: Academic (President, Princeton University 1902–1910)
Political Party: Democratic
Government Service: Governor (NJ) 1911–1913
Military Service: None
Preceded by: William Howard Taft (antagonizes women's suffrage movement; Theodore Roosevelt's progressive reforms moderated; Sixteenth Amendment ratified legalizing income taxes; Roosevelt breaks away and creates Progressive Party, known as the Bull Moose Party; Republican split puts Democrat Wilson into White House)

Woodrow Wilson was a student of history and, as a boy in Virginia's Shenandoah Valley, a witness to war, the tragedy of the American Civil War. Such study and firsthand experience should have guided his views on military preparedness. They did not.

Wilson's first presidential year, 1913, was the last year of the world he knew and a turning point in 126 years of America's foreign relations because an alarming and ominous shift in the European balance of power, which British Prime Minister Benjamin Disraeli claimed had been "entirely destroyed," was about to play out in "iron and blood."

In 1890, Germany's new, young Kaiser Wilhelm II requested the resignation of Chancellor Otto von Bismarck, the man who had enunciated his nation's "iron and blood" policy, and manipulated Austria into the 1866 Seven Weeks War, France into the 1870-71 Franco-Prussian War, and thereafter succeeded in uniting the German states with Prussia to form the most powerful nation on the European continent: the German Empire. What followed, in the words of Winston Churchill was "the era of armed peace."

Until then, the British-German connection had been one of alliances, not belligerence. George I of Hanover spoke not a word of English when he became Britain's king in 1714. His descendant Queen Victoria married German Prince Albert of Saxe-Coburg and Gotha, and their eldest daughter married the son of Kaiser Wilhelm I and bore a son, Wilhelm II, who was thereby the first cousin of Britain's King George V. Further, the connection consisted of much more than royal marriages as was amply demonstrated by the British-Prussian alliance of 1815 that defeated Napoleon at Waterloo.

In 1882, Bismarck created the Triple Alliance with Austria and Italy to ward off the potential threat of a two-front war with France and Russia. It was also a new age of empires, especially the Second British Empire, and the Race for Africa was on. Initially, Bismarck was a reluctant participant in this game of empires, and he cautioned against tweaking the British lion's mastery of the seas. The British fleet was the largest and most powerful in the world, serving both as the first line of defense for that island nation and as the safeguard of its critical seaborne commerce, its national lifeline. Wilhelm I paid attention; Wilhelm II did not. And Bismarck, the hawk, soon became the dove to Wilhelm II's increasing war mania.

This was in part driven by Wilhelm's irrational Anglophobia as expressed just before ascending the throne: "But that our family shield should be besmirched and the Reich brought to the brink of ruin by an English princess who is my mother—that is the most terrible thing of all. . . . One cannot have enough hatred for England." The sentiment became imbedded like a disease, spreading from event to event. He snubbed his uncle, Britain's future King Edward VII and set off a firestorm among the British with his 1885 Kruger Telegram, congratulating Boers who defeated the Cecil Rhodes–sponsored Jameson Raid in southern Africa. Four years later, he openly praised the Boers in the Second Anglo-Boer War, which evoked a comment from Queen Victoria, who told Lord Salisbury "to remonstrate at the presence of so many German officers and men with the Boers. It is monstrous."

President Woodrow Wilson
LIBRARY OF CONGRESS

Yet, for all this diplomatic immaturity, one single decision changed all and led to a war that would devour human life by the millions. In 1897, Kaiser Wilhelm II initiated a costly program of ship building to create the *Kaiserliche Marine*, an imperial navy to rival Britain's until-then unrivaled fleet. From the harrowing days of the Spanish Armada in 1588 to Napoleon's planned invasion in 1805, the navy had kept the British Isles safe from invasion. Then, after the mid-nineteenth century, when wood and sail were replaced by faster, stronger steel and steam, the British Navy became that nation's great worldwide force-projecting deterrent of the age, and the British government intended to maintain the advantage.

Adm. Alfred Thayer Mahan was the foremost naval theorist of the age despite his fear of the sea and his famously incompetent handling of ships. (Every vessel but one of those he commanded collided with other vessels or objects.) His 1890 seminal work, *The Influence of Sea Power Upon History*, which was widely read and influenced naval thinking in the United States, Europe, and Japan, asserted that sea power was the primary determinant of national power, a philosophy at odds with the Bismarckian and Napoleonic concepts of land-based strength. As if on cue, American and Japanese naval victories proved decisive in the 1898 Spanish-American War and the 1904-05 Russo-Japanese War.

Soon, Mahan realized the scope of his influence as the Anglo-German naval-building race upset the European balance of power at sea even more than the unification of Germany had upset it on land. Britain countered with the construction of the first super battleship, HMS *Dreadnought*, in 1906 and the formation the following year of the Anglo-Russo-French Triple Entente in direct response to Wilhelm's Triple Alliance.

In that year, President Theodore Roosevelt wrote Admiral Mahan: "Your position is a peculiar one, and without intending to treat this as a precedent, I desire you to have a free hand to discuss this in any way you wish the so-called peace proposals. You have a deserved reputation as a publicist which makes this proper from the public standpoint. Indeed, I think it important for you to write just what you think of the matter."

Woodrow Wilson took a different approach.

Shortly after his inauguration in 1913, top advisor and confidante Col. Edward House (the rank being honorary, not military) sailed for Europe, unsuccessfully seeking a means of throttling back the nearly two-decade-old arms race. This was the explosive situation the president relegated to the realm of words, while ignoring substantive deterrence in both his Inaugural Address and later in his First Annual Message to Congress on December 2, 1913:

> *The country, I am thankful to say, is at peace with all the world, and many happy manifestations multiply about us of a growing cordiality and sense of community of interest among the nations, foreshadowing an age of settled peace and good will. More and more readily each decade do the nations manifest their willingness to bind themselves by solemn treaty to the processes of peace, the processes of frankness and fair concession. So far the United States has stood at the front of such negotiations. She will, I earnestly hope and confidently believe, give fresh proof of her sincere adherence to the cause of international*

friendship by ratifying the several treaties of arbitration awaiting renewal by the Senate. In addition to these, it has been the privilege of the Department of State to gain the assent, in principle, of no less than 31 nations, representing four-fifths of the population of the world, to the negotiation of treaties by which it shall be agreed that whenever differences of interest or of policy arise which cannot be resolved by the ordinary processes of diplomacy they shall be publicly analyzed, discussed, and reported upon by a tribunal chosen by the parties before either nation determines its course of action.

There is only one possible standard by which to determine controversies between the United States and other nations, and that is compounded of these two elements: Our own honor and our obligations to the peace of the world. A test so compounded ought easily to be made to govern both the establishment of new treaty obligations and the interpretation of those already assumed.

There is but one cloud upon our horizon. That has shown itself to the south of us, and hangs over Mexico.

Colonel House tried again in May 1914, this time meeting with Kaiser Wilhelm II, chief of the German Navy Admiral Alfred von Tirpitz, as well as with British Foreign Secretary Sir Edward Grey. His report to the president was dire: "[S]ome spark might be fanned into a blaze," and in Berlin "the situation is extraordinary. It is jingoism run stark mad."

The "spark" soon came with the assassination of Austrian Archduke Franz Ferdinand and his wife in Sarajevo on June 28, 1914. Threats and ultimatums were followed by mobilizations, and World War I broke out during the first week of August, with the German, Austro-Hungarian, and Ottoman Empires facing Serbia, the British Empire, the Russian Empire, France, Belgium, and Luxembourg. Italy did not join its Triple Alliance partners, and instead later joined the Entente. Other countries, such as Greece, Bulgaria, and Romania, would also be drawn into the conflict.

On August 6, 1914, Wilson's wife, Ellen, passed away in the White House, and the president became despondent, a situation that lingered for months, all while Europe was descending into the depths of wholesale slaughter.

On the day of her death, Wilson silenced Admiral Mahan, writing to Secretary of the Navy Joseph Daniels:

The White House,
Washington,

August 6, 1914.

I write to suggest that you request and advise all officers of the Service, whether active or retired, to refrain from public comment of any kind upon the military or political situation on the other side of the water. I would be obliged if you would let them know that the request and advice comes from me. It seems to me highly unwise and improper that officers of the Navy and Army of the United States should make any public utterances to which any color of political or military criticism can be given where other nations are involved.

Cordially and faithfully yours,
Woodrow Wilson

Four months later, the admiral was dead, and his brother, Col. Frederick Mahan, wrote from Paris in May 1915 to a friend in New York: "There is no doubt in the minds of our family that the President's 'muzzling order' forbidding officers in the Army or Navy to write anything in connection with the war hastened greatly his death, because—so my sister writes me—he chafed much at not being able to call the attention of our people to the **great danger of being unprepared** [boldface by author]."

Woodrow Wilson may have refused to build up the nation's armed forces, but a preparedness movement was afoot among others, including Franklin Roosevelt, newly appointed assistant secretary of the Navy, the same position held by his cousin Theodore at the outbreak of the Spanish-American War. Both Roosevelts were avid readers of Mahan's works and frequently consulted with the admiral. However, other factors were at play. The United States had flirted with imperialism in 1898, only to recoil from the idea. Simultaneously, the Women's suffrage movement was gaining momentum, and many of its adherents were also advocating prohibition and pacifism. Meanwhile, millions of German-Americans and Irish-Americans were openly supporting Germany. All this had a dampening effect on military spending.

In 1916, Wilson was barely able to eke out a reelection victory with the help of surrogates who captured the American mood with a phrase Wilson never said, but never refuted: "He kept us out of the war." With such a prevailing sentiment dominating the public psyche, a major defense buildup would have been difficult to finesse, unless, of course, it was deemed more important than reelection. Wilson had other issues on his mind. Like Republican Theodore Roosevelt, Democrat Wilson was a progressive. He had already achieved success in that arena with programs such as establishment of the Federal Reserve to manage the nation's monetary policy, a groundbreaking accomplishment that would forever change the US economy. He believed he could do more, if only time and neutrality allowed.

So, unlike John Adams, who dealt with the British and French contest for domination of the seas by conducting the Quasi War with France, Wilson initially ignored the threat to American shipping posed by the British and German blockades. He even accepted the loss of American lives, most tragically the 128 Americans who went down with the *Lusitania* in 1915, sunk by German torpedoes in that country's unrestricted submarine warfare.

Germany stopped the practice for a time, but when it was resumed and Germany was simultaneously caught trying to entice Mexico into hostilities with the United States, as revealed in the British-intercepted Zimmerman Telegram, war was declared on April 6, 1917. Congress passed the Selective Service Act on May 18, drafting men for the US military buildup several years late. Gen. Erich Ludendorff, by then the true power in Germany, was unconcerned, looking upon "the almost non-existent American Army with derision." It would take more than a year for US forces to be trained, transported, and brought into the fight in any meaningful way.

Meanwhile, as in the War of 1812, Russia played a crucial role, this time by signing an armistice with Germany after Lenin's Bolsheviks gained the reins of power there in 1917. With Russia out of the war, massive numbers of German troops were transferred from the Eastern Front to the Western Front in 1918 while American troop transport ships were doing likewise from the opposite direction, finally providing 250,000 soldiers a month. Germany launched the Second Battle of the Marne and was on the verge of taking Paris, when the offensive finally stopped short, Ludendorff admitting that Americans "became the deciding factor in the war."

It had been a near thing. Germany came close to incorporating Europe, including Britain, into the German Empire, which could only have reverberated across the Atlantic in unknown ways, all due to America's unpreparedness, Wilson's unpreparedness.

This marked the United States' true entrance on the world stage and the beginning of the end for the nation's adherence to the warnings of George Washington and Thomas Jefferson, respectively: "It is our true policy to steer clear of permanent alliance with any portion of the foreign world" and "Peace, commerce, and honest friendship with all nations—entangling alliances with none." Isolationism would reappear after the war, and once again have a dampening effect on military preparedness, but the next war and modern science would finally convince most Americans that the days of wooden ships and wide seas were over.

FRANKLIN DELANO ROOSEVELT—WORLD WAR II
1933–1945

Born/Died: 1882 Hyde Park, NY–1945 Warm Springs, GA
Education: Harvard University, Columbia Law School (did not graduate)
Occupation: Lawyer, professional politician
Political Party: Democratic
Government Service: Governor (NY) 1929–1932, Assistant Secretary of the Navy 1913–1920, State Senator (NY) 1911–1913
Military Service: None

President Franklin Delano Roosevelt meeting with Soviet Premier Joseph Stalin
and British Prime Minister Winston Churchill in Tehran, 1943
LIBRARY OF CONGRESS

Preceded by: Herbert Hoover (one of America's most admired men due
to his Belgian relief efforts during World War I; turns 1929 Stock Market
Crash into the Great Depression by raising income taxes and passing the
Smoot-Hawley Tariff; defense spending is lowered while Germans rearm)

Ever since the days of Andrew Jackson, presidential candidates generally
identified themselves with the common man. Aristocratic William Henry
Harrison ran as a hard-cider, log-cabin candidate, defeating Martin Van
Buren, whose detail to dress conveyed the opposite impression. Even
Franklin Roosevelt's cousin Theodore joined cowboys in the West and
later recruited them as Rough Riders in the Spanish-American War to
blur the patina of his privileged upbringing. FDR made no such attempt.
He was an unabashed aristocrat, from upturned cigarette and cigarette

holder to regal, initials-only signature and Ivy League accent. While most of his predecessors honed man-of-the people personas, FDR was more akin to the Marquis de Lafayette offering his services to the American and French Revolutions. A true practitioner of noblesse oblige, FDR could not identify with the masses. He could and did care for them and, for countrymen suffering from the worst economic crisis in the nation's history, that seemed to suffice for a start.

Polio had made him generally wheelchair-bound. The public did not see this. They only saw him sitting or standing, not realizing braces were propping him up. The president did not play on this one feature of his being that could have gained the sympathy of the electorate. Quite the contrary, he projected a confident, jaunty, even cocky demeanor. In contrast to his dour predecessor, FDR was a cockeyed optimist, perhaps a model for a number from the 1949 Rodgers and Hammerstein musical, *South Pacific*. In 1932, though, FDR had his own theme song: "Happy Days Are Here Again." He also had his themes: a New Deal, which was unclear, and an end to Prohibition, which was both clear and compelling. However, in actual campaign rhetoric, he sounded more like Herbert Hoover than Hoover.

Hoover's budgets had run up deficits, not because he believed in deficit spending, but because the more he cut the budget, the more the economy faltered, which he countered with higher tax rates, all of which led to lower and lower tax revenues. Roosevelt decried these deficits and proposed a balanced budget himself, claiming, "Let us stop borrowing to meet continuing deficits" and "too often in recent history, liberal governments have been wrecked on the rocks of loose fiscal policy." It passed the House with Republican support, then stalled in the Senate under the threat of a Democratic filibuster, which he broke with political astuteness: Prohibition was still the law of the land, so the new president quickly asked Congress to pass a law allowing for the sale of beer and light wines. The ploy worked. The Senate passed the budget to make way for passage of the Beer and Wine Revenue Act. The politics were brilliant; the budget was not. Like Hoover and his budgets, FDR was ignoring John Maynard Keynes's deficit-spending advice (see Chapter 8, Hoover).

Roosevelt was not a farmer, banker, businessman, labor leader, or economist, yet with the country in the throes of the Great Depression, these were the front-burner professions demanding his attention, which he addressed without regard to ideology. He was not a wild-eyed socialist invoking the nanny state. In fact, he was accused during his first year in office of being a fascist when his National Recovery Administration (NRA) attempted to impose a state-controlled economy upon the country. On the one hand, the NRA encouraged collective bargaining and an end to child labor, while also establishing "codes" that allowed more than 550 industries to establish collective pricing, better known today as price fixing. In the end, with wages stagnating, consumer prices rising, and raw material prices rising even more, no one was happy, and within a year the US Supreme Court struck down the NRA as unconstitutional. There were few tears at its demise.

The NRA came out of FDR's famous first Hundred Days (actually the first hundred days after Congress convened), that whirlwind period when his Brain Trust of people from divergent political and economic persuasions experimented with methods to end the financial crisis. Without an ideological underpinning or attachment to constitutional restraints, the program lacked both cohesion and foundation. He called it the New Deal, though instead of a single program, it was an amalgam of unconnected programs. There was a positive psychological effect because the public realized the new president was at least open to a wide array of possible solutions. His Brain Trust was brainstorming, and as with most such sessions, there were an abundance of ideas, some good, some bad. What was unusual in the Hundred Days was that in the urgency of the times, FDR rushed fifteen major bills through an initially compliant Congress before the brainstorming had been given sufficient time to analyze and debate and cull the good from the bad. This and the absence of a philosophical grounding created conflicting initiatives. Nowhere was this more apparent than in his first budget.

His Brain Trust busted the budget with programs to help homeowners (Home Owners' Loan Act), farmers (Farm Credit Administration), railroads (Emergency Railroad Transportation Act), and the ten million unemployed (Federal Emergency Relief Act). Some of the financial shortfall was met through defense cuts (see chart below), this when Germany's newly elected Chancellor Adolf Hitler was unabashedly remilitarizing in defiance of the World War I Versailles Treaty, and the Japanese were overrunning Manchuria. At least Roosevelt, this former assistant secretary of the Navy, believing that branch of the service to be the bulwark of the nation's two-ocean moat defense, presciently authorized the building of thirty-two ships, including aircraft carriers *Yorktown* and *Enterprise*, vessels that would supplant battleships as the primary capital ships in the coming war. Indeed, these were two of the three carriers that narrowly tipped the balance in the 1942 Battle of Midway, the turning-point in the Pacific.

Meanwhile, the Army and the Army Air Corps (predecessor of the Air Force) languished. Was this because as a former assistant secretary of the Navy and disciple of Admiral Mahan's theories of naval superiority he convinced himself that ground forces were secondary, even irrelevant? Had this advocate of preparedness in the Wilson Administration learned the wrong lesson from World War I? Had he become an isolationist who thought only in defensive terms of fleets and oceans to protect the nation rather than expeditionary armies to protect our allies? The answers to these questions do not matter. What Roosevelt thought does not matter. What matters is what he did, or in the case of military preparedness, what he did not do. The phrase of the era was "Fortress America," a defensive mind-set reminiscent of a moat and drawbridge mentality. In line with this, he virtually turned the US Army into a cadre, a stand-by skeleton force capable of training large numbers of draftees if the need arose. It was a deeply flawed concept as Madison discovered in the War of 1812 and Wilson discovered in World War I.

Armies are not created overnight. As with any organization, military efficiency is rooted in skilled, motivated management from sergeants to generals and in well-trained, well-equipped enlisted personnel. The US Army of the 1930s was not such an organization. Promotion was so slow that middle-aged officers were captains and majors instead of colonels and generals, and compensation was commensurate. In 1935, forty-five-year-old Dwight D. Eisenhower and forty-two-year-old Omar Bradley were majors, and fifty-year-old George S. Patton had only been promoted from major to lieutenant colonel the year before. All three would become key generals in the coming war. Much of the equipment was obsolete and in short supply. Underfunded, technology lagged. Richard Winslip wrote in *American Military History: The United States Army in a Global Era, 1917–2003*: "Consequently, Army tanks would not compare favorably in firepower, one on one, to World War II German . . . models."

In 1935, Congress authorized an enlisted force of 165,000 men, of whom fifty thousand were assigned to coastal artillery units. By the end of World War II in 1945, the number would grow to 8,267,958 Army personnel and to a total of 12,209,238 in all branches.

According to Keynes, Roosevelt had not comprehended his economic advice, even as the president saw it put into practice by Germany, Italy, and Japan, where deficit spending was creating large, modern military organizations. All the while in America, people scrounging in garbage cans could not understand why the government was paying farmers to plow under crops and slaughter livestock while they were going hungry. The NRA was creating hardship instead of relief, and FDR's balanced budget brought deflation in a deflationary period. Then, 1937 brought another major downturn before 1939 and the start of World War II in Europe spurred exports.

The president was learning from his first year, and his successes began to multiply throughout the 1930s. The Glass-Steagall Act passed in 1933 forbade banks from speculating in the stock market (the overturning of which in the Clinton Administration was a major factor leading to the Great Recession of 2008). The act also created the Federal Deposit Insurance Corporation (FDIC), which has remained intact as bank depositors' major safety net. Securities were regulated, and Joe Kennedy, a market speculator and father of a future president, was selected to head the new Securities and Exchange Commission, with Roosevelt commenting, "Set a thief to catch a thief." The Tennessee Valley Authority brought electric power and economic relief to a broad swath of states. Within two years, Social Security was enacted to lift the elderly out of poverty.

FDR entered office at one of the critical moments in American history. Fascism and communism were on the rise abroad, and the Great Depression was eroding confidence in both the American political and economic systems at home. He started off with a great deal of activity, promising much, delivering little, and the bad times persisted. He did have a willingness to learn, and the public elected him four times with the expectation that he would eventually get it right, and so he did. After a decade of suffering, the massive Keynesian budget deficits of World War II finally restored prosperity.

Never truly neutral, Roosevelt continually edged the nation toward a war he knew must be won, completely concurring with British Prime Minister Winston Churchill, who addressed Parliament following the British evacuation from Dunkirk in June 1940:

> *Hitler knows that he will have to break us in this Island or lose the war. If we can stand up to him, all Europe may be free and the life of the world may move forward into broad, sunlit uplands. But if we fail, then the whole world, including the United States, including all that we have known and cared for, will sink into the abyss of a new Dark Age made more sinister, and perhaps more protracted, by the lights of perverted science. Let us therefore brace ourselves to our duties, and so bear ourselves that if the British Empire and its Commonwealth last for a thousand years, men will still say, "This was their finest hour."*

Serving from 1933 to 1945, no president was given a longer time to get it right. His initial steps were misplaced. He cut when he should have spent, and his famous Hundred Days lacked a cohesive philosophical basis. Unlike Churchill, who throughout much of the 1930s warned about German rearmament, but did not take his country's helm until 1940, Roosevelt largely ignored the growing European crisis. This came in part from domestic concerns about the economy and in part from the political reality of the nation's strong isolationism. In fact, had Roosevelt not been reelected in 1936, he would have been remembered for a few programs such as Social Security, though more negatively as the man who was unable to take the country out of the Great Depression, which actually worsened in 1937. Unlike Churchill, Roosevelt would have been blamed for the nation's lack of military preparedness. However, he was reelected, and the Roosevelt of 1937–1945 was quite different from the man who took office in 1933. In time he became the right man for the job.

Blame Keynes—US vs. German Military Spending 1932–1945
(in billions of US$)

Year	US	Germany	Comments
1929			Hoover becomes president; stock market crashes
1930			Great Depression begins
1931			
1932	$.702	$.250	US income taxes dramatically increased
1933	$.621	$.290	FDR succeeds Hoover; Hitler comes to power
1934	$.541	$.292	
1935	$.728	$2.415	
1936	$.916	$4.352	
1937	$.968	$4.704	
1938	$1.021	$6.908	
1939	$1.294	$12.048	World War II commences in Europe
1940	$1.567	$16.550	
1941	$5.875	$24.180	Hitler invades USSR; US enters World War II
1942	$22.633	$31.120	
1943	$60.882	$36.590	
1944	$74.670	$44.500	
1945	$80.616	$25.780	World War II ends

SOURCES: US DEPARTMENT OF COMMERCE, BUREAU OF THE CENSUS, *HISTORICAL STATISTICS OF THE UNITED STATES, COLONIAL TIMES TO 1970*, PART 2; CHARLES MAIER, *THE ECONOMICS OF FASCISM AND NAZISM: IN SEARCH OF STABILITY* (CAMBRIDGE: CAMBRIDGE UNIVERSITY PRESS, 1987)

HARRY S.* TRUMAN—THE BOMB AND JAPAN; KOREA AND CHINA 1945–1953

Born/Died: 1884 Lamar, MO–1972 Kansas City, MO
Education: Spalding's Commercial College (withdrew), University of Kansas City School of Law (withdrew)
Occupation: Farmer, small businessman
Political Party: Democratic
Government Service: Vice President 1945, Senator (MO) 1935–1945, Judge (Jackson County, MO) 1922–1924, 1926–1933, Director Federal Re-Employment (MO) 1933–1935
Military Service: Colonel; Reserves, World War I, National Guard 1905–1911
Preceded by: Franklin D. Roosevelt (New Deal programs—including Social Security and the SEC—contend with the Great Depression; Navy built up; Army languishes; Pearl Harbor attack brings United States into World War II; massive deficit military spending ends Depression; Manhattan Project builds atomic bomb)

Much was expected of Harry S. Truman, more than had ever been expected of a freshman president except for John Kennedy in the Cuban Missile Crisis. During the first month, he would oversee the defeat of Germany. In the following three months, he would be confronted with the decision to use or not use the atomic bomb against Japan. And from the beginning to the end of his presidency, he would be compelled to contend with Soviet expansion. When he agreed to be FDR's running mate, the president's health was obviously precarious. Even so, Truman was stunned when the presidency fell to him. Roosevelt, apparently in mortal denial, made no attempt to prepare his new vice president, unconscionably keeping him ignorant of the secret Manhattan Project even though atomic bomb development was nearing success. But Roosevelt

---

* "S." does not represent a name; it is used in accordance with the Truman Library usage.

President Harry S. Truman meeting with British Prime Minister Clement Attlee and Soviet Premier Joseph Stalin in Potsdam, July 1945
LIBRARY OF CONGRESS

was mortal, and Truman was sworn in on April 12, 1945, whereupon he immediately allowed himself to become burdened with paperwork, reading and answering a mountain of memos that grew faster than he could absorb or handle them. It was his presidency writ small.

Truman was the only president since Grover Cleveland to lack a college education. In fact, he was widely considered a political hack, a product of the Kansas City, Missouri, Pendergast Machine that propelled him into a Senate-seat victory in 1934. Once there, free from machine dictates, he made a name for himself with the Truman Committee, saving the nation billions of defense dollars during World War II. Yet he was utterly unprepared for the highest office, and no president ever received less time to learn.

Truman seemed to be in awe of both the job and of high-ranking military men, and this led to a history-changing mistake. Just before his death, FDR had returned from the Yalta Conference with the Soviet Union's Josef Stalin and Britain's Winston Churchill, but the agreement concluded there did not last the trip home. On April 18, Churchill wired

Truman a warning: The Soviets were already violating its terms, installing communist governments in countries overrun by their armies in Eastern Europe. He urged Truman to also ignore the agreement's provisions and allow the British, Free French, and American armies to proceed as far as Berlin—not a difficult task since German troops much preferred surrendering to them than to the Russians. The warning was reinforced by US Ambassador to the Soviet Union Averell Harriman, who flew to Washington, sounding the alarm of "a barbarian invasion of Europe."

All this led to a stern presidential meeting with Soviet Foreign Minister Vyacheslav Molotov. Ignoring decorum and the Russian's surprise, the president bluntly took him to task, ending with: "Carry out your agreements and you won't get talked to like that." It was a hollow demand. The new president understood the threat, but ignored the solution. His military chiefs and experts said the war in Europe would last another six months (primarily due to belief in the fictional National Redoubt Germany had built and manned in the Alps), and the war with Japan would go on for another year. Further, Truman's highest-ranking military advisor, Fleet Adm. William D. Leahy, discounted and ridiculed the Manhattan Project as "the biggest fool thing we have ever done. The bomb will never go off, and I speak as an expert in explosives."

In the end, Truman relegated the critical geopolitical decision to Gen. Dwight D. Eisenhower, commander of the European Theater of Operations (ETO). In 1944, Chief of Staff of the Army Gen. George C. Marshall (who would become Truman's secretary of State) had issued Eisenhower his orders on the eve of the June 6 D-Day landings: "You will enter the continent of Europe and, in conjunction with the other United Nations [a reference to the World War II alliance, not to the later UN], undertake operations aimed at the heart of Germany and the destruction of her armed forces." A broad bold order in theory, it came up short in practice. On April 19, 1945, Eisenhower responded, "Berlin itself is no longer a particularly important objective," and he halted his advance at the Elbe River when both Berlin and Prague were within his reach, thus ensuring the Soviet occupation and communization of East Germany and Czechoslovakia, events that would help create or at least prolong the coming Cold War. Half the continent of Europe would not be free. This was Truman's first big mistake. Eisenhower disagreed, claiming a clear demarcation line such as the Elbe was necessary to avoid unintentional military confrontations with the Soviet armies closing in from the east. In the final analysis, he did agree it was a political decision—in other words, Truman's decision.

Germany surrendered not in six months, but in less than one month, on May 8, 1945.

What followed in July was even more controversial. Truman met with Stalin, Churchill, and Churchill's successor, Clement Atlee, just outside Berlin in Potsdam. While there, the word "Trinity" was cabled to Truman indicating success of the first nuclear test at Alamogordo, New Mexico. The president approached Stalin with the news, only to find him unsurprised, and apparently unconcerned. Stalin calmly said he hoped America would use the bomb. It turned out Stalin's spies had kept tabs on the "Project" long before Truman was ever in the loop.

By August 1945, Japan's navy was sunk, its air force destroyed, and US submarines were successfully imposing a strangling blockade, cutting off critical oil and food for the island nation. The only choice left was to sue for peace, and Japan had attempted to do so with the Soviet Union as mediator. Stalin had other ideas, and the overtures were not passed on to the Americans, although codebreakers were already keeping Truman in the loop. Instead, having agreed to declare war on Japan and open a second front there once Germany was defeated, vulture-like, Stalin loosed his armies upon the already-defeated nation. As in Eastern Europe, Stalin's eye was turned toward territorial gain and the spread of communist ideology.

Truman was then faced with one of the most critical decisions in human history: Should the United States use the most destructive weapon ever devised against the Japanese? If so, against what targets? Andrew J. Rotter wrote in *Hiroshima: The World's Bomb*, "A kind of bureaucratic momentum impelled the bomb forward . . . It would have taken a president far more confident, far less in awe of his office and his predecessor, to reflect on the matter of whether the atomic bomb should be used. . . [because] ethical erosion had long collapsed the once-narrow ledge that had prevented men from plunging into the abyss of heinous conduct during war."

Advice descended upon the president from those few people who knew the secret. Drs. Leo Szilard and Albert Einstein had proposed the Manhattan Project to FDR. Now, Szilard and fifty-eight other scientists petitioned Truman, but he did not receive the document until he returned from Potsdam after the bombs had been dropped.

A PETITION TO THE PRESIDENT OF THE UNITED STATES

Discoveries of which the people of the United States are not aware may affect the welfare of this nation in the near future. The liberation of atomic power which has been achieved places atomic bombs in the hands of the Army. It places in your hands, as Commander-in-Chief, the fateful decision whether or not to sanction the use of such bombs in the present phase of the war against Japan.

We, the undersigned scientists, have been working in the field of atomic power for a number of years. Until recently we have had to reckon with the possibility that the United States might be attacked by atomic bombs during this war and that her only defense might lie in a counterattack by the same means. Today with this danger averted we feel impelled to say what follows:

The war has to be brought speedily to a successful conclusion and the destruction of Japanese cities by means of atomic bombs may very well be an effective method of warfare. We feel, however, that such an attack on Japan could not be justified in the present circumstances. We believe that the United States ought not to resort to the use of atomic bombs in the present phase of the war, at least not unless the terms which will be imposed upon Japan after the war are publicly announced and subsequently Japan is given an opportunity to surrender.

If such public announcement gave assurance to the Japanese that they could look forward to a life devoted to peaceful pursuits in their homeland and if Japan still refused to surrender, our nation would then be faced with a situation which might require a re-examination of her position with respect to the use of atomic bombs in the war.

Atomic bombs are primarily a means for the ruthless annihilation of cities. Once they were introduced as an instrument of war it would be difficult to resist for long the temptation of putting them to such use.

The last few years show a marked tendency toward increasing ruthlessness. At present our Air Forces, striking at the Japanese cities, are using the same methods of warfare which were condemned by American public opinion only a few years ago when applied by the Germans to the cities of England. Our use of atomic bombs in this war would carry the world a long way further on this path of ruthlessness.

Atomic power will provide the nations with new means of destruction. The atomic bombs at our disposal represent only the first step in this direction and there is almost no limit to the destructive power which will become available in the course of this development. Thus a nation which sets the precedent of using these newly liberated forces of nature for purposes of destruction may have to bear the responsibility of opening the door to an era of devastation on an unimaginable scale.

In view of the foregoing, we, the undersigned, respectfully petition that you exercise your power as Commander-in-Chief to rule that the United States shall not, in the present phase of the war, resort to the use of atomic bombs.

Scientists from the Manhattan Project led by project head Dr. J. Robert Oppenheimer weighed in:

Recommendations on the Immediate Use of Nuclear Weapons, by the Scientific Panel of the Interim Committee on Nuclear Power, June 16, 1945.

The opinions of our scientific colleagues on the initial use of these weapons are not unanimous: they range from the proposal of a purely technical demonstration to that of the military application best designed to induce surrender. Those who advocate a purely technical demonstration would wish to outlaw the use of atomic weapons, and have feared that if we use the weapons now our position in future negotiations will be prejudiced. Others emphasize the opportunity of saving American lives by immediate military use, and believe that such use will improve the international prospects, in that they are more concerned with the prevention of war than with the elimination of this specific weapon. We find ourselves closer to these latter views;

we can propose no technical demonstration likely to bring an end to the war; we see no acceptable alternative to direct military use.

Adm. William D. Leahy, the highest-ranking officer, who served in a position equivalent to today's Chairman of the Joint Chiefs of Staff, later wrote:

Once it had been tested, President Truman faced the decision as to whether to use it. He did not like the idea, but he was persuaded that it would shorten the war against Japan and save American lives. It is my opinion that the use of this barbarous weapon at Hiroshima and Nagasaki was of no material assistance in our war against Japan. The Japanese were already defeated and ready to surrender because of the effective sea blockade and the successful bombing with conventional weapons. . . . My own feeling was that in being the first to use it, we had adopted an ethical standard common to the barbarians of the Dark Ages. I was not taught to make wars in that fashion, and that wars cannot be won by destroying women and children.

Amid the debate about necessity, use, and targets was the ongoing issue of morality and even bigotry. Japanese racial epithets were common in a way never employed against the Germans, and this led to deeply ingrained hatred. Whatever the motivation or reason, Truman authorized the use of atomic bombs against two civilian centers, Hiroshima and Nagasaki. It was the culmination of the "total war" and "strategic bombing" concepts, euphemisms for massive attacks against civilian populations.

The bombs were dropped on August 6 and 9, 1945, to utterly devastating effect. In an instant, eighty thousand people were killed in Hiroshima and forty thousand in Nagasaki, with more dying later from the effects of wounds and radiation. Clearly, this same slaughter would never have been inflicted by ground force personnel, most of whom would never have carried out an unlawful order calling for the wholesale killing of noncombatant men, women, children, and babies.

With the deed done, the most revealing communication came from Truman himself:

The White House

Washington
August 11, 1945

My Dear Mr. Cavert:
I appreciated very much your telegram of August ninth.
    Nobody is more disturbed over the use of atomic bombs than I am but I was greatly disturbed over the unwarranted attack by the Japanese on Pearl Harbor and their murder of our prisoners of war. The only language they seem to understand is the one we have been using to bombard them.
    When you have to deal with a beast you have to treat him as a beast. It is most regrettable but nevertheless true.

Sincerely yours,

HARRY S. TRUMAN

Truman was prone to hyperbole, and it is difficult to comprehend a description of old men, women, and children as "beasts." Of course, he was referring to Japanese soldiers and politicians, and lamenting the loss of "kids." He did halt the planned August 17 attack. Very few soldiers had died at Hiroshima and Nagasaki; it had been nothing less than the wholesale slaughter of civilians.

Would he have done so later, once he had learned the intricacies and awesome responsibilities of the presidency? In fact, when Chinese communist forces were overrunning US-led UN troops in Korea five years later and Gen. Douglas MacArthur pleaded for nuclear intervention, Truman refused, perhaps because the Soviet Union, China's ally, then had the bomb; more likely because he was haunted by the ghosts of Hiroshima and Nagasaki.

In 1963, two years after leaving the presidency, Dwight D. Eisenhower succinctly said the obvious: "It wasn't necessary to hit them with that awful thing." This was consistent with his 1945 dissent, when he "rather forcefully" told Secretary of War Henry Stimson it was "completely unnecessary" and would be "shocking [to] world opinion" to use the bomb when Japan was already defeated and seeking peace.

This was Truman's second big—very big—first-year mistake. Another was on the way.

Within a year of becoming president in 1945, Truman, at the behest of Congress and the public, virtually demobilized the nation's armed forces despite a growing communist threat. In 1948, Gen. Omar Bradley, replacing General Eisenhower as Chief of Staff of the Army, was stunned: "It seemed to me there was a fundamental dichotomy in the containment policy. . . . Getting tough with the Russians . . . clearly demanded a concurrent buildup of our conventional military forces, especially the U.S. Army. It may seem hard to believe, but exactly the opposite was taking place. Truman had placed a firm ceiling on military spending. . . . Actually, the Army in 1948 could not fight its way out of a paper bag."

It was an invitation for aggression, and the communists accommodated. In 1950, with Soviet and Chinese support, North Korea invaded South Korea and nearly overran the understrength US forces rushed there. Truman's freshman mistakes of '45 created the fiasco of '50. Mistake number three.

On the other hand, once his presidential bearings were gained, good and great deeds followed. The Truman Doctrine saved Greece and began the policy of containment, virtually surrounding the USSR with US allies and alliances, foremost being the North Atlantic Treaty Organization (NATO), while the Marshall Plan, which he generously allowed to be named for his secretary of State George C. Marshall, saved friends and former foes alike in Europe. A similar plan did likewise for Japan, creating in the process peace, prosperity, and security for six decades and counting.

Harry Truman was a complex man. Struggling with biases, inadequate education, and limited experience, he was thrust onto a global and scientific stage unlike any other president in history. That he stumbled was not surprising. The American political system of the times vaulted him to an initially untenable height. That he overcame these handicaps was surprising.

Are Governorships the Best Preparation for the Presidency?

In theory, governors should make the best presidents because governorships require leadership, political acumen, managerial skill, and especially governmental budgeting prowess. It is the last of these where trouble looms. State budgets and federal budgets are different animals, and presidents who failed to recognize this ran into trouble. Unlike the federal government, states cannot print money, nor do they have the same access to tax revenue such as assessing tariffs on foreign goods. Further, states have a limited ability to borrow money due to varying degrees of credit-worthiness and economies that lack the depth and diversification of the national economy. Neither are states allowed to conduct foreign affairs or deploy armed forces outside of their states, which means their experience in these areas is generally inferior to that of US secretaries of State or War (later Defense).

However, when compared to individuals whose experience is limited to non-managerial congressional offices or non-managerial civilian occupations such as small law offices, governors are immeasurably better qualified for the presidency. The names of governors who reached the White House include many of the most admired presidents. The four who were appointed as military or territorial governors, Andrew Jackson, William Henry Harrison, Andrew Johnson, and William Howard Taft, are in a category apart and can only be judged by their particular circumstances. The others may be divided by century. Governors who became nineteenth-century presidents included Thomas Jefferson, James Monroe, John Tyler, James K. Polk, Rutherford B. Hayes, and Grover Cleveland. Governors who served as twentieth-century presidents included William McKinley, Theodore Roosevelt, Woodrow Wilson, Calvin Coolidge, Franklin Roosevelt, Jimmy Carter, Ronald Reagan, William Clinton, and George W. Bush.

A majority of the former governors are regarded as successful presidents, though every one of them had to undergo a foreign policy and federal budget learning curve. In answer to the question, "Are governorships the best preparation for the presidency?" the answer is, in general, yes.

THE FRESHMAN PRESIDENT'S
EPILOGUE

THE WORLD'S MOST EXCLUSIVE
UNIVERSITY

In modern times, all newly elected presidents and vice presidents receive briefings before taking office. It is all part of the unofficial curriculum of the unofficial White House University, although it has never been near enough. They dive into briefing papers, receive one-on-one input, and delegate learning to various subordinates. Some have insatiable appetites for learning; others are less hungry. Either way, the pathway from election to the oath of office has been inconsistent, which is why the freshman year has always been the only true educational forum for new presidents.

This patchwork presidential education needs a conversion from pre-office briefings and first-year, on-the-job training into an actual—albeit, voluntary—institution of higher learning for two: newly elected presidents and vice presidents. Between the November election and January inauguration, that pseudo-interregnum period when the outgoing president is a lame duck—or, in some cases, inappropriately active with last-minute appointments, pardons, and other mischief—presidents-elect are exceptionally busy forming Cabinets and engaging in numerous meetings, sometimes with prospective appointees or experts or even with foreign leaders, but nothing could be more important than preparing for an assumption of responsibility and power like no other in the world.

Prior to taking office, these new executives should have at hand succinct, organized, non-public presentations from experts in every pertinent field, especially economics and military strategy/history. Public opinion and public pressure would be the incentive for attendance, even for ego-charged politicians who have reached the pinnacle of the political ladder.

There is another, often overlooked font of knowledge. Former presidents are a squandered national resource. They should be formally engaged in the briefing of new presidents and also tapped for continued public service up to age eighty, whether by their choice as permanent voting members of the US Senate—where they would provide an informed counterweight to partisanship and continue to be addressed as president—or as permanent members of a presidential advisory council—a Presidential Brain Trust as it were—that regularly meets, is regularly briefed on national security and other issues, and, in turn, offers the sitting president the benefit of their deliberations.

The path from freshman president to former president is the most exclusive, responsibility-laden, and currently squandered course in America.

APPENDIX A

Details for Income Tax as a Percentage of Gross Income 1913–2013

(Incomes for a family of four adjusted for inflation to 2013 dollars)

	$1,000,000 Gross	Taxable Income	Tax Rate	OASDIHI	TAX % of Gross	$500,000 Gross	Taxable Income	Tax Rate	OASDIHI	TAX % of Gross
1913	40,000	32,000	2.0%		2%	20,000	16,000	1.0%		1%
1918	60,000	48,000	34.0%		27%	30,000	24,000	22.0%		18%
1925	80,000	64,000	21.0%		17%	40,000	32,000	13.0%		10%
1932	60,000	48,000	29.0%		23%	30,000	24,000	17.0%		14%
1936	60,000	48,000	31.0%		25%	30,000	24,000	21.0%		17%
1944	80,000	64,000	81.0%	60	65%	40,000	32,000	65.0%	60	52%
1955	120,000	96,000	72.0%	168	58%	60,000	48,000	59.0%	168	47%
1965	140,000	112,000	62.0%	348	50%	70,000	56,000	53.0%	348	43%
1972	180,000	144,000	66.0%	936	53%	90,000	72,000	55.0%	936	45%
1975	230,000	184,000	69.0%	1,650	56%	115,000	92,000	60.0%	1,650	49%
1980	350,000	280,000	70.0%	3,175	57%	175,000	140,000	64.0%	3,175	53%
1988	510,000	408,000	28.0%	6,759	24%	255,000	204,000	28.0%	6,759	25%
1993	620,000	496,000	39.6%	11,057	33%	310,000	248,000	36.0%	11,057	32%
2003	790,000	632,000	35.0%	33,698	32%	395,000	316,000	35.0%	33,698	35%
2013	1,000,000	800,000	39.6%	43,099	35%	500,000	400,000	39.6%	43,099	39%

	$100,000 Gross	Taxable Income	Tax Rate	OASDIHI	TAX % of Gross	$50,000 Gross	Taxable Income	Tax Rate	OASDIHI	TAX % of Gross
1913	4,000	0	1.0%		0%	2,000	0	1.0%		0%
1918	6,000	3,600	6.0%		4%	3,000	600	6.0%		1%
1925	8,000	3,700	1.5%		1%	4,000	0	1.5%		0%
1932	6,000	2,700	4.0%		2%	3,000	0	4.0%		0%
1936	6,000	2,700	4.0%		2%	3,000	0	4.0%		0%
1944	8,000	6,733	33.0%	60	28%	4,000	3,117	25.0%	60	21%
1955	12,000	8,600	26.0%	168	20%	6,000	3,017	20.0%	168	13%
1965	14,000	10,600	22.0%	348	19%	7,000	3,914	17.0%	348	14%
1972	18,000	13,700	25.0%	936	24%	9,000	4,700	19.0%	936	19%
1975	23,000	18,100	28.0%	1,650	28%	11,500	6,600	19.0%	1,346	21%
1980	35,000	27,600	32.0%	3,175	33%	17,500	10,100	18.0%	2,146	21%
1988	51,000	38,200	28.0%	6,759	32%	25,500	12,700	15.0%	3,830	21%
1993	62,000	46,700	28.0%	8,940	33%	31,000	15,700	15.0%	4,743	21%
2003	79,000	57,300	25.0%	12,087	31%	39,500	17,800	15.0%	6,044	20%
2013	100,000	72,200	15.0%	15,300	24%	50,000	22,200	15.0%	7,650	20%

	Std. Deduct. $100,000	Std. Deduct. $50,000	Four Exempt.	OASI	DI	OASIDI Limit	HI	HI Limit	OASDIHI x 2
1913			4,000						
1918			2,400						
1925			4,300						
1932			3,300						
1936			3,300						
1944	767	383	500	1.000%		3,000			2.0%
1955	1,000	583	2,400	2.000%		4,200			4.0%
1965	1,000	686	2,400	3.375%	0.250%	4,800			7.3%
1972	1,300	1,300	3,000	4.050%	0.550%	9,000	0.60%	9,000	10.4%
1975	1,900	1,900	3,000	4.375%	0.575%	14,100	0.90%	14,100	11.7%
1980	3,400	3,400	4,000	4.520%	0.560%	25,900	1.05%	25,900	12.3%
1988	5,000	5,000	7,800	5.530%	0.530%	45,000	1.45%	45,000	15.0%
1993	6,200	6,200	9,100	5.600%	0.600%	57,600	1.45%	135,000	15.3%
2003	9,500	9,500	12,200	5.300%	0.900%	87,000	1.45%	no limit	15.3%
2013	12,200	12,200	15,600	5.300%	0.900%	113,700	1.45%	no limit	15.3%

APPENDIX B

THE ANACONDA PLAN

HEADQUARTERS OF THE ARMY,
Washington, May 3, 1861.

Maj. Gen. GEORGE B. MCCLELLAN,
Commanding Ohio Volunteers, Cincinnati, Ohio:

SIR: I have read and carefully considered your plan for a campaign, and now send you confidentially my own views, supported by certain facts of which you should be advised.

First. It is the design of the Government to raise 25,000 additional regular troops, and 60,000 volunteers for three years. It will be inexpedient either to rely on the three-months' volunteers for extensive operations or to put in their hands the best class of arms we have in store. The term of service would expire by the commencement of a regular campaign, and the arms not lost be returned mostly in a damaged condition. Hence I must strongly urge upon you to confine yourself strictly to the quota of three-months' men called for by the War Department.

Second. We rely greatly on the sure operation of a complete blockade of the Atlantic and Gulf ports soon to commence. In connection with such blockade we propose a powerful movement down the Mississippi to the ocean, with a cordon of posts at proper points, and the capture of Forts Jackson and Saint Philip; the object being to clear out and keep open this great line of communication in connection with the strict blockade of the seaboard, so as to envelop the insurgent States and bring them to terms with less bloodshed than by any other plan. I suppose there will be needed from twelve to twenty steam gunboats, and a sufficient number of steam transports (say forty) to carry all the personnel (say 60,000 men) and material of the expedition; most of the gunboats to be in advance to open the way, and the remainder to follow and protect the rear of the expedition, &c. This army, in which it is not improbable you may be invited to take an important part, should be composed of our best regulars for the advance and of three-years' volunteers, all well officered, and with four months and a half of instruction in camps prior to (say) November 10. In the progress down the river all the enemy's batteries on its banks we of course would turn and capture, leaving a sufficient number of posts with complete garrisons to keep the river open behind the expedition. Finally, it will be necessary that New Orleans should be strongly occupied and securely held until the present difficulties are composed.

Third. A word now as to the greatest obstacle in the way of this plan—the great danger now pressing upon us—the impatience of our patriotic and loyal Union friends. They will urge instant and vigorous action, regardless, I fear, of consequences—that is, unwilling to wait for the slow instruction of (say) twelve or fifteen camps, for the rise of rivers, and the return of frosts to kill the virus of malignant fevers below Memphis. I fear this; but impress right views, on every proper occasion, upon the brave men who are hastening to the support of their Government. Lose no time, while necessary preparations for the great expedition are in progress, in organizing, drilling, and disciplining your three-months' men, many of whom, it is hoped, will be ultimately found enrolled under the call for three-years' volunteers. Should an urgent and immediate occasion arise meantime for their services, they will be the more effective. I commend these views to your consideration, and shall be happy to hear the result.

With great respect, yours, truly,
WINFIELD SCOTT

Union Correspondence, Orders, And Returns Relating To Operations In Maryland, Eastern North Carolina, Pennsylvania, Virginia (Except Southwestern), And West Virginia, From January 1, 1861, To June 30, 1865.—#3 Official Records—SERIES I—VOLUME LI/1 [S# 107]

APPENDIX C

THE LINCOLN-GREELEY LETTER

Executive Mansion,
Washington, August 22, 1862.
Hon. Horace Greeley [editor of the *New York Tribune*]:
Dear Sir.

I have just read yours of the 19th. addressed to myself through the New-York Tribune. If there be in it any statements, or assumptions of fact, which I may know to be erroneous, I do not, now and here, controvert them. If there be in it any inferences which I may believe to be falsely drawn, I do not now and here, argue against them. If there be perceptable in it an impatient and dictatorial tone, I waive it in deference to an old friend, whose heart I have always supposed to be right.

As to the policy I "seem to be pursuing" as you say, I have not meant to leave any one in doubt.

I would save the Union. I would save it the shortest way under the Constitution. The sooner the national authority can be restored; the nearer the Union will be "the Union as it was." If there be those who would not save the Union, unless they could at the same time *save* slavery, I do not agree with them. If there be those who would not save the Union unless they could at the same time *destroy* slavery, I do not agree with them. My paramount object in this struggle *is* to save the Union, and is *not* either to save or to destroy slavery. If I could save the Union without freeing *any* slave I would do it, and if I could save it by freeing *all* the slaves I would do it; and if I could save it by freeing some and leaving others alone I would also do that. What I do about slavery, and the colored race, I do because I believe it helps to save the Union; and what I forbear, I forbear because I do *not* believe it would help to save the Union. I shall do *less* whenever I shall believe what I am doing hurts the cause, and I shall do *more* whenever I shall believe doing more will help the cause. I shall try to correct errors when shown to be errors; and I shall adopt new views so fast as they shall appear to be true views.

I have here stated my purpose according to my view of *official* duty; and I intend no modification of my oft-expressed *personal* wish that all men every where could be free.

Yours,
A. Lincoln.

APPENDIX D

THE NIXON PARDON

By the President of the United States of America

A Proclamation

Richard Nixon became the thirty-seventh President of the United States on January 20, 1969 and was reelected in 1972 for a second term by the electors of forty-nine of the fifty states. His term in office continued until his resignation on August 9, 1974.

Pursuant to resolutions of the House of Representatives, its Committee on the Judiciary conducted an inquiry and investigation on the impeachment of the president extending over more than eight months. The hearings of the Committee and its deliberations, which received wide national publicity over television, radio, and in printed media, resulted in votes adverse to Richard Nixon on recommended Articles of Impeachment.

As a result of certain acts or omissions occurring before his resignation from the Office of President, Richard Nixon has become liable to possible indictment and trial for offenses against the United States. Whether or not he shall be so prosecuted depends on findings of the appropriate grand jury and on the discretion of the authorized prosecutor. Should an indictment ensue, the accused shall then be entitled to a fair trial by an impartial jury, as guaranteed to every individual by the Constitution.

It is believed that a trial of Richard Nixon, if it became necessary, could not fairly begin until a year or more has elapsed. In the meantime, the tranquility to which this nation has been restored by the events of recent weeks could be irreparably lost by the prospects of bringing to trial a former President of the United States. The prospects of such trial will cause prolonged and divisive debate over the propriety of exposing to further punishment and degradation a man who has already paid the unprecedented penalty of relinquishing the highest elective office of the United States.

Now, Therefore, I, Gerald R. Ford, President of the United States, pursuant to the pardon power conferred upon me by Article II, Section 2, of the Constitution, have granted and by these presents do grant a full, free, and absolute pardon unto Richard Nixon for all offenses against the United States which he, Richard Nixon, has committed or may have committed or taken part in during the period from January 20, 1969 through August 9, 1974.

In Witness Whereof, I have hereunto set my hand this eighth day of September, in the year of our Lord nineteen hundred and seventy-four, and of the Independence of the United States of America the one hundred and ninety-ninth.

GERALD R. FORD

ACKNOWLEDGMENTS

I am indebted and grateful to those individuals who directly contributed to this project as well as to those who indirectly contributed throughout years of interaction, most of the latter not realizing the extent or impact of their influence. Life is made of memories, and the images of people fondly remembered are of those who created them.

Senior Editor: Keith Wallman

Literary Agent: Douglas Grad

Research Assistant: Kathryn Cohn

Reviewers: Eleanor Clift, James Locher III, Evan Thomas

Editing: Michael Black, Brian Cohn, Colleen Elkins, Garret Elkins, Alda Finn, Thomas Finn, Elaine Gallagher, Thomas Gallagher, Col. Charles Giasson, USA (Ret.), Phyllis Giasson, Craig Jacobsen, Dave Klein, Rachael Klein, Natalie McKean

Insights and facilitation: Critical Issues Roundtable, Maj. Gen. Alan Salisbury, USA (Ret.) chairman, Jill Schwartzman

Indirect Contributors: Carol Anderson, Lt. Col. Stott Carleton, USA (Ret.), Henry, Carter, H.J., and Kelly Cohn, Scott, Linda, Connor, and Carson Cohn, Col. J. Brian Copley, USA (Ret.), Jan Copley, Col. Jonathan Dodson, USA (Ret.), Kathleen Duval, Linda Easthope, Serena, Graham, and John Elkins, James and Ryan Gallagher, Dr. Anthony Garvey, David Gerard, Michael Hageman, Thomas and Sandy Hageman, Barbara Hanan, Suzanne Jacobsen, Jade, Lt. Gen. Larry Jordan, USA (Ret.), Mary Kennard, Michael and Susan Kennard, Barney and Karen Keep, Sydney and Kenzie Klein, Dr. Thomas Laipply, James, Julie, and Scott McKean, Fred Mihm, Lt. Gen. David Ohle, USA (Ret.), Jay and Maureen Oliverio, Col. LeRoy Outlaw, USA (Ret.), John and Barbara Pattillo, Lt. Col. Gordon Sayre, USA (Ret.), Col. Ann Shaklee, USAF (Ret.), John Slonaker, Linda Smull, Camille Taylor-Sullivan, Judy Thompson, Col. Ralph Tildon, USA (Ret.), Janet Vehring, Elsa Verbyla, Brig. Gen. John Walsh, USA (Ret.).

Brothers-in-Arms: 2nd Platoon B Co. and Recon Platoon E Co., 5th Bn., 7th Regiment, 1st Cavalry Division, Vietnam 1969-70: Sylvester Amey, Al Bruns, James Clark (Hillbilly), Dan Dilts, Robert Dodge, Larry Eaton (Lucky), Eldon Erlenbach, Leo Fiegel, Ricardo Garza, Tony Gutierrez, Marcus Henson, Boyd Hines, David Larson, John (Doug) McInnes, Jim Mitchell, Mike Price, Bill Rowley, Rick Sonnenberg, William Starkey, Jack Thomas, Frank Thurston, Steve Tresemer, as well as those we unfortunately only remember as Arney, Butch, Doc, Hunley, Johnson, and Zeke, and those we remember **In Memoriam:** Captain Barry Mullineaux (company commander), Pvt. Charles Boxler, SP4 Richard Brueck, Sgt. Darrel Burns, Jim Carrel, Rick Colbert (Shorty), Leroy Conners (Pumpkin), SFC Joseph Sanchez, and James Sizemore

In Memoriam:
Annabel Ashley, Brig. Gen. John Eisenhower, 1st Lt. William Ericson II, William and Elizabeth (Buzz) Headlee, Donald and Marilyn Kauffman, 1st Lt. Peter Lantz, John Kennard, Millard and Henrietta Cohn, Ole Johnson, Warren Rogers, Gen. H. Norman Schwarzkopf Jr., G. L. and Louise Shaw, Col. Harry Summers Jr.

ENDNOTES

INTRODUCTION: THE FRESHMAN PRESIDENT

1. "I don't know that anyone . . ." Wayne Meyer, ed., *Clinton on Clinton: A Portrait of the President in His Own Words* (New York: Avon, 1999), 93.

3. "Boys, if you ever pray . . ." Harry Truman to reporters April 13, 1945, Harry S. Truman Library and Museum, Independence, MO.

3. "No man on earth . . ." Evan Thomas, *Ike's Bluff* (New York: Little, Brown and Company, 2012), 261.

3. "Franklin is such poor stuff . . ." "Teddy & Frank," *Time*, September 12, 1932.

3–4. "My movements to the chair of Government . . ." *George Washington Papers* at the Library of Congress, 1741–1799: Series 2 Letterbooks, "George Washington to Henry Knox, April 1, 1789"—Letterbook 22, Image 54 of 361.

4. Like the proverbial . . . Henry Wotton Sr., 1568–1639: *"An ambassador is a man of virtue. . ."* www.quotes.net/quote/19243, accessed January 10, 2015.

4. "A republic, if you can keep it" Dr. James McHenry, *American Historical Review*, vol. 11 (1906): 618.

6. fifty million more . . . S. Knobler, A. Mack, A. Mahmoud, S. Lemon, eds., "1: The Story of Influenza," in *The Threat of Pandemic Influenza: Are We Ready?* (Washington Workshop Summary, DC: 2005), 60–61.

CHAPTER 1: THE MODEL OTHERS FAILED TO FOLLOW

George Washington—Precedents

11. "I will not . . ." Letter, Martha Washington to Mercy Otis Warren, December 26, 1789, in Martha Washington, Item #25, http://marthawashington.us/items/show/25, accessed December 4, 2014.

11. "I walk on . . ." John C. Fitzpatrick, ed., *George Washington Writings*, 39 vols. (Washington, DC: Library of America, 1931–1944), XXXI, 493; John C. Fitzpatrick, ed., *George Washington Diaries*, 4 vols. (Boston and New York: 1925), IV, 128.

12. (derived in part . . . John Locke, *The Second Treatise of Civil Government*, http://faculty.history.wisc.edu/sommerville/367/locke%20decindep.htm, accessed January 23, 2015.

14. Having actively . . ." Woody Holton, "Abigail Adams, Bond Speculator," *William and Mary Quarterly*, 3rd series, 64:821–38, October 2007.

14. "I have thought whether . . ." James C. Taylor et al., eds., "Abigail Adams to Cotton Tufts, 17 January 1790," *The Adams Papers, Adams Family Correspondence*, vol. 9, January 1790–December 1793 (Cambridge, MA: Harvard University Press, 2009), 5–7.

15. *I do not mean however* . . . Dorothy Twohig, Mark A. Mastromarino, and Jack D. Warren, eds., "From George Washington to David Stuart, 15 June 1790," *The Papers of George Washington*, Presidential Series, vol. 5, 16 January 1790–30 June 1790 (Charlottesville: University Press of Virginia, 1996), 523–28.

17. "found himself deficient . . ." Gaillard Hunt, ed., *James Madison Writings*, 9 vols. (New York: 1900–1910), vol. VI, 1060n–1100.

17. "greatest character of the age," Richard Brookhiser, *Founding Father: Rediscovering George Washington* (New York: Free Press, 1996), 103.

18. *His mind was great* . . . Merrill Peterson, ed., *Thomas Jefferson, Writings* (New York: The Library of America, 1984), 1318–21.

CHAPTER 2: WITCH HUNTERS: SEDITION AND MCCARTHYISM

John Adams—Sedition

24. "Mr. Adams is vain, suspicious . . ." Frederick J. Turner, ed., *Correspondence of the French Ministers to the United States, 1791–1797* (Washington, DC: Annual Report of the American Historical Association for the year 1903, vol. II (1904), 1030.

24–25. "As to do nothing. . ." James Morton Smith, ed., *The Republic of Letters: The Correspondence between Thomas Jefferson and James Madison 1776–1826, Vol. Three 1804–1836* (New York: W.W. Norton & Co., 1995), 1029.

25. "write, print, utter or publish . . ." *A Century of Lawmaking for a New Nation: U.S. Congressional Documents and Debates, 1774–1875*, Statutes at Large, 5th Congress, 2nd Session, page 596 of 755, Library of Congress, http://memory .loc.gov/cgi-bin/ampage?collId=llsl&fileName=001/llsl001.db&recNum=719, accessed December 16, 2014.

25–26. "His highness, the President . . ." James C. Alexander, "Off to a Bad Start: John Adams's Tussle over Titles," *Vanderbilt Undergraduate Research Journal*, vol. 4 (2008), abstract.

26. "continued grasp for power . . ." John C. Miller, *Crisis in Freedom: The Alien and Sedition Acts* (New York: Little Brown and Company, 1951), 211–20.

26. "There were two regular . . ." Mary Tyler Peabody Mann, *Life of Horace Mann by His Wife* (Boston: Walker, Fuller, and Co., 1854), 277.

27. "Yet daringly do the vile incendiaries . . ." David McCullough, *John Adams* (New York: Simon & Schuster, 2001), 506.

27. "the blind, bald, crippled, toothless . . ." Miller, *Crisis in Freedom*, 27–29.
27. "guilty of any disloyal practice," Don E. Fehrenbacher, ed., *Abraham Lincoln Speeches and Writings 1859–1865* (New York: Viking Press, 1989), 511–12.
27. "[T]he First Amendment protects the publication . . ." *New York Times v. Sullivan*, The Oyez Project at IIT Chicago–Kent College of Law, www.oyez.org/cases/1960-1969/1963/1963_39, accessed March 11, 2014.
27. "dangerous to the peace and safety . . ." An Act Respecting Alien Enemies, 5th Cong., 2d Sess., in 1 Public Statutes at Large 577–78 (Little, Brown, 1845).

Dwight D. Eisenhower—McCarthyism

29. "Marshall should not be confirmed . . ." Mark Perry, *Partners in Command: George Marshall and Dwight Eisenhower in War and Peace* (New York: Penguin Books, 2007), 394.
31. "Here I have a case in mind. . . ." Dwight D. Eisenhower speech, October 3, 1952, Dwight D. Eisenhower Presidential Library, Museum and Boyhood Home, Abilene, KS.
32. "She gave him solace." Brig. Gen. John D. Eisenhower, Author's Interview, Military History Institute, Carlisle Barracks, PA, 1984.
32. "Good night! There are lots of things . . ." Autograph note, in pencil, written on the verso of an envelope printed "Souvenir from the Garden of Gethsemane," ca. June 1944–May 1945, which was found in Kay Summersby's wallet after her death, creased and wrinkled. Sotheby's.
32. *Their close relationship is quite accurately portrayed* . . . Omar N. Bradley and Clay Blair, *A General's Life* (New York: Simon and Schuster, 1983), 133.
33. *So when I would come down* . . . Neil M. Johnson, "Oral History with General Louis W. Truman, December 7, 1991," Harry S. Truman Library & Museum, 1991.
33. "I have no feelings . . ." James Chace, *Foreign Affairs*, May/June 1997.
34. "Nothing will be so effective . . ." Jeffrey Frank, *Ike and Dick: Portrait of a Strange Political Marriage* (New York: Simon & Schuster, 2013), 74.
34. his favorite film, *High Noon*, was an allegory . . . J. Hoberman, *New York Times*, April 25, 2004.
35. "The only cross I have to bear . . ." Martin Gilbert, *Churchill: A Life* (New York: Henry Holt & Co., 1991), 646.

Table: Well-Known Names from the Hollywood Blacklists
36. Ellen Schrecker, *The Age of McCarthyism: A Brief History with Documents* (New York: Palgrave, 2002); Erik Barnouw, *Tube of Plenty: The Evolution of American Television* (New York: Oxford University Press, 1990).

Chapter 3: The Loners

38. "I think this is the most extraordinary . . ." Gerhard Peters and John T. Woolley, "John F. Kennedy Remarks at a Dinner Honoring Nobel Prize Winners of the Western Hemisphere, April 29, 1962," The American Presidency Project, www.presidency.uc sb.edu/, accessed November 29, 2014.

38. "I hire people who are much smarter . . ." Andrew Farrell, "Ask a Billionaire," *Forbes*, July 15, 2008.

Thomas Jefferson—Louisiana Purchase

39. In *The Prospect Before Us* . . . John Davison Lawson, ed., *American State Trials* (St. Louis: F.H. Thomas Law Book Co., 1918), 837.

42. assume $7 million in American merchantmen claims . . . E. B. Potter, ed., *Sea Power: A Naval History* (Annapolis: Naval Institute Press, 1981), 89.

44. "reduced the army and navy to what is barely necessary." Merrill D. Peterson, *Thomas Jefferson and the New Nation: A Biography* (New York: Oxford University Press, 1970), 702.

44. "immorality personified." Brig. Gen. Vincent J. Esposito and Col. John R. Elting, *A Military History and Atlas of the Napoleonic Wars* (New York: Frederick A. Praeger, 1964), Biographical Sketches.

46. "The day that France takes possession of New Orleans . . ." Dumas Malone, *Jefferson the President: First Term, 1801–1805*, vol. IV (Boston: Little, Brown and Company, 1970), 249–61.

Jimmy Carter—Stagflation

47. "I can't deny . . ." David Cook, *Christian Science Monitor*, November 4, 2005.

48. "the trouble began with Carter . . ." Jules Witcover, *Party of the People* (New York: Random House, 2003), 603.

49. *With the exception of preventing war* . . . Jimmy Carter, *The President's Proposed Energy Policy*, April 18, 1977, *Vital Speeches of the Day*, vol. XXXXIII, no. 14, May 1, 1977, 418–20.

50. *On November 4, 1979, Iranian students* . . . US Department of State, Office of the Historian, https://history.state.gov/departmenthistory/short-history/iraniancrises, accessed July 7, 2015.

52. "I have nothing to offer but blood . . ." Gilbert, *Churchill: A Life*, 646.

52. "It's morning again in America," "Prouder, Stronger, Better," 1984 commercial, *Time*, http://content.time.com/time/specials/packages/article/0,28804,1842516_1842514_1842575,00.html, accessed December 5, 2014.

Chart: Prime Rate 1955–2014

51. Board of Governors of the Federal Reserve, www.federalreserve.gov/bankinforeg/bcreg20131101a1.pdf, accessed January 17, 2015.

Barack Obama—Obamacare

53. "decision-making apparatus . . ." David Ignatius, "Book Review: Leon Panetta's 'Worthy Fights,'" *Washington Post*, October 6, 2014.

53. "Obama has surrounded himself . . ." Todd Purdum, "Team of Mascots," *Vanity Fair*, July 2012.

54. *Thus, in economic policy making* . . . James P. Pfiffner, Professor of Public Policy at George Mason University, *Decision Making in the Obama White House* (College Station: Texas A&M Press, May 12, 2015), http://pfiffner.gmu.edu/files/pdfs/Articles/Obama%20Decision%20Making,%20PSQ.pdf, accessed July 7, 2015.

55. "electronic cash." "What is Quantitative Easing?" *The Economist*, January 14, 2014.

55. "economists have called for 40 years . . ." Jake Tapper, November 14, 2014, CNN, www.cnn.com/2014/11/14/politics/gruber-update-friday-white-house-obamacare, accessed December 6, 2014.

56. "Too often, Mr. [Iraqi Prime Minister Nuri . . ." Ramzy Mardini and Emma Sky, *New York Times*, October 13, 2013.

CHAPTER 4: CONFLICTS THEY MIGHT HAVE PREVENTED, AVOIDED, OR WON: 1812, VIETNAM, 9/11, AFGHANISTAN, AND IRAQ

James Madison—The War of 1812

59. "He is said to have been a master of the small arena." Miller Center, University of Virginia, *American President: A Reference Resource* (Charlottesville: Rector and Visitors of the University of Virginia, 2014), http://millercenter.org/president/madison/essays/biography/9, accessed December 4, 2014.

60. "a Russian [and Austrian] army of 76,000 . . ." George Bourne, *The History of Napoleon Bonaparte: The Emperor of the French and King of Italy* (Baltimore: Warner and Hanna, 1806), 360.

60. "They [Britain] never made . . ." James Morton Smith, ed., *The Republic of Letters: The Correspondence between Thomas Jefferson and James Madison 1776–1826*, vol. 3, 1804–1836 (New York: W.W. Norton & Co., 1995), 1585.

63. Among their demands . . . Witcover, *Party of the People*, 119–20.

63. *Finally, if the Union be destined* . . . "Hartford Convention Resolutions," Connecticut State Library, Historical Notices of Connecticut (Boston: Wells and Lilly, 1815), www.fofweb.com/History/MainPrintPage.asp?iPin=E12150&DataType=AmericanHistory&WinType=Free, accessed December 17, 2014.

64. "The United States of America engage . . ." Yale Law School—Lillian Goldman Law Library—The Avalon Project: Documents in Law, History and Diplomacy, http://avalon.law.yale.edu/19th_century/ghent.asp, accessed December 16, 2014.

Lyndon Baines Johnson—The Vietnam War
67. "Instead of concentrating . . ." Col. Harry G. Summers Jr., *On Strategy: A Critical Analysis of the Vietnam War* (Novato, CA: Presidio Press, 1982), 44.
68. "U.S. forces should have been . . ." Ibid., 119.
68. "You know you never defeated us . . ." Ibid., 1.

George W. Bush—9/11, Afghanistan, and Iraq

Chart: 9/11 Comparative Time Sequence
72–73. Thomas H. Kean and Lee H. Hamilton, *Without Precedent the 9/11 Commission Report* (New York: Vintage Books, 2007), multiple pages.

74. "there's no documentary evidence" Peter Dale Scott, *The Road to 9/11* (Los Angeles: University of California Press, 2007), 227.
74. *If the military had* . . . Kean and Hamilton, *Without Precedent*, 266.

Essay: Is the Vice Presidency the Best Preparation for the Presidency?
76. vice presidential literature . . . *Washington Post*, October 3, 2014.
76. "My country has . . ." "Quotes: US Vice Presidency," *Deseret News*, September 28, 2008.
76. "[It is a] tranquil and unoffending station . . ." Ibid.
76. "Once there were two brothers . . ." Ibid.
76. "[Taking the job] was the worst . . ." Ibid.
76. "Look at all the vice presidents . . ." Ibid.
76. "President Bush gave me . . ." Ibid.

CHAPTER 5: AMERICA'S ORIGINAL SIN: SLAVERY
77. "Given his continued dependence . . ." James Oakes, *Slavery and Freedom: An Interpretation of the Old South* (New York: Alfred A. Knopf, Inc., 1990), 103.
78. "equality in slavery . . ." Alexis de Tocqueville, Henry Reeve, trans., and Jim Manis, ed., *Democracy in America, Volumes One and Two by Alexis de Tocqueville* (Hazelton: Pennsylvania State University Press, 2013), 72.

James Monroe—Missouri Compromise of 1820
83. "The crop of 1824 was 30 million pounds . . ." Worthy Putnam Sterns, *The Foreign Trade of the United States from 1820 to 1840* (Chicago: The University of Chicago Press, 1900), 453.

Zachary Taylor and Millard Fillmore—Compromise of 1850
85. "wholly unqualified . . ." Frank B. Williams Jr., *Tennessee's Presidents* (Knoxville: University of Tennessee Press, 1981), 66.

85. "He really is a most . . ." Mann, *Life of Horace Mann by His Wife*, 292.
85. "People of the North need have . . ." John D. Eisenhower, *Zachary Taylor* (New York: Times Books, Henry Holt and Co., 2008), 99.
85–86. "taken in rebellion . . ." Frank Freidel and Hugh Sidey, *Presidents of the United States of America* (Washington, DC: White House Historical Association, 2006), 30.
86. "[S]end a fleet to blockade . . ." Mann, *Life of Horace Mann by His Wife*, 292.
86. "facilitating and protecting . . ." Peters and Woolley, "Millard Fillmore: 'First Annual Message,' December 2, 1850," The American Presidency Project, www .presidency.ucsb.edu, accessed November 29, 2014.
87. "They were adopted . . ." Ibid.

Franklin Pierce—Kansas-Nebraska Act of 1854
89–90. *If the Federal Government* . . . James D. Richardson, *A Compilation of the Messages and Papers of the Presidents, Volume 5, part 3: Franklin Pierce* (a Public Domain Book, 2011), 201.
90. "I hold that the laws . . ." Ibid., 203.
90–91. "The Commonwealth of Massachusetts . . ." James G. Blaine, *Twenty Years of Congress: From Lincoln to Garfield* (Norwich, CT: The Henry Bill Publishing Co., 1884), 264.

James Buchanan—Secession
94. "The United States are . . ." *Washington Post*, April 24, 1887, 4.
94. "The whole Territorial question . . ." Peters and Woolley, "James Buchanan Inaugural Address, March 4, 1857," The American Presidency Project, www .presidency.ucsb.edu/, accessed November 29, 2014.

Andrew Johnson—Reconstruction
99. "With malice toward none . . ." Fehrenbacher, *Abraham Lincoln Speeches and Writings 1859–1865*, 687.
100. "He was a man of few talents . . ." Clinton Rossiter, *The American Presidency* (New York: Harcourt, Brace & World, 1956), 101.

CHAPTER 6: PROFESSIONAL GENERALS OF THE NINETEENTH CENTURY: COUNTERWEIGHTS OF THE WEST
101–2. *The smaller the society* . . . James Madison, *The Federalist Papers*, No. 10, "The Same Subject Continued: The Union as a Safeguard Against Domestic Faction and Insurrection," *New York Daily Advertiser*, November 22, 1787.

Andrew Jackson—Trail of Tears

104–5. *A portion, however, of the Southern tribes* . . . Peters and Woolley, "Andrew Jackson, First Annual Message, December 8, 1829," The American Presidency Project, www.presidency.ucsb.edu/, accessed December 5, 2014.

106. "the decision of the Supreme Court . . ." Jon Meacham, *American Lion: Andrew Jackson in the White House* (New York: Random House, 2008), 205.

106. "Do the obligations of justice . . ." Ibid., 96.

106. "a man of violent character . . ." Michael S. Kimmel, *The History of Men: Essays on the History of American and British Masculinities*, quoting de Tocqueville (Albany: State University of New York, 2005), 95.

106. *The charter of the Bank of the United States* . . . Peters and Woolley, "Andrew Jackson, First Annual Message, December 8, 1829," The American Presidency Project, www.presidency.ucsb.edu/, accessed December 5, 2014.

William Henry Harrison—Health of the President

108. "Give him a barrel . . ." Gregory Alan Borchard, *The Firm of Greeley, Weed, and Seward: New York Partisanship and the Press, 1840–1860* (Gainesville: University of Florida Press, 2003), 46.

109. "The fact is that I am so much harassed . . ." "The Ultimate Presidential Rarity; An Autograph Letter of the Sick, Soon to Die, William Henry Harrison," March 10, 1841, Shapell Manuscript Foundation, www.shapell.org/manuscript.aspx?letter-of-ill-soon-to-die-president-william-henry-harrison-suffering-harassed, accessed November 12, 2014.

Ulysses S. Grant—Trust and Distrust

110. "fell into dissipated habits . . ." Edward J. Wheeler, ed., *Current Literature*, vol. XLV, July–December 1908 (New York: The Current Literature Publishing Co.,1908), 10.

110. A substantial body of evidence . . . Lloyd Lewis, *Captain Sam Grant* (Boston: Little, Brown, 1950), 291–93.

110. "[W]hiskey-drinking was . . ." Wheeler, *Current Literature*, 10.

112. "You have not faced Bobby Lee yet." Maj. Gen. Grenville Mellen Dodge, *Personal Recollections of Abraham Lincoln, General Ulysses S. Grant and William T. Sherman* (Glendale: The Arthur H. Clark Company, 1914), 70.

112. running against black suffrage . . . Lewis L. Gould, *Grand Old Party: A History of the Republicans* (New York: Random House, 2003), 54.

112. "The earlier generation . . ." Ibid., 63.

112. "found politicians intimidating . . ." William Gienapp, *Origins of the Republican Party* (New York: Oxford University Press, 1987), 302.

113. One of his first missions . . . John Y. Simon, ed., *Ulysses S. Grant: The Papers of Ulysses S. Grant: January 1–October 31, 1876* (Carbondale: Southern Illinois University Press, 1967–2012), 47.

114. "It was my fortune, or misfortune . . ." Miller Center, Gleaves Whitney, ed., *American Presidents: Farewell Messages to the Nation, 1796–2001*, Ulysses S. Grant Final Annual Message (Lanham, MD: Lexington Books, 2003), 201.

Essay: None of the Twelve General/Presidents Took the Country into a Major War

114. "I hate war as only a soldier who has lived it can . . ." Eisenhower Address before the Canadian Club, Ottawa, Canada, January 10, 1946, Dwight D. Eisenhower Presidential Library, Museum and Boyhood Home, 1946.

114–15. *The long gray line* . . . Sylvanus Thayer Award Acceptance Address, Gen. Douglas MacArthur, May 12, 1962, West Point, NY, www.americanrhetoric .com/speeches/douglasmacarthurthayeraward.html, accessed December 21, 2014.

115. "Although a soldier by education and profession . . ." John Y. Simon, ed., *The Papers of Ulysses S. Grant: November 1, 1876–September 30, 1878*, Speech in London, June 15, 1877 (Carbondale: Southern Illinois University Press, 2005), 217.

CHAPTER 7: TAXATION WITH REPRESENTATION: TARIFFS TO INCOME TAXES

John Quincy Adams—Tariff of Abominations

119–20. *I told [South Carolina Sen. John C.] Calhoun* . . . Allan Nevin, ed., *The Diary of John Quincy Adams, 1794–1845* (New York: Charles Scribner's Sons, 1951), 225–32.

121. "rebaptized Federalism," Arthur Schlesinger Jr., *The Age of Jackson* (New York: Little, Brown and Company, 1988), 12.

121. "a Federalist in sheep's clothing." Ibid., 19.

121. "out of tune with the party . . ." John F. Kennedy, *Profiles in Courage* (New York: Harper & Brothers, 1956), 28–29, 31–32.

122. *BEFORE we proceed* . . . *The Federalist Papers*, No. 35, "The Same Subject Continued: Concerning the General Power of Taxation," Yale Law School— Lillian Goldman Law Library—The Avalon Project: Documents in Law, History and Diplomacy, http://avalon.law.yale.edu/18th_century/fed35.asp, accessed December 22, 2014.

Benjamin Harrison—1890 McKinley Tariff and the Panic of 1893

124. never understanding how the protective tariff was harming . . . Foster Rhea Dulles, *The United States since 1865* (Binghamton, NY: The University of Michigan Press, 1959), 139.

William Howard Taft—Income Tax and Suffrage

126. "If I could be sure . . ." Eleanor Clift, *Founding Sisters and the Nineteenth Amendment* (Hoboken, NJ: John Wiley & Sons, 2003), 88.

126–27. "The theory that Hottentots . . ." Mary Walton, *A Woman's Crusade: Alice Paul and the Battle for the Ballot* (New York: Palgrave MacMillan, 2010), 39.

Ronald Reagan—Flat Tax

128. "We will bury you . . ." http://rt.com/news/159524-sukhodrev-interpreter-khrushchev-cold-war/ May 16, 2014, accessed January 3, 2015.

128. "A review of CIA's estimates . . ." Gerald K. Haines and Robert E. Leggett, eds., *Watching the Bear: Essays on CIA's Analysis of the Soviet Union* (Washington, DC: CIA Center for the Study of Intelligence, 2008), xiii.

130. "I mean, Kemp-Roth . . ." William Greider, "The Education of David Stockman" *The Atlantic* Online, December 1981, 47.

131. "Stockman's Revenge . . ." Joe Klein, *The Natural: The Misunderstood Presidency of Bill Clinton* (New York: Random House, 2002), 49.

131. "In his first year in office . . ." Peter Drier, National Housing Institute, Issue #135, May/June 2004, www.nhi.org/online/issues/135/reagan.html, accessed January 18, 2015.

George H. W. Bush—"No New Taxes"

136. "Read my lips; no new taxes" George H. W. Bush, Transcript of Acceptance Speech at the Republican National Convention, August 18, 1988, http://millercenter.org/president/bush/speeches/speech-5526, accessed November 28, 2014.

136–37. "It is clear to me . . ." Andrew Rosenthal, "Bush Now Concedes a Need for Tax Increases to Reduce Deficit in Budget," *New York Times*, June 27, 1990.

137. The odd part about the recanted pledge . . . Liu Pin, *China Times*, March 10, 2011.

138. five deferments . . . Katharine Seelye, "Cheney's Five Draft Deferments during the Vietnam Era Emerge as a Campaign Issue," *New York Times*, May 1, 2004.

138. "High diddle, diddle . . ." *Frontline*, "Oral History: Norman Schwarzkopf, 1995–2014," www.pbs.org/wgbh/pages/frontline/gulf/oral/commanders.html, accessed December 5, 2014.

Chapter 8: Panic, Laissez Faire, and Depression

Martin Van Buren—Panic of 1837

144. "secret, sly, selfish, cold . . ." Edward Sylvester Ellis, *The Life of Colonel David Crockett: Comprising His Adventures as Backwoodsman and Hunter* (Classic Reprint—Forgotten Books, 2012) (original from New York Public Library—Porter & Coates, 1861), 13.

144. "The less Government interferes . . ." Edward Morse Shepard and John T. Morse, eds., *American Statesmen Martin Van Buren* (Boston: Houghton, Mifflin and Co., 1896), 332.

Essay: Physical Traits and Whether They Matter

145. "Height should not matter . . ." Dr. James Le Fanu, "The Benefits of Height," *Telegraph*, September 8, 2013.

Calvin Coolidge—The Road to Depression

146. "a politician who . . ." Amity Shlaes, *Coolidge* (New York: Harper Collins, 2013), 224.

146. "Please accept my sincerest sympathy." Ibid., 202.

146. "I believe in budgets . . ." Calvin Coolidge, *Foundations of the Republic: Speeches and Addresses* (New York: Scribner, 1926), 172.

147. "Three presidents served under Mellon." John Steele Gordon, *Hamilton's Blessing: The Extraordinary Life and Times of Our National Debt* (New York: Walker Publishing Company, 2010), 103.

148. He had voted for women's suffrage . . . Shlaes, *Coolidge*, 114.

148. contraction of the money supply . . . Ben S. Bernanke, *Essays on the Great Depression* (Princeton, NJ: Princeton University Press, 2000), 7.

148. "Well, they're going to elect that superman Hoover . . ." Col. Edmund W. Starling and Thomas Sugrue, *Starling of the White House: The Story of the Man Whose Secret Service Detail Guarded Five Presidents from Woodrow Wilson to Franklin D. Roosevelt* (New York: Simon and Schuster, 1946), 263.

148. "The expenditure of money . . ." Shlaes, *Coolidge*, 443.

Herbert Hoover—The Great Depression

149. "If a man has not made a fortune by 40 . . ." George H. Nash, *The Life of Herbert Hoover: The Engineer 1874–1914* (New York: W. W. Norton & Co., 1983), 509.

150. "Napoleon of mercy . . . responsible for saving more lives . . ." George H. Nash, "Herbert Hoover and Belgian Relief in World War I," *Prologue* magazine, Spring 1989, vol. 21, no.1.

150. "Twelve Greatest American Men," *New York Times*, July 23, 1922.
152. "He left a whole rigamarole of figures." John Maynard Keynes, *The General Theory of Employment, Interest, and Money* (New Delhi: Atlantic Publishers & Dist., 2006), and Nathan Miller, *F.D.R., An Intimate History* (New York: Doubleday, 1983), 408.
153. "A huge work relief program . . ." Robert S. McElvaine, *The Great Depression: America 1929–1941* (New York: Crown Publishing Group, 2010), 200.

Chart: Significant US Tariffs
154. "espoused the extreme protective policy . . ." F. W. Taussig, *The Tariff History of the United States* (New York: G.P. Putnam's Sons, 1910), 243.

CHAPTER 9: IN DEFIANCE OF PARTY

John Tyler—The Man without a Party
156. "He is the creature . . ." "John Tyler—Replying to an Invitation Sent by Mr. & Mrs. Rosevelt," Shapell Manuscript Foundation, www.shapell.org/manuscript.aspx?john-tyler-president-jokes, accessed November 10, 2014.
156. "His Accidency" "President John Tyler, Says He Is a Creature of Accidents, 'Being an Accident Himself'" Ibid.
158. "I was forced to make a cabinet . . ." John Tyler—Original Handwritten Letter to a Friend November 25, 1852, "John Tyler: His Cabinet Problems, James Pierce's Election, and Presidential Etiquette," Shapell Manuscript Foundation, www.shapell.org/manuscript.aspx?john-tyler-presidency-james-pierce, accessed December 18, 2014.

Rutherford B. Hayes—The Great Swap
159. "My task was to wipe out the color line . . ." Harry Barnard, *Rutherford Hayes and His America* (Newtown, CT: American Political Biography Press, 2005), 418.
161. "If citizens of one race . . ." Anonymous, *United States Circuit Courts of Appeals Reports: With Key-Number Annotations . . . V. 1–171 [1891–1919]* (Ulan Press, 2011) (original from Harvard University—West, 1903), digitized in *Atlantic Reporter*, August 4–October 20, 1921, vol. 114 (St. Paul: West Publishing Co., 1921), 845.
161. "No Negro or Mulatto shall come into . . ." State of Indiana, *Year Book of the State of Indiana* (original from the University of California, 1918) (digital: RareBooksClub.com, 2012) (Indiana Historical Bureau), www.in.gov/history/2858.htm, accessed December 13, 2014.

161. The 1847 Illinois Constitution . . . Roger D. Bridges, *The Illinois Black Codes* (Illinois Periodicals Online, 1996), www.lib.niu.edu/1996/iht329602 .html, accessed December 13, 2014, and The Legal Map for Interracial Relationships (1662–1967), www.lovingday.org/legal-map, Loving Day 2012, accessed December 10, 2014.

162. electing governors in Indiana, Colorado . . . National Governors Association (official site), Washington, DC, 2011, multiple governors under Ku Klux Klan, www.nga.org/cms/searchResults.html?jcrMethodToCall=get&src_ originSiteKey=NGA&src_nodeType=jmix%3AeditorialContent&src_ terms%5B0%5D.term=ku+klux+klan+Indiana+governor&src_terms%5B0%5D .applyFilter=true&src_pagePath.value=%2Fsites%2FNGA%2Fhome&src_ pagePath.valueView=Home&src_pagePath.includeChildren=true&search-go=go, accessed January 3, 2015.

William J. Clinton—A President for All Reasons
162. "The chief business of the American . . ." David John Farmer, *Public Administration in Perspective* (Armonk, NY: M.E. Sharpe, Inc., 2010), 39.

163. "I'm not sure how different this presidency . . ." Klein, *The Natural*, 160.

163. "The mismanagement in 1993 . . ." Tim Russert, *Meet the Press*, September 27, 2007.

165. "Part of it is growing pains . . ." *Newsweek*, vol. 122, issues 18–26, 1993.

165. "What do we do now?" Jeremy Larner, *The Candidate*, DVD. Directed by Michael Ritchie (Warner Brothers, 1972).

165. "The internal mayhem . . ." Klein, *The Natural*, 59.

CHAPTER 10: EMPIRE WARS: MEXICO AND SPAIN
168. "The White Man's Burden." Rudyard Kipling, Thomas James Wise, poem: "The White Man's Burden" (New York: Doubleday and McClure Company, *McClure's* magazine, February 12, 1899).

James K. Polk—The Mexican-American War
169. "an unsigned [1845] article in . . ." Donald M. Scott, *The Religious Origins of Manifest Destiny. Divining America*, TeacherServe©, National Humanities Center, http://nationalhumanitiescenter.org/tserve/nineteen/nkeyinfo/man destiny.htm, accessed January 17, 2015.

171. "We have not sought to extend . . ." John Stilwell Jenkins, *The Life of James Knox Polk: Late President of the United States* (Hudson, NY: P.S. Wynkoop, 1850), 1845.

William McKinley—The Spanish-American War

173. "Just because they are my sons . . ." Dennis Gaffney and Peter Gaffney, *The Presidents* (New York: Hachette Books, 2012), 169.

173. "There is no use of my writing about Quentin . . ." Peter Collier with David Horowitz, *The Roosevelts: An American Saga* (New York: Simon & Schuster, 1994), 239.

173. the Spanish-American War would claim 2,446 . . . US Department of Veterans Affairs Fact Sheet, Washington, 2014.

Chapter 11: Invade or Blockade: Fort Sumter, the Bay of Pigs, and the Cuban Missile Crisis

Abraham Lincoln—Fort Sumter and the Civil War

176. *My paramount object* . . . Fehrenbacher, *Abraham Lincoln: Speeches and Writings 1859–1865*, 357–58.

178. "My first impulse would be to free . . ." Ibid., 508–27.

178. *I will say then that I am not* . . . Ibid., 636–84.

179. "We have just carried an election . . ." Ibid., 196–97.

179. "So all is over . . ." Chris DeRose, *The Presidents' War: Six American Presidents and the Civil War that Divided Them* (Guilford, CT: Lyons Press, 2014), 114.

180. *The provision of the Constitution* . . . Fehrenbacher, *Abraham Lincoln: Speeches and Writings, 1859–1865*, 175–76.

181. I. Throw off the old . . . Transcribed and Annotated by the Lincoln Studies Center, Knox College, *Abraham Lincoln Papers at the Library of Congress* (Galesburg, IL, Letter from Winfield Scott to William H. Seward, March 3, 1861).

182. *I have always regarded the dissolution of the Union* . . . J. G. de Roulhac Hamilton, ed., *The Correspondence of Jonathan Worth* (Raleigh, NC: North Carolina Historical Commission, 1909), 145–48.

182–83. "I think to lose Kentucky . . ." Fehrenbacher, *Abraham Lincoln: Speeches and Writings 1859–1865*, 268–70.

183. "You and I, Mr. Stanton . . ." Jonathan Brown Bright, *The Bookman*, vol. 21 (New York: Dodd, Mead and Co., 1905), 35.

184. "all persons held as slaves . . ." Fehrenbacher, *Abraham Lincoln: Speeches and Writings, 1859–1865*, 368–70.

184. "We show our sympathy . . ." Donn Piatt, *Memories of the Men Who Saved the Union* (New York: Belford, Clark & Co., 1887), 150.

185. *Perhaps you have long been free* . . . Fehrenbacher, *Abraham Lincoln: Speeches and Writings 1859–1865*, 353–57.

Chart: If the Upper South Had Not Seceded
186. The Upper South made up . . . E. B. Long, *The Civil War Day by Day: An Almanac 1861–1865* (New York: Doubleday & Co., 1971), 701.
186. "sustained about one fourth . . ." Mark Mayo Boatner, *The Civil War Dictionary* (New York: David McKay Co., 1959), 598.
186. "Federals . . . outnumbered . . ." Long, *The Civil War Day by Day*, 704.
187. "It is also unsatisfactory . . ." Fehrenbacher, *Abraham Lincoln: Speeches and Writings 1859–1865*, 397–401.

Essay: Secessions
188. "'Self determination' is not a mere phrase . . ." D. Rai'c, *Statehood and the Law of Self Determination* (The Hague: Kluwer Law International, 2002), 182.
188. "To invoke the general principle of self-determination . . ." David Fromkin, "Self-Determination: Origins and Meaning," *Wall Street Journal*, March 31, 1999.
188–89. "It is for us the living . . ." Fehrenbacher, *Abraham Lincoln Speeches and Writings 1859–1865*, 536.

John F. Kennedy—The Bay of Pigs and the Cuban Missile Crisis
189. Former President Harry S. Truman famously said . . . Robert Dallek, *Harry S. Truman: The American Presidents Series* (New York: Henry Holt & Co., 2008), 148.
192. "There's an old saying . . ." Theodore C. Sorensen, *Kennedy* (New York: Harper & Row, 1965), 308–9.
192. "How could I have been so . . ." Robert Dallek, *An Unfinished Life: John F. Kennedy, 1917–1963* (New York: Back Bay Books, reprint edition, 2004), 367.
192. "In part they arose . . ." Sorensen, *Kennedy*, 304.
193. "You're damn right, he does. . . "Aleksandr Fursenko and Timothy Naftali, *One Hell of a Gamble: Khrushchev, Castro, and Kennedy, 1958–1964* (New York: W.W. Norton & Co., 1997), 261–66.

CHAPTER 12: MACHINE MEN

James Garfield—Gender-Biased Suffrage
198–99. *The free enjoyment of equal suffrage . . .*"William Ralston Balch, *James Garfield Late President of the United States* (Philadelphia: McCurdy, 1881), 562.
199. "I am a Stalwart . . ." Burton T. Swaney Doyle and H. Homer, *Lives of James A. Garfield and Chester A. Arthur* (Washington, DC: R. H. Darby, 1881), 61.

Chester A. Arthur—Conkling's Man

200. "[T]here is no place . . ." Michael Harwood, *In the Shadow of Presidents* (New York: J.B. Lippincott Company, 1966), 115.

200. "Garfield has not been square . . ." Ibid., 117.

201. "Madam, I may be president . . ." H. Wayne Morgan, *From Hayes to McKinley: National Party Politics, 1877–1900* (Syracuse, NY: Syracuse University Press, 1969), 56.

CHAPTER 13: REFORM MEN

Grover Cleveland—The Veto President

203. "We are told . . ." H. Paul, *An Honest President: The Life and Presidencies of Grover Cleveland* (New York: Harper Collins, 2000), 117.

204. "Public money appropriated . . ." Grover Cleveland, *The Public Papers of Grover Cleveland: Twenty-Second President of the United States. March 4, 1885, to March 4, 1889* (US Government Printing Office, 1839) (Ulan Press, 2011), 110.

205. "ineffective" being the most common term . . . Paul Klinghard, *The Nationalization of American Political Parties, 1880–1896* (New York: Cambridge University Press, 2010), 154.

205. "The consensus of Cleveland biographers . . ." Paul, *An Honest President*, 127.

205. "I cannot look upon the prospect of success . . ." Ibid., 116.

Theodore Roosevelt—Panic of 1907

206. "He endorsed women's suffrage . . . Long Island and the Woman Suffrage Movement, September 15, 2013, http://longislandwomansuffrage.com/?p=461, accessed December 19, 2014.

Essay: Why We Should Not Rank the Presidents

208. "Entangling alliances." William Safire, *Safire's Political Dictionary* (New York: Oxford University Press, 2008), 217.

CHAPTER 14: UNPARDONABLE SCANDALS: TEAPOT DOME, DIRTY TRICKS, AND AN UNPARDONABLE PARDON

Warren G. Harding—Teapot Dome

210. "I am not fit for this office . . ." Nicholas Murray Butler, President of Columbia University, *Across the Busy Years: Recollections and Reflections* (New York: Charles Scribner's Sons, 1939), 410–11.

211. "You see, White, what really interests me . . ." Ibid., 351.

211. "the general atmosphere . . ." Alice Roosevelt Longworth and Mrs. Michael L. Teague, *Conversations with Alice Roosevelt Longworth* (New York: Doubleday, 1981), 170.

212. "low taxes, [high] tariffs, less central government." Shlaes, *Coolidge*, 209.

Richard M. Nixon—Dirty Tricks

213. "Pink Lady," and "Tricky Dick." Greg Mitchell, *Tricky Dick and the Pink Lady: Richard Nixon vs. Helen Gahagan Douglas—Sexual Politics and the Red Scare, 1950* (New York: Random House, 1998), xvi.

214. "delicate and tenuous." Julie Nixon Eisenhower, *Pat Nixon: The Untold Story* (New York: Simon & Schuster, 1986), 151.

214. "Eisenhower was always telling Nixon . . ." Frank, *Ike and Dick*, 339.

214. "We understand that the power . . ." Press conference, August 24, 1960; transcript: www.presidency.ucsb.edu.

215. "He oughtn't be doin' this . . ." LBJ White House Tape 6811.01, November 2, 1968, and Frank, *Ike and Dick*, 314.

215. "was not, to put it charitably . . ." Frank, *Ike and Dick*, 314.

215. "You know, I know Dick . . ." Ibid., 323.

Gerald R. Ford Jr.—Pardoning the Unpardonable

217. *It is believed that . . . The Code of Federal Regulations of the United States of America* (Washington, DC: The Office of the Federal Register, National Archives and Records Section, 1975), 66.

218. "Well, when the president does it . . ." From the third Nixon-Frost interview, *New York Times*, May 20, 1977, A16.

218. "Actions which otherwise . . ." Robert S. Hirschfield, *The Power of the Presidency: Concepts and Controversy* (Piscataway, NJ: Aldine Transaction, 3rd edition, 1982), 273.

218. Ford responded by requesting . . . Yanek Mieczkowski, *Gerald Ford and the Challenges of the 1970s* (Lexington: University Press of Kentucky, 2005), 283–84, 290–94.

218. "He's the weakest president in U.S. history . . ." Lewis Sorley, *A Better War* (New York: Harcourt Brace, 1999), 374.

CHAPTER 15: AN ABSENCE OF DETERRENCE: WORLD WAR I AND WORLD WAR II

Woodrow Wilson—World War I

22. "entirely destroyed," *Hansard Parliamentary Debates*, Ser. III, vol. cciv, February–March 1871, speech of February 9, 1871, 81–82.

222. "iron and blood." Otto von Bismarck, Wilhelm Schüßler, ed., *Reden 1847–1869* [*Speeches, 1847–1869*], vol. 10, *Bismarck: Die gesammelten Werke* [*Bismarck: Collected Works*], Hermann von Petersdorff, ed. (Berlin: Otto Stolberg, 1924–1935), 139–40.

222. "the era of armed peace." Winston S. Churchill, *The Great Democracies* (New York: Dodd, Mead & Co., 1958), 282.

222. "But that our family shield . . ." John Rohl and Nicolaus Sombart, eds., *Kaiser Wilhelm II New Interpretations: The Corfu Papers* (New York: Cambridge University Press, 1982), 33.

223. "to remonstrate at the presence . . ." Byron Farwell, *The Anglo-Boer War* (New York: Harper & Row, 1976), 254.

224. "Your position is a peculiar one . . ." Charles Carlisle Taylor, *The Life of Admiral Mahan, Naval Philosopher, Rear-Admiral United States Navy* (London: Forgotten Books, 2013), 276–77.

224–25. *The country, I am thankful to say* . . . Peters and Woolley, "Woodrow Wilson: 'First Annual Message,' December 2, 1913," The American Presidency Project, www.presidency.ucsb.edu/, accessed December 12, 2014.

225. "[S]ome spark might . . ." Justus D. Doenecke, *Nothing Less Than War: A New History of America's Entry Into World War I* (Lexington: University Press of Kentucky, 2011), 94.

226. *I write to suggest* . . . Taylor, *The Life of Admiral Mahan*, 275.

226. "There is no doubt. . ." Ibid., 277.

227. a phrase Wilson never said. . . "He kept us out of the war." Dan Balz and John Maxwell Hamilton, "In 2016, We're Going to Party Like It's 1916," *Washington Post*, January 4, 2015.

227. "the almost non-existent . . ." Virginia Cowles, *The Kaiser* (New York: Harper & Row, 1963), 376.

228. "became the deciding factor . . ." J. F. C. Fuller, *A Military History of the Western World* (New York: Funk & Wagnalls, 1956), 275.

228. "It is our true policy to steer clear of permanent alliances . . ." George Washington, "Washington's Farewell Address 1796," Yale Law School—Lillian Goldman Law Library—The Avalon Project: Documents in Law, History and Diplomacy, http://avalon.law.yale.edu/18th_century/washing.asp, accessed January 20, 2015.

228. "Peace, commerce, and honest friendship . . ." Thomas Jefferson, "First Inaugural Address, March 4, 1801," *The Papers of Thomas Jefferson* (Princeton, NJ: Princeton University, 1801).

Franklin Delano Roosevelt—World War II
230. "Let us stop borrowing . . ." Gordon, *Hamilton's Blessing*, 114.

233. "Consequently, Army tanks would not compare . . ." Richard Winslip, *American Military History: The United States Army in a Global Era, 1917–2003*, vol. II (Washington, DC: Center of Military History, United States Army, 2005), 67.

233. to 8,267,958 Army personnel . . . The National World War II Museum, New Orleans, 2015.

233. "Set a thief to catch a thief." Michael R. Beschloss, *Kennedy and Roosevelt* (New York: Norton, 1980), 88.

234. *Hitler knows that* . . . Gilbert, *Churchill: A Life*, 664.

Chart: Blame Keynes—US vs. German Military Spending 1933–1939

235. US Department of Commerce, Bureau of the Census, *Historical Statistics of the United States, Colonial Times to 1970*, Part 2; and Charles Maier, *The Economics of Fascism and Nazism: In Search of Stability* (Cambridge: Cambridge University Press, 1987), 242.

Harry S. Truman—The Bomb and Japan; Korea and China

238. "a barbarian invasion of Europe." David McCullough, *Truman* (New York: Simon and Schuster, 1992), 458.

238. "Carry out your agreements . . ." Ibid., 461.

238. "the biggest fool thing . . ." Harry S. Truman, *Memoirs of Harry S. Truman: Year of Decisions, Vol. 1* (Cambridge, MA: Da Capo Press, 1986), 11.

238. "You will enter the continent of Europe . . ." Walter Bedell Smith, *Eisenhower's Six Great Decisions* (London: Longmans, Green & Co., 1956), 15.

238. "Berlin itself is no longer . . ." Dwight D. Eisenhower, *Crusade in Europe* (Garden City, NY: Doubleday & Co., 1948), 402.

239. "A kind of bureaucratic momentum . . ." Andrew J. Rotter, *Hiroshima: The World's Bomb* (New York: Oxford University Press, 2008), 236.

240–41. *A PETITION TO THE PRESIDENT* . . . US National Archives, Record Group 77, Records of the Chief of Engineers, Manhattan Engineer District, Harrison-Bundy File, folder #76.

241–42. *Recommendations on the Immediate Use* . . . Ibid.

242. *Once it had been tested* . . ." William Leahy, *I Was There* (New York: Whittlesey House, 1950), 441.

243. *My Dear Mr. Cavert* . . . Correspondence between Harry S. Truman and Samuel Cavert, August 11, 1945, "The Decision to Drop the Bomb, Official File," *Truman Papers*, Harry S. Truman Library and Museum, Independence, MO.

243. "It wasn't necessary to hit them . . ." Dwight D. Eisenhower, "Ike on Ike," *Newsweek*, November 11, 1963.

243–44. "rather forcefully" told Secretary of War . . . Bradley and Blair, *A General's Life*, 444.
244. "It seemed to me there was a fundamental . . ." Ibid., 473–74.

APPENDICES

253–54. Appendix C: Roy P. Basler, ed., *Collected Works of Abraham Lincoln*, 2006, http://quod.lib.uMIedu/l/lincoln.
255–56. Appendix D: Peters and Woolley, "The Nixon Pardon Gerald R. Ford: Proclamation 4311—Granting Pardon to Richard Nixon September 8, 1974," The American Presidency Project, www.presidency.ucsb.edu, accessed December 17, 2014.

SELECTED BIBLIOGRAPHY

Alexander, James C. "Off to a Bad Start: John Adams's Tussle over Titles," *Vanderbilt Undergraduate Research Journal*, vol. 4, 2008.

American Historical Association, Annual Report for the Year 1903.

Anonymous. *United States Circuit Courts of Appeals Reports: With Key-Number Annotations . . . V. 1–171 [1891–1919]*. Ulan Press, 2011, original from Harvard University—West, 1903.

Atlantic Reporter, August 4–October 20, 1921, vol. 114. St. Paul: West Publishing Co., 1921.

Balch, William Ralston. *James Garfield Late President of the United States*. Philadelphia: McCurdy, 1881.

Balz, Dan, and John Maxwell Hamilton. "In 2016, We're Going to Party Like It's 1916," *Washington Post*, January 4, 2015.

Barnard, Harry. *Rutherford Hayes and His America*. Newtown, CT: American Political Biography Press, 2005.

Barnouw, Erik. *Tube of Plenty: The Evolution of American Television*. New York: Oxford University Press, 1990.

Bernanke, Ben S. *Essays on the Great Depression*. Princeton, NJ: Princeton University Press, 2000.

Beschloss, Michael R. *Kennedy and Roosevelt*. New York: Norton, 1980.

von Bismarck, Otto, Wilhelm Schüßler, ed. *Reden 1847–1869 [Speeches, 1847–1869]*, vol. 10, *Bismarck: Die gesammelten Werke [Bismarck: Collected Works]*, Hermann von Petersdorff, ed. Berlin: Otto Stolberg, 1924–1935.

Blaine, James G. *Twenty Years of Congress: From Lincoln to Garfield*. Norwich, CT: The Henry Bill Publishing Co., 1884.

Blum, John M. *The National Experience: A History of the United States*. New York: Harcourt Brace, 1989.

Board of Governors of the Federal Reserve, www.federalreserve.gov/bankinfo reg/bcreg20131101a1.pdf, accessed January 17, 2015.

Boatner, Mark Mayo. *The Civil War Dictionary*. New York: David McKay Co., 1959.

Borchard, Gregory Alan. *The Firm of Greeley, Weed, and Seward: New York Partisanship and the Press, 1840–1860*. Gainesville: University of Florida Press, 2003.

Bourne, George. *The History of Napoleon Bonaparte: The Emperor of the French and King of Italy*. Baltimore: Warner and Hanna, 1806.

Bradley, Omar N., and Clay Blair. *A General's Life*. New York: Simon and Schuster, 1983.

Bridges, Roger D. *The Illinois Black Codes*. Illinois Periodicals Online, 1996.

Bright, Jonathan Brown. *The Bookman*, vol. 21. New York: Dodd, Mead and Co., 1905.

Brookhiser, Richard. *Founding Father: Rediscovering George Washington*. New York: Free Press, 1996.

Bush, George H. W. Transcript of Acceptance Speech at the Republican National Convention, August 18, 1988.

Butler, Nicholas Murray, President of Columbia University. *Across the Busy Years: Recollections and Reflections*. New York: Charles Scribner's Sons, 1939.

Chace, James. "Marshall Plan Commemorative Section: An Extraordinary Partnership: Marshall and Acheson," *Foreign Affairs*, May–June 1997. www.foreignaffairs.com/articles/europe/1997-05-01/marshall-plan -commemorative-section-extraordinary-partnership-marshall, accessed August 11, 2015.

Churchill, Winston S. *The Great Democracies*. New York: Dodd, Mead & Co., 1958.

Cleveland, Grover. *The Public Papers of Grover Cleveland: Twenty-Second President of the United States. March 4, 1885, to March 4, 1889*. US Government Printing Office, 1839, Ulan Press, 2011.

Clift, Eleanor. *Founding Sisters and the Nineteenth Amendment*. Hoboken, NJ: John Wiley & Sons, 2003.

CNN. Jake Tapper, November 14, 2014.

Cole, Donald B. *Martin Van Buren and the American Political System*. Princeton, NJ: Princeton University Press, 1984.

Collier, Peter, with David Horowitz. *The Roosevelts: An American Saga*. New York: Simon & Schuster, 1994.

Connecticut State Library, Historical Notices of Connecticut, "Hartford Convention Resolutions." Boston: Wells and Lilly, 1815.

Constitutional Rights Foundation, Los Angeles, www.crf-usa.org.

Cook, David. *Christian Science Monitor*, November 4, 2005.

Coolidge, Calvin. *Foundations of the Republic: Speeches and Addresses*. New York: Scribner, 1926.

Cowles, Virginia. *The Kaiser*. New York: Harper & Row, 1963.

Dallek, Robert. *Harry S. Truman: The American Presidents Series*. New York: Henry Holt & Co., 2008.

Dallek, Robert. *An Unfinished Life: John F. Kennedy, 1917–1963*. New York: Back Bay Books, reprint edition, 2004.

DeRose, Chris. *The Presidents' War: Six American Presidents and the Civil War that Divided Them*. Guilford, CT: Lyons Press, 2014.

Deseret News, "Quotes: US Vice Presidency," September 28, 2008.

Dodge, Maj. Gen. Grenville Mellen. *Personal Recollections of Abraham Lincoln, General Ulysses S. Grant and William T. Sherman*. Glendale: The Arthur H. Clark Company, 1914.

Doenecke, Justus D. *Nothing Less Than War: A New History of America's Entry into World War I*. Lexington: University Press of Kentucky, 2011.

Doyle, Burton T. Swaney, and H. Homer. *Lives of James A. Garfield and Chester A. Arthur*. Washington, DC: R. H. Darby, 1881.

Drier, Peter. National Housing Institute, Issue #135, May/June 2004.

Dulles, Foster Rhea. *The United States since 1865*. Binghamton, NY: The University of Michigan Press, 1959.

The Economist. "What Is Quantitative Easing?" January 14, 2014.

Eisenhower, Dwight D. *Crusade in Europe*. Garden City, NY: Doubleday & Co., 1948.

Eisenhower, Dwight D. "Ike on Ike," *Newsweek*, November 11, 1963.

Eisenhower, Dwight D. Presidential Library, Museum and Boyhood Home, Abilene, KS.

Eisenhower, John D. *Zachary Taylor*. New York: Times Books, Henry Holt and Co., 2008.

Eisenhower, Julie Nixon. *Pat Nixon: The Untold Story*. New York: Simon & Schuster, 1986.

Ellis, Edward Sylvester. *The Life of Colonel David Crockett: Comprising His Adventures as Backwoodsman and Hunter*. Classic Reprint—Forgotten Books, 2012, original from New York Public Library—Porter & Coates, 1861.

Esposito, Brig. Gen. Vincent J., and Col. John R. Elting. *A Military History and Atlas of the Napoleonic Wars*. New York: Frederick A. Praeger, 1964.

Farmer, David John. *Public Administration in Perspective*. Armonk, NY: M.E. Sharpe, Inc., 2010.

Farrell, Andrew. "Ask a Billionaire," *Forbes*, July 15, 2008.

Farwell, Byron. *The Anglo-Boer War*. New York: Harper & Row, 1976.

Fehrenbacher, Don E., ed. *Abraham Lincoln Speeches and Writings 1859–1865*. New York: Viking Press, 1989.

Fitzpatrick, John C., ed. *George Washington Diaries*, 4 vols. Boston and New York: 1925.

Fitzpatrick, John C., ed. *George Washington Writings*, 39 vols. Washington: Library of America, 1931–1944.

Founders Online, National Archives.

Frank, Jeffrey. *Ike and Dick: Portrait of a Strange Political Marriage*. New York: Simon & Schuster, 2013.

Freidel, Frank, and Hugh Sidey. *Presidents of the United States of America*. Washington, DC: White House Historical Association, 2006.

Fromkin, David. "Self-Determination: Origins and Meaning," *Wall Street Journal*, March 31, 1999.

Frontline. "Oral History: Norman Schwarzkopf, 1995–2014."

Fuller, J. F. C. *A Military History of the Western World*. New York: Funk & Wagnalls, 1956.

Fursenko, Aleksandr, and Timothy Naftali. *One Hell of a Gamble: Khrushchev, Castro, and Kennedy, 1958–1964*. New York: W.W. Norton & Co., 1997.

Gaffney, Dennis, and Peter Gaffney. *The Presidents*. New York: Hachette Books, 2012.

Gienapp, William. *Origins of the Republican Party*. New York: Oxford University Press, 1987.

Gilbert, Martin. *Churchill: A Life*. New York: Henry Holt & Co., 1991.

Gordon, John Steele. *Hamilton's Blessing: The Extraordinary Life and Times of Our National Debt*. New York: Walker Publishing Company, 2010.

Gould, Lewis L. *Grand Old Party: A History of the Republicans*. New York: Random House, 2003.

Greider, William. "The Education of David Stockman." *The Atlantic* Online, December 1981.

Gruber, Dr. Jonathan. At the 2011 Pioneer Institute's 5th Annual Hewitt Health Care Lecture at Harvard Medical School.

Haines, Gerald K., and Robert E. Leggett, eds. *Watching the Bear: Essays on CIA's Analysis of the Soviet Union*. Washington, DC: CIA Center for the Study of Intelligence, 2008.

Hamilton, J. G. de Roulhac, ed. *The Correspondence of Jonathan Worth*. Raleigh: North Carolina Historical Commission, 1909.

Hansard Parliamentary Debates, Ser. III, vol. cciv, February–March 1871, speech of February 9, 1871.

Harwood, Michael. *In the Shadow of Presidents*. New York: J.B. Lippincott Company, 1966.

Hirschfield, Robert S. *The Power of the Presidency: Concepts and Controversy*. Piscataway, NJ: Aldine Transaction, 3rd edition, 1982.

Holt, Michael. *The Rise and Fall of the American Whig Party: Jacksonian Politics and the Onset of the Civil War*. New York: Oxford University Press, 1999.

Holton, Woody. "Abigail Adams, Bond Speculator," *William and Mary Quarterly*, 3rd series, 64:821–38, October 2007.

Hunt, Gaillard, ed. *James Madison Writings*, 9 vols. New York: 1900–1910.

Ignatius, David. "Book Review: Leon Panetta's 'Worthy Fights,'" *Washington Post*, October 6, 2014.

Indiana, State of. *Year Book of the State of Indiana*. Indiana Historical Bureau. Original from the University of California, 1918.

Jefferson, Thomas. "First Inaugural Address, March 4, 1801." *The Papers of Thomas Jefferson*. Princeton, NJ: Princeton University, 1801.

Jenkins, John Stilwell. *The Life of James Knox Polk: Late President of the United States*. Hudson, NY: P.S. Wynkoop, 1850.

Johnson, Neil M. Oral History with General Louis W. Truman. Independence, MO, Harry S. Truman Library and Museum, December 7, 1991.

Kean, Thomas H., and Lee H. Hamilton. *Without Precedent, the 9/11 Commission Report*. New York: Vintage Books, 2007.

Kennedy, John F. *Profiles in Courage*. New York: Harper & Brothers, 1956.

Keynes, John Maynard. *The General Theory of Employment, Interest, and Money*. New Delhi: Atlantic Publishers & Dist., 2006.

Kimmel, Michael S. *The History of Men: Essays on the History of American and British Masculinities*. Albany: State University of New York, 2005.

Kipling, Rudyard, and Thomas James Wise. Poem: "The White Man's Burden." New York: Doubleday and McClure Company, *McClure's* magazine, February 12, 1899.

Klein, Joe. *The Natural: The Misunderstood Presidency of Bill Clinton*. New York: Random House, 2002.

Klinghard, Paul. *The Nationalization of American Political Parties, 1880–1896*. New York: Cambridge University Press, 2010.

Knobler, S. A., A. Mahmoud Mack, and S. Lemon, eds. "1: The Story of Influenza," in *The Threat of Pandemic Influenza: Are We Ready?* Washington, DC: Workshop Summary, 2005.

Larner, Jeremy. *The Candidate*, DVD. Directed by Michael Ritchie. Warner Brothers, 1972.

Lawson, John Davison, ed. *American State Trials*. St. Louis: F.H. Thomas Law Book Co., 1918.

Leahy, William. *I Was There*. New York: Whittlesey House, 1950.

The Legal Map for Interracial Relationships, 1662–1967, www.lovingday.org/legal-map, Loving Day 2012, accessed December 10, 2014.

Lewis, Lloyd. *Captain Sam Grant*. Boston: Little, Brown, 1950.

Lincoln Studies Center, Knox College. *Abraham Lincoln Papers at the Library of Congress*. Galesburg, IL, Letter from Winfield Scott to William H. Seward, March 3, 1861.

Locke, John, *The Second Treatise of Civil Government*, 1690.

Long, E. B. *The Civil War Day by Day: An Almanac 1861–1865*. New York: Doubleday & Co., 1971.

Longworth, Alice Roosevelt, and Mrs. Michael L. Teague. *Conversations with Alice Roosevelt Longworth*. New York: Doubleday, 1981.

Los Angeles Times, November 2, 2010.

MacArthur, Gen. Douglas. Sylvanus Thayer Award Acceptance Address. West Point, NY, May 12, 1962.

Madison, James. *The Federalist Papers*, No. 10. "The Same Subject Continued: The Union as a Safeguard Against Domestic Faction and Insurrection." *New York Daily Advertiser*, November 22, 1787.

Maier, Charles. *The Economics of Fascism and Nazism: In Search of Stability.* Cambridge: Cambridge University Press, 1987.

Malone, Dumas. *Jefferson the President: First Term, 1801–1805*, vol. IV. Boston: Little, Brown and Company, 1970.

Manis, Jim, ed., trans. Henry Reeve. *Democracy in America*, vol. 1 and 2 by Alexis de Tocqueville. Hazelton: Pennsylvania State University Press, 2013.

Mann, Mary Tyler Peabody. *Life of Horace Mann by His Wife.* Boston: Walker, Fuller, and Co., 1854.

Mardini, Ramzy, and Emma Sky. *New York Times*, October 13, 2013.

McCullough, David. *John Adams.* New York: Simon & Schuster, 2001.

McCullough, David. *Truman.* New York: Simon & Schuster, 1992.

McElvaine, Robert S. *Franklin Delano Roosevelt.* Washington: CQ Press, 2002.

McElvaine, Robert S. *The Great Depression: America 1929–1941.* New York: Crown Publishing Group, 2010.

McHenry, Dr. James. *The American Historical Review*, vol. 11, 1906.

Meacham, Jon. *American Lion: Andrew Jackson in the White House.* New York: Random House, 2008.

Meyer, Wayne, ed. *Clinton on Clinton: A Portrait of the President in His Own Words.* New York: Avon, 1999.

Mieczkowski, Yanek. *Gerald Ford and the Challenges of the 1970s.* Lexington: University Press of Kentucky, 2005.

Miller Center, University of Virginia. *American President: A Reference Resource.* Charlottesville: Rector and Visitors of the University of Virginia, 2014.

Miller, John C. *Crisis in Freedom: The Alien and Sedition Acts.* New York: Little Brown and Company, 1951.

Miller, Nathan. *F.D.R.: An Intimate History.* New York: Doubleday, 1983.

Mitchell, Greg. *Tricky Dick and the Pink Lady: Richard Nixon vs. Helen Gahagan Douglas—Sexual Politics and the Red Scare, 1950.* New York: Random House, 1998.

Morgan, H. Wayne. *From Hayes to McKinley: National Party Politics, 1877–1900.* Syracuse, NY: Syracuse University Press, 1969.

Nash, George H. "Herbert Hoover and Belgian Relief in World War I." *Prologue* magazine, Spring 1989, vol. 21, no.1.

Nash, George H. *The Life of Herbert Hoover: The Engineer 1874–1914.* New York: W.W. Norton & Co, 1983.

National Archives and Records Section, The Office of the Federal Register. *The Code of Federal Regulations of the United States of America.* Washington, DC: 1975.

NationalAtlas.gov, 1970 print edition.

National Governors Association (official site), www.nga.org. Washington, DC, 2011.

National Park Service, US Department of the Interior, www.nps.gov/liho/history culture/debate4.htm.

The National World War II Museum, New Orleans, 2015.

Nevin, Allan, ed. *The Diary of John Quincy Adams, 1794–1845.* New York: Charles Scribner's Sons, 1951.

New York Times, December 23, 2003.

Oakes, James. *Slavery and Freedom: An Interpretation of the Old South.* New York: Alfred A. Knopf, 1990.

Oates, Stephen B. *Abraham Lincoln: The Man Behind the Myths.* New York: Harper & Row, 1984.

The Oyez Project at IIT Chicago–Kent College of Law.

Oynangen, Knut. Iowa State University Center for Agricultural History and Rural Studies, American Agricultural History Primer, "The Cotton Economy of the Old South," http://rickwoten.com/CottonEconomy.html, accessed August 11, 2015.

Paul, H. *An Honest President: The Life and Presidencies of Grover Cleveland.* New York: Harper Collins, 2000.

Perry, Mark. *Partners in Command: George Marshall and Dwight Eisenhower in War and Peace.* New York: Penguin Books, 2007.

Peters, Gerhard, and John T. Woolley. The American Presidency Project, www .presidency.ucsb.edu/ws/?pid=29471.

Peterson, Merrill D. *Thomas Jefferson and the New Nation: A Biography.* New York: Oxford University Press, 1970.

Peterson, Merrill, ed. *Thomas Jefferson, Writings.* New York: The Library of America, 1984.

Piatt, Donn. *Memories of the Men Who Saved the Union.* New York: Belford, Clark & Co., 1887.

Pin, Liu. *China Times*, March 10, 2011.

Potter, E. B., ed. *Sea Power: A Naval History.* Annapolis: Naval Institute Press, 1981.

Public Statutes at Large. *An Act Respecting Alien Enemies, 5th Cong., 2d Sess.* Washington, DC: Little, Brown, 1845.

Rai'c, D. *Statehood and the Law of Self Determination.* The Hague: Kluwer Law International, 2002.

Richardson, Albert D. *Personal History of Ulysses S. Grant.* Hartford: American Publishing Co., 1868.

Richardson, James D. *A Compilation of the Messages and Papers of the Presidents. Volume 5, part 3: Franklin Pierce.* A Public Domain Book, 2011.

Rohl, John, and Nicolaus Sombart, eds. *Kaiser Wilhelm II New Interpretations: The Corfu Papers.* New York: Cambridge University Press, 1982.

Rosenthal, Andrew. "Bush Now Concedes a Need for Tax Increases to Reduce Deficit in Budget." *New York Times,* June 27, 1990.

Rossiter, Clinton. *The American Presidency.* New York: Harcourt, Brace & World, 1956.

Rotter, Andrew J. *Hiroshima: The World's Bomb.* New York: Oxford University Press, 2008.

Russert, Tim. *Meet the Press,* September 27, 2007.

Safire, William. *Safire's Political Dictionary.* New York: Oxford University Press, 2008.

Schlesinger, Arthur, Jr. *The Age of Jackson.* New York: Little, Brown and Company, 1988.

Schrecker, Ellen. *The Age of McCarthyism: A Brief History with Documents.* New York: Palgrave, 2002.

Schüßler, Wilhelm. *Bismarck: Die gesammelten Werke* [*Bismarck: Collected Works*], vol. 10, ed. Hermann von Petersdorff. Berlin: Otto Stolberg, 1924–1935.

Scott, Donald M. *The Religious Origins of Manifest Destiny. Divining America.* TeacherServe©, National Humanities Center, http://nationalhumanities center.org/tserve/nineteen/nkeyinfo/mandestiny.htm.

Scott, Peter Dale. *The Road to 9/11.* Los Angeles: University of California Press, 2007.

Seelye, Katharine. "Cheney's Five Draft Deferments during the Vietnam Era Emerge as a Campaign Issue," *New York Times,* May 1, 2004.

Shapell Manuscript Foundation permanent exhibition at the Beverly Hills City Library in Los Angeles, California.

Shepard, Edward Morse, and John T. Morse, eds. *American Statesmen Martin Van Buren.* Boston: Houghton, Mifflin and Co., 1896.

Shlaes, Amity. *Coolidge.* New York: Harper Collins, 2013.

Simon, John Y., ed. *Ulysses S. Grant: The Papers of Ulysses S. Grant: January 1–October 31, 1876.* Carbondale: Southern Illinois University Press, 1967–2012.

Smith, James Morton, ed. *The Republic of Letters: The Correspondence between Thomas Jefferson and James Madison 1776–1826,* vol. 3 1804–1836. New York: W.W. Norton & Co., 1995.

Smith, Walter Bedell. *Eisenhower's Six Great Decisions.* London: Longmans, Green & Co., 1956.

Sorensen, Theodore C. *Kennedy*. New York: Harper & Row, 1965.

Sorley, Lewis. *A Better War*. New York: Harcourt Brace, 1999.

Starling, Col. Edmund W., and Thomas Sugrue. *Starling of the White House: The Story of the Man Whose Secret Service Detail Guarded Five Presidents from Woodrow Wilson to Franklin D. Roosevelt*. New York: Simon and Schuster, 1946.

Stearns, Worthy Putnam. *The Foreign Trade of the United States from 1820 to 1840*. Chicago: The University of Chicago Press, 1900.

Summers, Col. Harry G., Jr. *On Strategy: A Critical Analysis of the Vietnam War*. Novato, CA: Presidio Press, 1982.

Taussig, F. W. *The Tariff History of the United States*. New York: G.P. Putnam's Sons, 1910.

Taylor, Charles Carlisle. *The Life of Admiral Mahan, Naval Philosopher, Rear-Admiral United States Navy*. London: Forgotten Books, 2013.

Taylor, James C., Margaret A. Hogan, Karen N. Barzilay, Gregg L. Lint, Hobson Woodward, Mary T. Claffey, Robert F. Karachuk, and Sara B. Sikes, eds. "Abigail Adams to Cotton Tufts, 17 January 1790," *The Adams Papers, Adams Family Correspondence*, vol. 9, January 1790–December 1793. Cambridge, MA: Harvard University Press, 2009.

Thomas, Evan. *Ike's Bluff*. New York: Little, Brown and Company, 2012.

Time, September 12, 1932.

de Tocqueville, Alexis, Henry Reeve, trans., and Jim Manis, ed. *Democracy in America, Volumes One and Two by Alexis de Tocqueville*. Hazelton: Pennsylvania State University Press, 2013.

Truman, Harry S., Library and Museum, Independence, MO.

Truman, Harry S. *Memoirs of Harry S. Truman: Year of Decisions, Vol. 1*. Cambridge, MA: Da Capo Press, 1986.

Turner, Frederick J., ed. *Correspondence of the French Ministers to the United States, 1791–1797*. Washington, DC: Annual Report of the American Historical Association for the year 1903, vol. II, 1904.

Twohig, Dorothy, Mark A. Mastromarino, and Jack D. Warren, eds. "From George Washington to David Stuart, 15 June 1790," *The Papers of George Washington*, Presidential Series, vol. 5, 16 January 1790–30 June 1790 (Charlottesville: University Press of Virginia, 1996), 523–28.

US Congressional Documents and Debates, 1774–1875.

US Department of Commerce, Bureau of the Census, *Historical Statistics of the United States, Colonial Times to 1970*, Part 2.

US Department of Veterans Affairs Fact Sheet, Washington, DC, 2014.

US National Archives, Record Group 77, Records of the Chief of Engineers, Manhattan Engineer District, Harrison-Bundy File, folder #76.

Vital Speeches of the Day, vol. XXXXIII, no. 14, May 1, 1977.

Walton, Mary. *A Woman's Crusade: Alice Paul and the Battle for the Ballot.* New York: Palgrave MacMillan, 2010.

Washington, George, Papers at the Library of Congress, 1741–1799.

Washington Post, October 6, 2014.

Williams, Frank B., Jr. *Tennessee's Presidents.* Knoxville: University of Tennessee Press, 1981.

Wilson, Woodrow. *First Annual Message.* December 2, 1913.

Winslip, Richard. *American Military History: The United States Army in a Global Era, 1917–2003*, vol. II. Washington, DC: Center of Military History, United States Army, 2005.

Witcover, Jules. *Party of the People.* New York: Random House, 2003.

Wotton, Henry, Sr. www.quotes.net/quote/19243, accessed January 10, 2015.

Yale Law School—Lillian Goldman Law Library—The Avalon Project: Documents in Law, History and Diplomacy.

INDEX